Werner Rügemer

Imperium EU

Labor Injustice,
Crisis,
New Resistances

WWW.TREDITION.DE

Layout: Susanne Junge
Coverdesign: Jasmin Grünau using an image by Elfie Hackl-Ceran
        (www.elfie-hacklceran.at)
Translation: Alexander John Maisner OBE
Printer & Publisher: tredition GmbH, Halenreie 40-44, 22359 Hamburg

978-3-347-37267-2 (Paperback)
978-3-347-37268-9 (Hardcover)
978-3-347-37269-6 (e-Book)

Bibliographic information published by the Deutsche Nationalbibliothek: The Deutsche Nationalbibliothek lists this publication in the Deutsche National-bibliographie; detailed bibliographic data are available in the internet at: http://dnb.d-nb.de..

Contents

Introduction   9
CORONA PANDEMIC IN THE EU
Pre-diseased systems: Health, economy, government

     Pre-diseased health systems   9

     Pre-diseased economy and "Reconstruction Europe"   19

     The alternatives   25

Part One
LABOR INJUSTICE IN THE EUROPEAN UNION

1. Work as a human right!   **29**

     Labor and labor injustice - the great taboo   29

     Labor rights as human rights: Suppressed   33

     The systemic crisis in the EU   36

2. The early days: Geopolitical configuration   **43**

     Suppression of the democratic resistance movements   44

     USA as regulatory power I: Marshall Plan   46

     United States as Regulatory Power II: NATO   54

     In convoy: Eastern Enlargement of EU and NATO   60

     Nationalism, ethno-politics   62

3. The seeds of the EU:
Coal and Steel Community, EEC, Euratom   **64**

     European Coal and Steel Community   66

     Action Committee for the United States of Europe   77

The European Atomic Energy Community (EURATOM)   78

European Economic Community (EEC)   80

4. Expansion to (almost) all of Europe   **89**

Single Market, EURO, Eastern Enlargement   89

Today's capitalist bureaucracy   99

Dominant capitalist players in the EU   103

5. Economic policy principles: Without labor rights   **111**

Privatization   111

Aid to companies: Prohibited, but lavishly distributed   113

Subsidies without conditions for labor rights   115

Free trade agreements and global supply chains   116

6. Labor injustice: Direct legal instruments   **117**

PRIMARY LAW   117

SECONDARY LAW I: DIRECTIVES   121

No collective labor law   127

Flexicurity: Flexibilization without security   129

Safety and health at work?   132

Equal rights for men and women at work?   133

Whistleblowers or corruption in EU bureaucracy   134

SECONDARY LAW II:
JUDGMENTS OF THE EUROPEAN JUDICIARY   136

European Court of Justice (ECJ)   136

European Court of Human Rights (ECtHR)   145

7. In the crisis: Even more labor injustice!   **147**

European Pillar of Social Rights (EPSR, 2017)   147

BlackRock & Co: Private pension provision   150

Eight EU institutions to enforce labor injustice   151

European Social Fund ESF as soft power   153

Labor migration between poor and even poorer states   156

European minimum wage?   158

Part Two
STIRRINGS
AGAINST EXPLOITATION AND DISENFRANCHISEMENT

On the situation of the working class in the EU   161

The new era of social and political organization   162

From the defensive against the capitalists   166

**1. UK: Where the new labor injustice began
and will not end with Brexit**   **171**

Rise of the working class and its humiliations   171

Bought Brexit Campaign:
The EU as a surrogate enemy   174

Gig workers are organizing themselves -
but with Soros' help   180

2. EU founding and core states   **182**

Benelux: Rich, at the expense of the other EU states   182

Germany: Leading labor injustice state   183

France: The leading movements against capitalist Europe   188

3. Later EU Member States   **190**

Spain: Migrant organization in EU vegetable garden   190

Ireland: Against Ryanair - First Europe-wide
organization of pilots   195

Austria: 30-hour week for carers!   201

4. Ex-Yugoslav states   **206**

   North Macedonia: A voice for women textile workers!   208

   Croatia: Shipyard workers - strikes and hopes
   pinned on China   213

5. Scandinavian states   **219**

6. Eastern European states   **223**

   Hungary 2019: Workers suddenly realize their strength   224

   Poland: Internationally networked against Amazon   230

7. Baltic States   **239**

   Lithuania: Logistics center of the EU   243

8. Associated states   **248**

   Switzerland: "We went on strike against our invisibility"   248

Abbreviations   253

Glossary   255

Bibliography (selection)   258

Annotations   262

Introduction

Corona pandemic in the EU

Pre-diseased systems:
Health, economy, government

How fragile, in some places, and at the same time (seemingly) steadfast the US-led West is, can be seen in the Covid-19 pandemic. This also applies to the EU, with differences in the Member States. The dependent employees, and among them again the weakest, the low-wage workers, the mini-jobbers, the temporary workers, the single mothers, the small self-employed and the pseudo self-employed, the migrant workers and refugees - they were and are hit the hardest - health-wise and economically. By contrast, the plummeting "people's" parties with their emergency regime were able to take refuge in their ability to take action, initially. And BlackRock, Amazon & Co, with the complicity of the EU and national governments, are becoming even more powerful than before.

Pre-diseased health systems
"EU health policy focuses on protecting and improving health, giving equal access to modern and efficient healthcare for all Europeans, and coordinating any serious health threats involving more than one EU country." Thus proclaims the EU.[1] That sounds good, doesn't it?

However, via the internal market, the EU promotes the access of private investors. In Germany, groups such as Asklepios, Rhön-Kliniken, Helios/Fresenius, Sana, Ameos and the rehab group Median have not only formed large hospital chains, but also sell numerous medical services throughout Europe via subsidiaries. The largest hospital in Europe, Berlin's Charité, may be a public corporation, but it is radically privatized.[2]

Health became a commodity on the capitalist market. Nursing positions were cut, the number of treatments increased. Local care, treatment of common ailments - unimportant. There were no reserves when Covid-19 arrived. Not even the cheapest test kits, protective masks and protective clothing were available, not even for hospital staff.

The scarce, overworked nursing staff are poorly paid. Other employees in the health care system are paid even less: As many positions as possible are outsourced to precarious jobs at subcontractors, for patient transport - also within the clinics - for cleaning, kitchen, laundry, warehousing, processing of medical records, sanitation, janitorial services, as Charité has done with the help of McKinsey.[3] Superficial cleaning under time pressure, even now with corona - hygiene especially in hospitals? Not so important.

Then, up to half of the beds in the hospitals are empty - as a pool for corona patients, who did not exist in this quantity. Short-time work was prescribed. This is the logically absurd consequence of shortage: demand increases, but the shortage is exacerbated. To that end, 1.6 million planned treatments and surgeries were interrupted or canceled in Germany for the seven weeks between the start of the pandemic measures on March 13 and May 4, 2020 alone.[4] According to estimates by the ten external corona experts at the Federal Ministry of the Interior, as many as 2.5 million treatments were canceled for the period mentioned.[5] How many people died and will subsequently die earlier because of this than if they had been treated?

How many there really are in total to date remains unexplained - that does not interest the Minister of Health and the responsible health authority and the state and private mainstream media, nor the oh so caring Chancellor. They remained fixated on "corona" with half-empty hospitals and GP surgeries and on expensive, unused intensive care beds for corona patients. There were also fewer screenings, fewer admissions to emergency departments, fewer doctor visits, for fear of infection. Alongside the corona hype, people were dying, unrecognized and uncounted.[6]

EU adopts flat rate per case from the USA
One element of the profit orientation is the flat rate per case, Diagnosis Related Groups (DRG). It was developed at the elite private US university Yale and introduced into the US healthcare system in 1983.

This does not reward remedial activity, but rather the most short-term and technology-intensive treatment of individual ailments. Every bed must be emptied quickly for the next operation. This was part of the neoliberal program of US President Ronald Reagan. This former Hollywood actor was ex-press spokesman of General Electric - the leading US manufacturer of medical equipment - and promised to cut costs. But the US health care system became the most expensive and antisocial in the world. It excludes a large, the poorer part of the dependent workforce and the unemployed, African Americans and Native Americans from medical treatments.

The EU funded the *EuroDRG* project. Smaller US-affine states, such as Ireland and the Netherlands, were the first to adopt the system. In Germany, the CDU/CSU/FDP government under Chancellor Helmut Kohl, during this time also advised by McKinsey in the Treuhandanstalt for the privatization of GDR companies, pushed through the Health Structure Act in 1993. This replaced the cost-covering principle with "performance-based remuneration". In the meantime, flat rates per case now apply throughout the EU.[7]

Many sick people never make it to hospital

In 2004, the SPD/Green government under Chancellor Gerhard Schröder added further measures to the flat-rate payments as part of Agenda 2010; Tony Blair with New Labour had shown the way in Great Britain. These include the relief of employers from social security contributions, also for health insurance, and the multiple burden on dependent employees through co-payments for medicines, screenings, treatments and hospital stays.

The upshot, even in normal times: many ailments remain undetected and untreated. The ardent corona crusaders are not fundamentally interested in the health of dependent employees, pensioners, unemployed. You are poor - you do not need all the teeth in your mouth, you can die earlier.

Privatized, bought science

Moreover, the EU is lulled into a sense of security by the top scientific authority on health, the Johns Hopkins University (JHU). The health institutes of this private US elite university are funded by the private foundations of multi-billionaires such as Michael Bloomberg, Stavros Niarchos and William Gates. It has far more funding than the World Health Organization (WHO) and the EU.[8]

This university produces the Global Health Security Index. It evaluates the health systems of all 193 UN states. The systems in the USA and Great Britain are ranked first and second: They are considered "best prepared" against pandemics! And the healthcare systems in EU countries such as France, Italy, Spain and Germany, in the upper rankings, are considered to be "well prepared" for all epidemics and pandemics![9]

This is one of the reasons why not only the US government under President Trump, but also the EU and the governments of the EU states lulled themselves into a sense of security. The German Minister of Health, Jens Spahn, also claimed as late as the end of February 2020: No danger! They took the countermeasures firstly unprepared, secondly too late, thirdly incorrectly.[10]

After the 2007 financial crisis: Even more untreated illnesses
The health care systems in Italy, Spain and Greece have been below normal EU standards for a decade. On top of this, after the financial crisis, came the measures of the European Commission (COM), the IMF and the ECB (Troika): they demanded drastic cuts to save the indebted domestic banks: Not in the military budget, however, but in the social and infrastructure sectors. In the health sector alone, the Troika demanded 63 cuts from these states between 2011 and 2018: Lay off doctors and nurses, sell hospitals![11]

The cuts in (contractual) wages, unemployment benefits and pensions demanded in addition by the Troika also mean that more and more medical treatments can no longer be afforded by dependent employees, the unemployed and pensioners.

EU: Eastern Europeans do not have to be healthy
In Eastern EU-influenced regions such as Poland, Hungary, Croatia, Bosnia and Kosovo, the two-tier system was expanded even more brutally than in the West: The nouveau riche turn to private clinics for care. At the same time, the public health care systems fall into disrepair and remain underfunded. Monthly salaries for doctors and nurses here range from EUR 400 to 1,200 - with a cost of living similar to that in the rich EU states. Younger people emigrate, older staff in particular hold out, overstretched.

The recurring strikes by doctors and nurses in Poland and Croatia, for instance, are ignored by EU bodies. Meanwhile, the German health minister had younger employees poached from there to the hospitals of the richest EU state, for example from Kosovo. Eastern Europeans don't need to be healthy. European solidarity?

Collective self-blinding of virologists and epidemiologists

Virologists and epidemiologists at Johns Hopkins University, the Robert Koch Institute and the Charité are probably not subjectively corrupt. They do not have to be handed envelopes with wads of money under the table. They have risen in the privatized health and research system, have state-related, systemically important functions. They are showered with praise, well paid, their institutions are financed by the state and at the same time receive private donations.

Mutual endorsement over decades, as with the mainstream economists. This is how the collective self-blinding of the ruling elite, its accomplices and its support staff comes about, in the scientific establishment as well. They are socially and scientifically blind and yet feel in possession of the truth: this possession is not called into doubt even by the ritual but non-binding invocation of scientifically necessary doubts.

Socially and environmentally blind pandemic science

Consequently, Western governments assume: The virus spreads evenly through the population, whether in the underfunded (still) public hospital or in the well-equipped private clinic, in the sprawling villa district of Hamburg-Blankenese or in the cramped mass accommodation of Romani-an meat cutters exhausted by 16-hour shifts at the Tönnies slaughterhouse.

People are viewed by the leading virologists merely as biological be-ings, the virus infection as merely a biological event. Therefore, the pandemic measures have a universal character, affect (ostensibly) all citizens equally - i.e. as far as possible everyone, instead of giving special protec-tion to those particularly at risk, testing them as a priority, setting up addi-tional treatment facilities and employing additional personnel for this purpose, as is done, for example, in South Korea and especially in China.

For this reason, in late March 2020, the Robert Koch Institute argued that "corona deaths" should not involve forensic medicine. This is in breach of current law: in the case of deaths, unusual ones certainly, an official death certificate must be issued: What is the main cause of death? That is: What role did the virus play? Is it the cause of death or just ran-dom by-catch or something in between?

A small number of forensic physicians, such as those in Hamburg, who nevertheless examined the "corona dead", found only a small amount of the virus in the vast majority of old patients, who also had chronic preconditions, and furthermore: This new virus variant acts differently than previous, already known variants. It attacks not only the lungs, as previously assumed, but also other organs, such as the kidney and brain. Therefore, the treatments of the infected would need to focus not only on intensive artificial respiration, but also, for example, on palliative measures.[12] It was not until the end of May that a few more forensic doctors ventured to examine the dead on their own initiative.[13]

The government and capitalist virologists admit at best on the biological level: Yes, the elderly, those over 80 with their two or three pre-existing conditions, are a high-risk group. But it is precisely in the nursing homes that testing was not done in the first year. And the reality is still quite different.

Highest risk groups: The multiple subclasses
Age is only one risk factor. And still the unasked question: Where do age-related pre-existing conditions come from, how are they amplified in one place, in one social milieu, and not in another? Are obesity, diabetes and heart disease equally distributed among rich and poor? No - but the Robert Koch and Charité virologists did not investigate this either. Among some medical sociologists, an insight germinated on the fringes of the scientific community - but it did not reach the government.[14]

Several of the corona dead are *young*. This was also evident in the US. African-Americans are much more likely to have chronic illnesses early on, are much more likely to be unemployed, live in more cramped quarters, are less likely to receive medical treatment, are underpaid and shunned in menial jobs, and live shorter lives. They are physically and emotionally battered - they were six times more likely to die with corona in the first US hotspot, New York - but were even less likely to be tested than whites.[15] Moreover, that is why the underreporting rate is high. Many young Americans are ill: The average age at death due to and with the new virus was 48, about two decades lower than in Europe.[16]

Working poor and working sick
Exploited African-Americans, "illegal" Latinos, migrants from Nepal and Bosnia at Smithfield Foods, Tyson Foods & Co meat plants were disproportionately infected and died at particularly high rates. In the first count, 16 percent of the 3,700 workers at Smithfield's three-shift meat plant in

South Dakota turned out to be infected.[17] Working poor is linked to working sick: extremely exploited, extremely sick.

Similarly, poor African-Americans, Latinos, and poor whites in the overcrowded mass incarceration facilities. The highest rates of infection and death, however, hit Native American communities. Among them, too, were many young people. "Decades of contempt, discrimination, exclusion" determined the physical and mental health status here, combined with unemployment and a particularly poor health care system.[18] About half of US cities with average annual household incomes below USD 35,000 have abysmal hospitals and no intensive care beds, and mortality rates are high.[19]

An evaluation of 17 million patients during the pandemic in the UK, which was not commissioned by WHO, JHU or the Gates Foundation, showed that infections with fatal consequences primarily affect underprivileged, poorly paid people with deficient health care, and these include many immigrants from Africa and Asia.[20]

By the way, what the so knowledgeable New York Times then does not report after all: BlackRock & Co are the main shareholders of the largest US pig slaughtering company Tyson. And incidentally: BlackRock & Co are also the main shareholders of the New York Times. Criticism of the otherwise so environmentally active and media-sensitive BlackRock CEO Lawrence Fink and the health missionary and co-financier of the Global Health Security Index, William Gates, was not disclosed.[21]

Germany: Denial of infection backdrop
If the fight against the pandemic had been scientifically conducted, it should have been done as follows:

- Immediately identify at-risk groups with underlying health conditions at the onset – according to work, living, environmental, age, and health conditions;
- test these groups as completely as possible;
- deploy forensic medicine on a broad scale;
- then align the measures with treatment, protective measures, quarantine. Instead of setting up additional treatment facilities, the German government paid hospitals premiums of EUR 500 per day for beds kept empty.

But that is exactly what was not done. In old people's homes, meat factories, social hotspots, etc., no tests were carried out in the USA or the EU - or only when the infections spread catastrophically from there to the surrounding area, as in the case of the Iduna Center in Göttingen, a run-down prefabricated building in which 700 migrants, the unemployed, the homeless and drug addicts were crammed into a very small space by official order.[22]

Or, for example, in the case of the hotspot Tirschenreuth, a Bavarian district with the highest proportion in Germany of infected (1,136) and dead (134, both figures as of May 25, 2020): a malt liquor festival was claimed to be the springboard of the infection, according to Bavaria's populist prime minister, Söder (CSU). But: 1. in the middle of the district, in the small town of Mitterteich with 6,500 inhabitants, the Schott AG glass factory with 1,250 employees, which belongs to a worldwide group and is the largest company in the district, emits invisible glass dust that can settle in the lungs; 2. In this apparent idyll on the border with the Czech Republic - or precisely for that reason - an economically supra-regionally important interim storage facility is still being operated for nuclear waste from laboratories, hospitals, industry and nuclear power plants: But that remains outside the interest and investigation methods of the government virologists. The Bavarian prime minister had a *tropical* physician investigate the situation - methodologically exactly missing the possible source of danger![23]

Or the unemployed, for example: a study by the Allgemeine Ortskrankenkasse AOK and the University Hospital of Düsseldorf, not commissioned by the German government, proved: unemployed people had an 84 percent higher risk of Covid-19 than the average population.[24]

Working poor and working sick
Thus, in Germany as in the USA, suppressed risk groups only came to light catastrophically, "surprisingly" and late: This was also the case with the numerous deaths in some old people's homes and the frequently infected migrant workers in the meat industry: Within the space of a few days, high infection rates were revealed: At the Westfleisch Group in NRW, at Müller Fleisch in Baden-Württemberg, at Vion in Schleswig-Holstein.[25] And then, with a particularly long delay, at the market leader

Tönnies in Europe's largest pig slaughterhouse, in Rheda-Wiedenbrück, on June 24: 1,500 infected.[26]

Only then did the authorities have the workers tested. Before that, like President Trump in the US, federal and state governments had declared meat production to be "systemically important". Migrant workers were forced to work even more extra shifts, uncontrolled and unprotected. Clemens Tönnies, owner of Tönnies Holding, could proudly announce: "My employees" are now doing additional 16-hour shifts on weekends.[27]

Actually, the EU, the federal government, the state governments are fully aware: Meat workers with the lowest status under labor law as contract workers often work shoulder to shoulder. The chilled air promotes infections. The work is exhausting, the time pressure is extremely high, shifts can last 16 hours and sometimes even longer. The bodies are weakened, their health is affected. Breaks are not always taken. That's why most of the Eastern European contract workers can only endure the stress for between two and four years and are then sent back by the intermediaries to Bulgaria, Romania, Poland, Hungary, Moldova and Ukraine, whether sick or healthy. This has been going on for two decades and is public knowledge.[28]

A virological study had already been published back in 2017, which showed that slaughterhouses are hotspots for bio-aerosols: They damage workers' lungs and favor the transmission of bacteria and viruses.[29] But such pertinent findings - they come from the University of Shiraz, i.e. a hostile or, for the West, scientifically non-existent state, namely Iran. This does not reach Western government virologists. And they themselves do not hit upon the idea to pursue this obvious question.

Synergistic threat: Migrant meat workers
The particular risk of infection arises from a combination of factors. For example, meat workers are usually also housed in cramped shared rooms. Six to eight workers in 30 square meters, with a communal small kitchen and shared sparse sanitary facilities. Because the subcontractors who rent out the accommodation want to rake in as much as possible, the standard of furnishings and hygiene remains derisory. Even during the pandemic, meat workers sat by the hundreds cramped together at narrow tables in the canteen at Tönnies - with no checks by the state. They are transported daily in overcrowded buses from their lodgings to work and back again.

Thus, several practices synergistically endanger the health of the at-risk group. The legal instrument is the contract for work. It enables further breaches of the law, exploitation and health hazards. And it increases profits at Vion, Westfleisch, Müller Fleisch, Wiesenhof, Anhalter Fleischwaren, Danish Crown, Tönnies. This has also been shown with similarly exploited migrant workers in Ireland, the Netherlands, the UK, Poland, Italy, France.[30]

The pandemic measures also reveal the class character of the EU: It organizes labor migration at the expense of the impoverished, economical-ly underdeveloped Member States and at the expense of the unemployed and underemployed there, in favor of the companies in the rich EU found-ing states in the West. The populace here also gets a few nuggets of this with cheap meat and also with cheap services in the cheap brothels sup-plied with young Eastern European women.[31]

No corona rules for companies

The police, who control with high precision social distancing rules in parks, streets, playgrounds and stores in Germany's urban public spaces and impose fines - they do not control any slaughterhouse. Likewise, the customs, the trade supervisory authority (responsible for industrial safety), the health offices – no one comes. None of the dozen EU agencies respon-sible for labor rights comes. Instead, they see to it that labor migration continues even under corona conditions: not only in the meat industry, but also in construction, haulage, private care for the elderly, seasonal agricul-tural work. Unions have to strike, for example, against the health hazards in Amazon's US and also European fulfillment centers to get a minimum of health protection - no national or EU health and safety agency steps in.

The German government also did not issue a rule for 'normal' compa-nies until August 2020, five months after the supposed general lockdown. It was only in July that the Ministry of Labor produced an initial draft of an occupational health and safety rule. The business lobby with BDA and Gesamtmetall even called for "a reduction in existing documentation re-quirements". It was not until August 20, 2020, that the Ministry of Labor announced the SARS-Covid-19 occupational health and safety rule: only a "rule", i.e. not a law, only non-mandatory provisions, no controls, no sanctions for violating the rules.[32]

Although the lockdown is not being implemented in companies, no further infections or indeed deaths have been reported - except in hotspots such as the meat industry. The Robert Koch Institute stated at the end of August 2020: 5,824 infections were known in companies, almost exclusively in the meat industry - the Tönnies site in Rheda-Wiedenbrück alone with 1,500 infected persons.[33] Whether any of them fell ill or died - unknown. There are two possible explanations: Either there were virtually no infections, sick people or deaths in the companies, or there were and they were hushed up. Both variants expose the "corona" management as a lie.

Immediately after the start of the lockdown, the German Ministry of Health commissioned the PR agency Scholz & Friends to design and advise on corona communications, with an initial fee of EUR 22 million (#wirbleibenzuhause). The contract runs for four years, until 2024.[34]

Pre-diseased economy and "Reconstruction Europe"

The border closures ordered because of the pandemic, the shutting of stores, restaurants, schools, kindergartens, universities and cultural institutions caused "the economy to crash," it was said. In fact, it was mainly temporary workers, low-wage workers, small self-employed and freelancers who became unemployed. In some businesses, work tailed off or came to a temporary standstill, such as in catering/hospitality, retail, aviation, the public transport system, and tourism.

Hyped-up crisis – "legal windfall gains"
In addition, a few million employees were dispatched to home office. The vast majority of employees in Germany, however, continued to work, contrary to the public staging by governments and Scholz & Friends that "we all stay at home". Even at the peak of the second lockdown, in January 2021, no more than 24 percent of employees were working from home, i.e. only about 10 million of the 44 million employees. And many of those who work from home often have to go in to work occasionally.

The number of people employed had stood at 45.1 million in February 2020, before the pandemic. At the end of July, after 18 weeks of corona lockdown, the number had fallen only to 44.5 million: only 1 percent more unemployment. The business rag FAZ reported this figure correctly, while otherwise bemoaning the dire corona consequences.[35]

One emergency measure is the short-time allowance. This exists in several EU countries. Because of the crisis, it was extended and slightly increased in Germany. But it is lower than normal earnings and is not enough to live on, especially for the lower wage groups, and many temporary employees and 450-euro jobholders do not receive it at all.

Companies had applied for short-time benefits for 10 million employees for May 2020 - but only 1.06 million were actually on short-time work, including fraud: Companies put people back to work when the stores opened, but pocketed the short-time allowance. "Companies sent parts of their workforce on short-time work, and it turns out afterwards that they worked anyway", notes the employment agency, but to its own regret it does not have the staff to check the majority of applications; the companies calculate on this.[36] These are "legal windfall profits", is how one business lawyer glosses over such fraud.[37]

Pre-diseased policy
Not only is the sick health care system being propped up, but also, with billions in state aid, the sick economic system. In so doing, the sick political system of the plummeting "people's" parties also wants to seek refuge in its role as crisis manager.

Breach of the constitution: State aid for shrinking economies
The debt brake, which was ostentatiously incorporated into the German constitution, was immediately suspended when corona arrived. In a manifest breach of the constitution, the government has borrowed an additional EUR 450 billion for 2020 and 2021 - in one fell swoop, that's a quarter more national debt than before. To be sure, the one-off modest payments of EUR 300 per child are welcome to single mothers and parents.

And the EUR 2,000 to 15,000 for the self-employed and up to EUR 150,000 for SMEs provide short-term help in times of need. Lasting solutions look different. Raising the minimum wage to at least a paltry EUR 12? - not even that. Abolition of rolling limited contracts? None of that. Expansion of the public transport system, also as a contribution to saving the environment?

Subsidies for innovation-hostile companies

By contrast, the large corporations are being subsidized in the long term. EUR 9 billion to rescue Lufthansa, initially until 2023: In the process, jobs are being cut or switched to part-time work, pensions slashed, unpaid vacations extorted - while multi-year guarantees take effect for the new Lufthansa shareholders such as multi-billionaire Heinz Hermann Thiele and investment bank Morgan Stanley, who only bought into the company speculatively at the beginning of the "corona crisis". Technically, it would be no problem to convert Lufthansa and the car factories to the development and production of collective local transport systems.[38]

But none of it. Repairing the 40,000 bridges, the majority of which are in poor condition? Repairing the leaky sewer systems that allow untreated sewage to seep into groundwater? Repairing the dilapidated school buildings?

Drosten, Gates&Co: Privatize health care systems even more!

And oh, the health care system: No expansion of capacities. Higher wages for hospital nurses? More nurses? None of that. But a few billions for digitization, that's also the solution for the health minister - and multimillionaire - Spahn, slotted timely into place as a privatization and digitization fundy. Google & Amazon had their offers ready, which the German, the French government and the COM (apparently) can't refuse.

Around EUR 500 billion are needed to improve healthcare in the EU by 2030, according to calculations by the Vienna Institute for International Economic Studies WIIW. But the EU's EUR 750 billion rescue package does not include any funds for this. And the hunt by private hospital operators in the rich EU states for cheap doctors and nurses from Kosovo, Serbia, Croatia and Bosnia continues.[39]

And, the foundation of the largest private media group in the EU, Bertelsmann, in complicity with the state government of North Rhine-Westphalia, repeats it: The 1,900 hospitals now left in Germany are to be slashed to between 600 and 400 mostly private super-hospital factories. This plan, already published in 2019, has now been reaffirmed. It overlaps with the plan of the Charité Institute Global Health, its virologist Prof. Drosten, the Gates Foundation and the Boston Consulting Group: By privatizing the hospital system even further, Germany is to be among the leaders in world health, alongside the WHO, according to the intention.[40]

Innovation on the environment front? Deferred
The economic crisis had already begun insidiously long before "corona".[41]
It was precisely in the three years 2017, 2018, and 2019 that DAX companies in Germany distributed by far the highest profits, i.e. during the looming crisis.[42] Or, more correctly, high profits that were not invested, and the innovations neglected as a result, fueled the crisis.

This was most visible in the leading German and Western industry, car production. Diesel engines had continued to be built fraudulently, innovation ignored for the benefit of profits. Car sales, starting in the USA, had been gradually declining for years. Orders for suppliers in Baden-Württemberg as well as in Mexico, Hungary, the Czech Republic and Poland were cut. Only production and sales in China, albeit with restrictions, kept and keep car companies like VW in the black, in 2021 as well.[43]

Such companies are now being "rescued" with the "corona" sticker. Conditions for jobs and labor rights? Requirements against tax evasion? None of it.

Cars with gasoline and diesel engines and hunky SUVs are still allowed to be produced - if equipped with an electric motor, then the state chips in with an additional EUR 6,000: Something for higher earners and their eco-conscience. The state also pays this subsidy for hybrid cars, i.e. for the backward-looking, environmentally harmful hybrid: gasoline engine with battery add-on. Now at least a speed limit on the highways? No. And criminal proceedings against the fraudulent VW board members are dropped in exchange for a few million in fines. The criminal proceedings for "gang fraud" against bankers who cheated the state out of billions for the benefit of the wealthy are at risk of being time-barred - because of "corona".[44]

Renewed state doctrine: State economy to excess
The coal, lignite and oil companies are not subjected to any conditions to speak of either, but receive billions in subsidies.[45] The business lobby has succeeded in ensuring that the state, even if it becomes a co-owner in order to save a company, as in the case of Lufthansa, retreats into a "silent partnership": paying heavily, giving guarantees, but the decisions remain with the previous innovation refuseniks and crisis perpetrators.

While in the USA and the EU the largest state programs are launched to bail out private companies, criticism of China as a "state economy" is intensified - China does not know such direct state aid at all, moreover without environmental and labor law requirements.

The neoliberal lie that the state must "stay out of the economy" is once again being reduced to absurdity, as it was with the bank bailout in 2008, and elevated to the status of open state doctrine, on an even larger scale: Without the state, this capitalist economy would be doomed.

EU also breaching the constitution: "Reconstruction" and over-indebtedness

Together with the COM, the governments of Germany and France have pushed ahead with an EUR 750 billion rescue program for the "recon-struction of Europe". Here, too, "corona" is the sticker. Poland, the EU's fossil-fuel monster - 80 percent of energy from coal, biggest importer of old used cars, 33 of Europe's 50 most air-polluted cities are in Poland - gets whopping subsidies.[46]

And because the largest capital organizer in the Western world, the US investor BlackRock, has already advised the European Central Bank so well so far - in order to make itself and its super-rich, anonymous clients the largest owners of the largest stock corporations in the EU - that is why BlackRock is again advising not only the US Federal Reserve Bank dur-ing "corona", but also the ECB. The ECB wants to buy up more than EUR 1 trillion in bonds from states and companies (Pandemia ¬Emergency Purchase Program, PEPP) and thus plunge itself, that is the EU states, into new debts. And because the COM itself does not really know how the EU's ambitious Green Deal program can be realized, none other than BlackRock again got the consulting mandate.[47]

Deadly EU-style state economy
For the EUR 750 billion, the EU is taking out loans, against current budg-etary law, i.e. also in breach of the constitution - until now, the budget has been financed by contributions from the Member States. These new loans will also be paid out in part as non-repayable grants to the states. But the 750 billion must be repaid at some point by the same EU states, in addi-tion to their current contributions. But this is being concealed from the citizens - repayment is not to begin until 2028, with the next EU budget, and is to be concluded by 2058. But how will the German state, for exam-

ple, repay its share of these EU loans, in addition to the 450 billion loans taken out directly at national level?

In this regard, a basic observation: a state can incur debt comfortably if

- it ensures new revenues, for example through taxes on those who have so far been the biggest tax evaders,
- it raises mass purchasing power or promotes it, for example through its own investments and through increased labor income and pensions,
- it ensures innovation and new good mass products by imposing conditions on private companies.

But neither the EU nor the Federal Government is doing any of this. This leaves only the dependent employees as debt redeemers.

Thus, an even larger, EU-wide "austerity" or cutback program looms, for decades to come: deadly EU-style state economy.

Digital colonialism
With "corona", the EU finally wants to achieve "European sovereignty" in digitization as well. This populist wish will not come true. Unfortunately, the German-French cloud and digitization initiative is getting entangled in the already established clouds and medical algorithms of the "apocalyptic horsemen of the Internet", Google, Amazon, Microsoft, Facebook, Apple, abbreviated GAMFA.[48]

It started with the "corona" app: Google and Apple were able to blackmail the German and other governments. Then came the further digitization and robotization of healthcare. Amazon added 82 new planes to its transport fleet during the crisis and 175,000 new employees, mostly low-wage workers. On their "corona" roll, GAMFA have bought up numerous companies, in the EU, in the USA, in Asia.[49]

Digitization of disenfranchised labor
The digital and platform corporations with their BlackRock&Co major shareholders continue to shrink national economies: the steady decline in the number of hours worked in the West has been evident since 2005, accelerated in 2019 and further since 2020 with "corona". But this does not distribute work equally in a fair way, rather it increases the number of unemployed, gig workers, precarious workers and unsecured solo self-employed, mass poverty grows, as the ILO sums up in its Covid-19-Monitor of January 25, 2021.

It continues with cashless payment, and then it really starts: Homeschooling and home office; state and business administration; driverless car and traffic systems; civil, military and intelligence surveillance and, last but not least, the further digitized fragmentation of work in the direction of gig- and crowdworking.

German state governments used the Microsoft Teams conferencing system for homeschooling. US intelligence agencies thus now have access to the data of students, teachers, parents. "Microsoft is required under US laws such as FISA (Foreign Intelligence Surveillance Act) and the Cloud Act to release the data to the US government."[50] The same is true, for example, for the most widely used video conferencing provider, Zoom.

GAMFA "are the winners of the corona crisis" and "with their enormous financial resources they are further expanding their power". This is "digital colonialism," even the business newspaper Handelsblatt says.[51] What Handelsblatt does not reveal: Where do "the enormous financial resources" come from? They come from the GAMFA major shareholders such as BlackRock, Vanguard, State Street & Co.

The alternatives

In order to draw the right consequences for public health from "corona" as well as from the catastrophic "normal state", others must take action, trade unions and health initiatives that have formed during the pandemic.[52]

Detachment from the USA!
With GAMFA, BlackRock & Co are also the winners of state and EU corona management. They are an active part of "America First", were already before President Trump, having risen under his predecessors Clinton, Bush and Obama and with the elated approval of, for example, the long-time COM President, Jean-Claude Juncker: He was previously the creator of the largest financial haven in the EU, Luxembourg, which is particularly popular with Amazon & Co.[53]

They cooperate with the US intelligence services and the US military. And no matter how vehemently the liberal milieu repeated its cheap criticism of former US President Trump, the EU, acting somewhat less militantly, tagged along with Trump's media-military-intelligence aggression against Russia, Iran, Afghanistan, Venezuela, Cuba, Syria and, above all, against the People's Republic of China. Under the new US President Joe Biden, the aggression against China and Russia will be intensified - militarily, economically, politically, and via the media.

One of the EU's "corona" measures, in the wake of the military policy demanded by the US, is the "European Peace Facility" (EPF): in future, this title will accommodate spending on EU military missions and for training and upgrading "friendly armies".[54]

Europe must free itself from this dependence!

"America's declaration of bankruptcy"

In the process, "corona" is debunking the USA's role as a model state even for its very last few fans: with the most expensive and antisocial healthcare system in the world, it is proving to be a deadly hotspot in the pandemic. These victims come on top of the victims of shooting sprees and police violence.

The Western model and leading state produces the most deaths, at home, but also abroad. Suicide and the killing of others are part of the same social model: the many private gun owners kill not only other citizens, but above all themselves.[55] The USA leads the world in the suicide rate among children and young people.[56]

The US model produces the most unemployed by Western standards and also the poorest, amplified in the pandemic. The US also produces the most severe economic collapse. The US is the most indebted state and is sliding ever deeper into debt for the "corona" bailout. This suicide-prone and homicidal state is expanding its military budget, already by far the highest in the world, is sending even more warships with 6,000-man crews off the coast of China. Even during the pandemic, it is pouring billions of dollars into the largest wall ever built by a state against other states - highly equipped with Israeli security technology and militarized border police. It is proving to be the world leader in racism and in violating human rights and international law. And the richest US capitalists, like Amazon's Bezos and Microsoft's Gates, got even richer during the crisis.

"America's declaration of bankruptcy," it is said even in business circles: "High mortality figures, economic collapse, political failure."[57] Admittedly, the impetus to part company with the crashing, dangerous colossus is unlikely to come from these circles.

BlackRock: Crisis advance of the "shadow banks"
BlackRock, the largest unregulated "shadow bank", headquartered in New York (and legally domiciled in the US state of Delaware, for which current US President Biden spent 40 years as a senator helping to expand its role as the Western world's largest financial haven), advises not only the EU and the ECB. BlackRock organizes the de-industrialization of the US and EU economies by buying up and merging companies.

BlackRock made itself the biggest monopolist in German housing, playing the vanguard in driving up rents and utility costs. The second-largest housing group in Germany, Deutsche Wohnen AG, owned by BlackRock & Co, was promoted to the DAX, the elite club of the 30 most important companies in Germany, in the middle of the pandemic - after the largest housing group in Germany, Vonovia, also owned by BlackRock & Co, had already achieved this promotion three years ago.[58]

This shadow bank - and it is only the largest of the several hundred US shadow banks that operate similarly - is also helping to Americanize labor relations in the EU.[59] And it is advising the EU on the Europe-wide introduction of private pensions. In the "corona" crisis, BlackRock CEO Fink, as spokesman for this new Western capitalist phenomenon, sees "tremendous opportunities"; Fink is also spokesman for the privately organized Great Reset of Capitalism at the World Economic Forum/Switzerland.[60]

No going back to "normal"! New beginning! Re-founding of the EU!
Europeans only have a future in economy, democracy, prosperity, peace, human rights including social and labor rights: they must break away from the multi-tentacled imperium of "America First".

What governing politicians are promising as a return to "normality" after "corona" cannot and will not and must not be allowed to happen, from any perspective. BlackRock, Google & Co as well as the COM and the federal German government and the French government do not want that either, in their way.

And we, the majority of the population, the dependent employees, the colorful bunch of the working class, we cannot want this out of our own, completely different interests either. Because: The present neoliberal "normal state", which has become even more pronounced since the financial crisis of 2007, has led to the current health, political, economic, media and also global security crisis, including the labor injustice described in this book.[61]

Stirrings against exploitation and disenfranchisement
No return to "normal"! The prevailing corona management is a new, acute reason for the reversal of the status quo, for the democratic, peaceful re-founding of Europe based on human rights.

In the second part of this book, people, activists, trade unionists and authors from a dozen EU Member States and candidate countries have their say. They have been fighting for human rights at work, against exploitation and disenfranchisement long before "corona". The reports date from the first quarter of 2020. Initiatives that have since grown in strength, such as the international organization of Amazon workers, of health workers in several EU countries, and many others, could not be included here.

Part One

Labor Injustice in the European Union

1.
Work as a human right!

If you desire peace, cultivate justice!

Motto of the International Labor Organization (ILO), part of the League of Nations, founded after the First World War. Since the founding of the United Nations UN after World War II, the ILO has been one of its subsidiary organizations.

Labor and labor injustice - the great taboo

In the European Union, labor injustice, exploitation, disenfranchisement, insecurity, impoverishment, multiple sickness prevail, especially among dependent employees. And this is the main reason for the political drift to the right: The EU promotes labor injustice and thus also the drift to the right in Europe. It is not the AfD, Le Pen and similar right-wing groupings that are responsible for this, but the leading parties and governments in the EU. In Germany, these are the Christian-painted parties CDU and CSU and the social-democrat-painted SPD, supported by the unabashedly neoliberal FDP, private and state-run mainstream media, consultants and other accomplices.

Labor injustice is not just about impoverished low-wage workers and cross-border wage dumping. Even the low statutory standards are violated millions of times and with impunity by capitalists and their highly paid aides/support staff, for example in the minimum wage, through chain-like subcontracting, in the exploitation of migrant workers and refugees. No area of law in the EU knows such a statutory injustice *and* such an enforcement deficit *and* such a gray and dark zone of systemic illegality –

except perhaps in the case of sexual abuse in the Catholic Church, which is systemically relevant to such a system of injustice.[62]

The majority of dependent employees - even in the most "modern" sectors of the gig economy - have been and continue to be not only financially degraded, but also disenfranchised, humiliated, worn down, made ill, silenced, and these days also increasingly monitored. This is true in the new EU states of Eastern Europe and the Balkans as well as in the rich founding nations of Western Europe - and in the EU's supply and production chains reaching as far as North Macedonia, Bangladesh, Mexico and Liberia.

Big capitalists -
today more invisible than ever before in the history of capitalism
This taboo also includes the media-political disappearance of big business and its coordinators such as BlackRock, Vanguard, State Street, Capital Group, Blackstone, KKR, PwC, Freshfields & Co. They hide the "beneficial owners", i.e. the owners of the companies and banks, in the occult parallel society of four dozen financial havens: The most important financial havens also include central founding states of the EU such as Luxembourg and the Netherlands. And the European Commission in Brussels takes advice from the organizers of the parallel society.

Today, the hidden, irresponsible capitalists are at the same time as invisible and as unproductively rich as never before in the history of capitalism.[63]

The extorted silence of the working class
And freedom of expression, this so highly esteemed value of the "free western community of values", it is occupied by the big private media, in Germany also by the state compulsory media ARD, ZDF and DLF. And in the working class there is extorted silence.

The arrest in Turkey of a journalist from the newspaper "Die Welt" from the private Springer group is denounced, but the arrest of striking Turkish trade unionists - also in German companies there such as Deutsche Post DHL - is ignored not only by the Springer media with complicit silence. Workers and their representatives should shut up everywhere, in Germany and in Turkey. If they protest, they are imprisoned in Turkey, in Germany they are "merely" dismissed, psychologically demoralized and vanish in the media-political darkness.

Talking tools

In the Western mainstream media, dependent employees sometimes do indeed pop up. They speak briefly about the labor injustice done to them. But, typically, it says "name changed". They are given different names, their faces are rendered unrecognizable, they speak behind a curtain, their voice is "dubbed": Fear reigns, there is no freedom of expression – at the heart of the cradle of "free expression". "Talking tools" – as the Greek tutor of slave owners, the philosopher Aristotle, referred to slaves. They must understand work instructions but are not allowed to speak publicly.

The lower they are in the hierarchy, the more dependent employees are left with only their mere body, the muted commodity of labor power, the hectic securing of existence, religious and cultural abandonment, the more or less joyless search for distraction in the jungle of target-group-specific entertainment production.

War refugees, who have somehow overcome the walls of death around the fortress of wealth after all, along with millions of labor migrants from impoverished EU states form in the middle of the rich EU founding states a "ghost army of labor without a face, without a name and without a history", as the migrant care worker Rev. Peter Kossen bemoans again and again, without being heard by Christian-painted politicians or the bishops of ecclesiastical Christianity.[64]

Women in the EU:
Capitalist leadership and cheap prostitution

The tabooing is also organized with the help of the "new values" such as "diversity", promotion of up-and-comers from ethnic and other minorities, through corporate programs for the free choice of sexual gender (LGBT, extended on Facebook to 40 sexual orientations), as well as through the perverted part of the women's movement: It promotes the rise of women to the upper echelons of business, the military and EU institutions - for example, the presidents of the European Commission and the ECB and the growing ranks of national 'defense' ministers.

The capitalist media promote the sexual empowerment of female celebrities and semi-celebrities and actresses, such as with quotas on corporate and party boards and with the display of prominent figures in the MeToo movement – while the same milieu humiliates, abuses and also sexually exploits precariously employed women in private households and companies by the millions, this moreover also in mafialike organized prostitution with minors from the EU periphery.

Individual as consumer: courted - Individual as worker: invisible
People are courted as consumers, celebrated, publicly portrayed in a highly professional manner in the happy enjoyment of the CO_2 guzzlers they buy. The right to consume is the highest value for the people.

Yet, as dependent employees these same people are not celebrated. Especially in the leading Western nation USA, where the richest capitalists are even richer and more brutal than elsewhere - there the dependent employees are more invisible than anywhere else.[65]

Yet "the customer is king" has always been a fake – the money is plucked from his pocket for feigned happiness, even if he piles up debt and plunges himself into despair and poverty. And, besides, today's mass consumer is surreptitiously even more tracked, manipulated, resold.

Selfie with laughing female colleagues at the boss's desk?
Ethnic, religious, and sexual affiliations are cultivated in the US-led West as the most important criteria of individual and collective identity. How do I live as a Muslim and as a Jew in Germany? Recently, the search for identity among gays and lesbians has been cultivated in the media, literature, and politics: How many years was I afraid to come out as gay and lesbian after all?

But the question is not asked how dependent employees are afraid throughout their whole lives and deny their identity as self-confident people and upright citizens. Instead of self-confidently beating their entrepreneurs and bosses around the ears about the humiliations, the mobbing, the low pay? Or: Where did the question appear so far in this warped discourse on identity: How did I overcome my fear as a dependent employee to come out as a candidate for the next works council election? With a nice little selfie - surrounded by laughing colleagues - at the desk of the stupidly grinning boss? And that totally regardless of denominational or sexual orientation.

The exploited as his own employer
Likewise, the taboo is organized by the perverse escalation of private entrepreneurship: Dependent employees are supposed to disavow their identity as dependent employees. Rather, they are supposed to become entre-

preneurs themselves, entrepreneurs of their labor power who, in competition with the other desperate entrepreneurs of their own labor power, expose and offer themselves on the market even more streamlined and at the same time cheaper. The unemployed person who, full of hope, transformed himself into a "Me plc" and would succeed as a me-entrepreneur was part of the original Hartz laws in Germany.[66]

Labor rights, conditions and incomes vary widely across EU countries. But everywhere, since the end of socialism in Europe, the average level has been lowered and additionally decoupled from growing productivity,[67] while incomes and rights of capitalist private owners and their managerial and advisory staff have been excessively - and at the same time hierarchically - increased.

Labor rights as human rights: Suppressed

The Treaty of Versailles after World War I regulated not only the much-discussed reparations in 1919. The International Labor Organization (ILO) was also founded. Their immediate program included: an 8-hour day, a weekly rest period of 24 hours, equal pay for equal work for men and women. Since 1919 the ILO's motto is "If you desire peace, cultivate justice". This insight and these rights were not simply granted by the capitalists to the workers of that time – it required class struggle. And even these rights are not yet or no longer reality, despite the fact that today's labor productivity makes quite other rights possible.[68]

ILO: If you desire peace, cultivate justice

To date, the ILO has adopted 189 labor rights. The best known of these are the eight core standards, especially the right to free trade unions, collective bargaining and strikes, equal pay for men and women, and the abolition of forced labor. Less well known, including among trade unions, are other labor rights: adequate wages that can support a family with dignity; paid leave and paid training; protection against dismissal (including for pregnant women and the disabled); protection against hazards at work; social insurance for unemployment, sickness and retirement; rights for migrants and domestic workers.[69]

At the same time, these rights have a completely different quality than the labor rights promoted in the EU from the very beginning: What is more, these relate to the labor *market*. In the EU, human labor is a capitalized commodity. *Note*: Those who speak of a labor 'market' negate human rights, no matter how much they may invoke them.

UNO: The right to work

In the UN Universal Declaration of Human Rights of 1948, labor rights are enshrined in Articles 23 and 24 as human rights: The right to work in general and the most important rights codified by the ILO; the right to education and further training; the right of working mothers to special care; the right to privacy in the workplace and the prohibition of discrimination of any kind.

The right to work can be realized under socialism, but also through full employment under capitalism.[70] The right to work as defined by the UN also does not mean that "any work" must be accepted; on the contrary, it must be in accordance with human rights. Today we can add new substantive criteria: The work must not serve the destruction of the environment nor the preparation of wars.

UN Social Covenant: Ratified - and forgotten

The most important ILO standards were incorporated into the UN Social Covenant of 1966 as an international treaty. The Western European states ratified the treaty - but with the help of the EU they have forgotten and suppressed it. The four Hartz laws in Germany in the 2000s, then the minimum wage delayed for decades, in truth a poverty wage, women still being paid less and treated worse - all this violates the Social Covenant.

The German Basic Law and the EU documents essentially only know civil "fundamental rights".[71] The UN's Universal Human Rights of 1948 and the labor and social rights[72] contained therein are not even mentioned. In the Basic Law, the terms trade unions and labor rights are scrupulously avoided. The most recent EU declaration "European Pillar of Social Rights" (2017) looks even worse.[73] (see page 125ff.)

Capitalism – the (dis)order of the capitalist minorities

The leading Western nation USA is the lonely leader when it comes to non-recognition of ILO standards, universal human rights and international law. In terms of the country's wealth and purchasing power it has the lowest statutory minimum wage in the world: USD 7.25, with exceptions down to USD 2.13 for occupations where tips are expected, such as restroom attendants and waiters.

Thus, at the current nadir of labor injustice, it is part of the necessary countermovement to emphatically demand the rights of dependent employees - including the many new forms of digitally organized (pseudo) self-employment - as universal human rights.

The perverted ILO
Today, however, it is no longer possible to simply appeal to the ILO. Like the UN itself during the time of UN Secretary General Kofi Annan, it was attuned by the global corporate lobby to the Western-defined "globalization".

For example, in 1998 the ILO adopted the "Declaration on Fundamental Principles and Rights at Work and its Follow-up". The "realities of the globalization of the economy (are to be) countered by a genuine minimum social base".[74] To this end, the 181 individual standards on social insurance, protection against dismissal and paid leave, protection against workplace hazards, etc. are omitted altogether. Reference is made only to the eight core standards: However, they are worded more generally and without the ILO's implementing provisions involving sanctions; and the two standards on equal pay for men and women and on the minimum age for dependent employment are omitted altogether.

The established trade unions, participants in the ILO tripartite system (the bodies are made up of representatives of governments, employers and trade unions), tag along, blackmailed and complicit.

Free trade agreements all refer to this diluted 1998 Declaration in a mandatory chapter. But the few standards are also exempt from all sanctions. In the context of a worldwide democracy movement, a new start is required.[75]

All people are born with equal rights
In many ways people are not equal. In many ways, they cannot and need not be equal at all. But they are born with equal rights. Equality before the law applies. In a democracy, there are no unmerited privileges.

In the EU, there are 240 million dependent employees, at least according to the official count, which is probably missing many millions who live in the EU gray areas and manage to work somehow or languish unemployed. But this also includes many millions more who depend on the work, rights and incomes of these 240 million, children and other family members. And dependent employees also include those who once had this status and now, dependent thereon, draw their more or less adequate pension. It is about the tabooed interests of these majorities of the population, the working class, i.e. about the fundamental question of democracy.

Human rights internationalism confronts minority-led globalization, also promoted by the EU. Ultimately, only a form of socialism can bring about the democratic, peace-securing equality of people before the law and in social reality. But, for the foreseeable future, we now have to prove ourselves in the difficult transitional phase.[76]

For work in accordance with human rights in a free, democratic and peaceful Europe!

The systemic crisis in the EU

The EU, contrary to its initial promises, is neither social nor peaceful nor democratic. The post-World War II promises of general prosperity, the rule of law and peace were accepted by majorities of the population. But these promises were merely populist maneuvers by those who then organized the EU with its precursors - with the Marshall Plan and NATO, the Coal and Steel Community, the Single Market, the euro, and eastward enlargement.

The German Chancellor: "At the crossroads" in the old direction
In post-war Europe, unlike anywhere else in the world, the extreme US-style contempt for and exploitation of dependent employees clashed with labor and trade union rights, which had been at least partially renewed in the wake of fascism - in the Western European states with the potency of the left and trade unions and in the socialist states with their fundamental orientation toward workers' interests. This conflict is not over. It is a key part of the systemic crisis that was inherent in the EU from the very beginning.

"Europe is at a crossroads," the German chancellor declared, repeating similar EU statements since 2017. "If we stand still, we will be crushed in the great global structures."[77] The populist was onto something there. But EU leaders continue to want to speak for the whole of Europe in a peace-threatening manner. Simulating independence, they want to remain vassals of the USA and NATO.[1] Correct: They are being crushed globally, and not only by the "global structures": The EU grinds down, disenfranchises even its own population majorities with the core of dependent employees and those farmers not yet expropriated by agribusiness. These crisis and crossroads proclaimers, including the new European Commission president von der Leyen, want to continue on the old crisis-spawning path, also in continuation of the Corona pandemic management. Self-blinded, they stick to the old path.

Thus, the "furies of hyperglobalization" have pushed the injustices in both the EU and in the US-led "Western community of values" as a whole even beyond the conditions that have hitherto been denounced as "neoliberal". The new capital organizers like BlackRock are preparing, along with companies like Google, Apple, Microsoft, Amazon and Facebook, in which they are the main shareholders, the even more direct control of society, in the shape of *stakeholder capitalism* (departure from *shareholder capitalism*, the superficial inclusion of workers, clients, municipalities…) that is to be combined with a *Green New Deal* and digitalized, global disease management and the *Great Reset* of a "sustainable" capitalism, such as that propagated by BlackRock CEO Lawrence Fink with the World Economic Forum.

Multi-class system between EU states and within EU states
In better times, there was talk of a "two-speed Europe": The wealthy founding states with Germany and France - and somewhere also Great Britain - at the top, and next to and below them and somewhat "slower" the rest.

---

[1] •Since the Roman Empire and the European Middle Ages, vassal by no means signifies total subservience. The relationship of the vassal to the master is often regulated by contract. For the master's recognition and his promised protection, the vassal must perform some services, such as providing soldiers and cheap labor, collecting taxes from his subjects, and preventing uprisings. In return, the vassal gets advantages: He or the vassal community may pursue their own interests, enrich themselves, expand regional power, oppress their own population. There are always minor conflicts between the vassals and the master. The master can change his preferences between the vassals, such as for some time Poland has been rated higher than Germany in certain respects.

Today, the EU states are entangled in a multifaceted over-, under- and against each other. The EU is led by Germany and France, with Germany competing with economic dominance and France with greater military-colonial pretensions.

The social democratic model of the welfare state - especially lauded in the Scandinavian countries - dissolved into a rich-poor divide and nationalist right-wing radicalism. And one level lower are Eastern European states like Poland, the Czech Republic, Hungary and Slovakia, with reactionary oligarchs and a wealthy upper class exploiting and nationalistically agitating their working class and relegated middle classes - mostly in the service of Amazon, VW & Co as well as a corrupt domestic bourgeoisie.

And yet lower still, again hierarchically tiered among themselves, the very poorest EU states such as the three Baltic states, Greece, Croatia, the EU protectorate Bosnia-Herzegovina and then those still standing as poor beggars in front of the door and offering themselves as future EU members with servile preparatory inputs, such as Serbia and, as an important US military base, the corrupt, impoverished US protectorate of Kosovo. The latter is ruled by the mafia and is supposed to serve no other purpose anyway and was separated from Serbia to this end in violation of international law.

This multiple split is being exacerbated by the management of the corona crisis. The Western states, and additionally through them the EU, are taking out by far the largest loans to date to bail out environmentally damaging, innovation-resistant corporations in the auto and coal industries resting fat on their profits. And the German government is not only taking out most of these loans, but also has to pay the lowest interest rates for them, or none at all. And for new outsourcing of operations to impoverished EU countries, German, French, Taiwanese and US companies are once again receiving the highest EU subsidies.

And across these divides, millions of migrant workers and refugees are herded back and forth in a gray and shadowy realm systemically linked to illegality, crime, and human rights violations: A multi-class system between and multi-class system within individual EU states.

Technological and economic decline

In the EU, all states are already so over-indebted that, according to current logic, no debt reduction can take place in their EU lifetime, accompanied by cuts in public-sector budgets ("debt brake"). For the majority of the population, vital infrastructure is falling into disrepair - or being privatized and made more expensive. With the pandemic management, this process is intensifying.

Moreover, not only states and public-sector budgets down to the municipalities are over-indebted, but also private companies and millions of individual private households – incidentally, unlike the enemy states Russia and China. In 2019, purchasing power-adjusted per capita government debt alone was USD 46,000 for the US, USD 41,000 for France, USD 33,000 for Germany, but only USD 7,000 for China and USD 4,000 for Russia.[78]

As a result of the inherent visible and invisible long-term, multifaceted government cutbacks, the purchasing power of the majority in the Western and EU states is sinking, including that of the middle classes that politically were previously deemed systemically relevant. And precisely the leading companies in the EU have fallen behind in environmental technology, especially in comparison with the innovative People's Republic of China, which has risen to become the world's largest economy. And against the dominance of the leading US digital corporations - and their tax evasion and breaches of the law - the EU is making no headway, despite constant new attempts.[79]

"Rebuilding Europe": The unjust crisis system is being perpetuated

If we subtract the environmentally destructive part of production and services - such as coal and lignite power, big cars with gasoline and diesel engines, plastic packaging, cheap mass textiles, cheap mass aviation and transcontinental free trade goods traffic, arms production and military operations and maneuvers - the meaningful economic performance in the EU shrinks far below the puny turnover success figures even further, also looking ahead. This also means that human skills are devalued, disqualified, perverted, abused. The potential for uplifting, meaningful, joyful, interlinked work and the products and services that result is demoralized, destroyed.

Precisely because the pandemic has exposed the vulnerability and obsolescence of the political and economic system, we need to do more than just "rebuild" the old system. But political innovation - i.e. democratization -, economic innovation - i.e. innovation in the environment and European sovereignty in technology, investment - and labor innovation - e.g. an end to organized working-poor migration - are being neglected, obstructed.

US military and geostrategic dominance

Contrary to the insipid declarations of intent by the German and French governments, for example, that they finally wanted to develop "more independence" vis-à-vis the US, the EU continues to submit to the military and geostrategic dictates of the US, even if the vassals did at times take potshots at Trumpkins up to 2020:

- Rapid, obedient increase in military budgets of European NATO members
- participation in military actions and wars in violation of international law, such as in Iraq, Afghanistan, Syria, Libya
- compliance with US economic boycotts of Russia, Iran, Cuba, and Syria, resulting in economic harm, including the loss of many jobs
- agitation and armament against Russia and now also against the People's Republic of China
- immediate support for US-sponsored coups in South America, such as Venezuela and Bolivia
- silent helplessness of the EU in the US-led construction of the "Eastern NATO" within NATO by the US with the help especially of the nationalist governments of Poland and the Baltic states (Visegrad states, Intermarium).

The geopolitical wealth fortress

The EU's involvement in the new US-led wars, beginning in Yugoslavia, then Iraq, Afghanistan, Libya, Syria, is driving millions of refugees from these impoverished war zones. The EU does not want to face these consequences - the EU is being turned into a fortress. The fundamental human right that drowning people be rescued is permanently being violated. Directly and indirectly, the EU organizes and provokes the death of refugees in the Mediterranean with police resources. The leading Western capitalist democracies in particular cause more war and economic refugees than any other states. None of the demonized states like Russia or China are driving refugees to their deaths on their shores and erecting walls and fences on their borders.

In the EU wealth fortress, only the wealth of a few is being defended. Walls are being built not only against refugees from the outside, but also walls of the gated communities of the super-rich against the poor at home.

At the same time, the EU is outsourcing its defense against refugees to states outside the EU. Thus, it promotes permanent conditions in breach of human rights in the immediate neighboring states, such as Turkey, Libya - which, moreover, was previously destroyed under US leadership - and other North African states. Where the slave trade flourishes.[80]

EU: Against international law and universal human rights
The EU stands in conflict with the democratically organized world community: In international law and universal human rights, especially individual and collective labor rights. Western EU countries in particular ratified the UN Social Covenant with its social and labor rights in the 1960s and 1970s, but undermine it through EU directives and national laws.

The International Convention on the Protection of the Rights of All Migrant Workers and Members of their Families (ICRMW): This international treaty has been in force since 2003. But the EU and its Member States reject it to this day.[81]

The EU also rejects the global supply chain law: this stipulates that the disregard of human rights by companies in the international production and service chains is an offence. The UN Human Rights Council had already adopted this binding treaty in 2011. The German government is also delaying such a mandatory and sanctioned supply chain law due to resistance from the business lobbyists of BDA, CDU, CSU.[82]

The UN Declaration on the Rights of Peasants and other People Working in Rural Areas was rejected by the small minority of the US and its closest friends Britain, Israel, New Zealand, Australia, Sweden and Hungary. By abstaining, the majority of EU states, including Germany and France, made it clear that they will not implement these rights either.[83]

The EU has also failed to ratify the ILO Convention on the Protection of Workers at Work adopted in June 2019: This convention - the importance of which also stems from the fact that it was adopted on the

100th anniversary of the ILO - is concerned, among other things, with equal treatment of the sexes in the workplace, with upper limits on working hours, with health and safety, and with the protection of privacy.[84]

The EU promotes hate, racism, nationalism
Since the war against Yugoslavia in the 1990s at the latest, the EU, in cooperation with NATO, has been promoting nationalist hatred, and in many cases Christian-based racism.

Anti-democratic and even fascist traditions were revived from the dustbin of history. Politicians of this ilk were maneuvered into government in the small new states split along ethnic lines, as in Croatia and Kosovo. Similarly, in Eastern European countries such as the Baltic States, Poland and Hungary, then Ukraine.

After the primary populists come the secondary populists
The political parties that helped build the EU have not been able to fulfill, have not wanted to fulfill, have not been allowed to fulfill their, from the very beginning, populist promises of prosperity and work for all, peace and democracy.

In particular, the systemic labor injustice for the working class and the actual, feared, claimed and ongoing restrictions on the middle classes have fueled the decline of these 'people's' parties. But because these primary populists, and with them the mainstream media, interpret this descent, they do not promote the rise of democratic and left-wing forces, but the emergence of secondary populists. The public utterances of the capitalist lobby and the private mainstream media gripe a bit about the style and choice of words of the new up-and-comers - that is typically "bourgeois": This attitude already promoted the rise of fascists and similar forces in Europe after World War I, starting in Italy, then Poland, Scandinavia, and finally Germany.

Thus, transatlantic capitalists turn up their noses at populist and nationalist liars and bullies like Donald Trump and Boris Johnson – but these are infinitely preferable to the democratic alternatives such as Corbyn's Labour Party in the UK, Bernie Sanders in the USA, La France Insoumise in France and Podemos in Spain.

The real crisis
The real crisis of the EU, as of the entire US-led West, is this: the democratic forces are not (yet) strong enough for change. They are stronger than they generally believe themselves to be. They have by no means brought their defeats to date on themselves - contrary to the prevailing legend, for which the guilt-ridden sociologist Didier Eribon, for example, is happy to let himself be used by the mainstream media.[85]

Rather, the democratic forces are preparing themselves, still tentatively, mostly unheard and uncoordinated. And the representatives of the old order attempt to stifle and/or instrumentalize or even integrate even small stirrings. But it is precisely such stirrings that point the way ahead.

2.
The early days: Geopolitical configuration

Labor injustice, its tabooization and the systemic crisis of the EU have deep roots. Their widespread obscurity, repression, distortion are part of this taboo and this crisis. The capitalists, with their new transatlantic links in and after World War II, did a great deal to prevent the liberation of labor that had become historically possible. The pro-capitalist, anti-communist and then failed reorganization of Europe led by Hitler was taken over and strategically reshaped by the new Western superpower, the United States of America, using more modern means.

Since the 1920s, US corporations and governments did everything they could to prevent Germany's economic, political, and technological alliance with the Soviet Union: Such an alliance, it was feared, would have created the largest competitor. For this reason, against the Rapallo Treaty of 1922 - establishment of diplomatic and economic relations of Germany with the Soviet Union - the USA installed the countermeasure: the Dawes Plan (1924): Generous loans were intended to help the German Reich, but also to promote US investment activity. With the intermediate step of the Young Plan of 1929, the Marshall Plan of 1947 was then the decisive sequel, subsequently further reinforced by NATO.

Like no other territory, West Germany, which was initially occupied by the Western Allies, and then the Federal Republic, which was further occupied from 1949 onward, could be rebuilt and rearranged according to the ideas of the US superpower. This was the cumulation of the pivotal decisive system conflict of world society at that time This was also part of the establishment of a global anti-communist, pro-American trade union movement on all continents, in other words, the global organization of labor *in*justice - with consequences to this day.[86]

Suppression of the democratic resistance movements

During World War II, anti-fascist movements in all countries occupied by Hitler's Wehrmacht had developed concepts for a democratic postwar order. This was particularly true of the Western European and Scandinavian countries, especially France and Italy, but also of Germany itself.[87]

Thus, the notion of a "Europe of Fatherlands", taken up by Charles de Gaulle and developed together with the Résistance against Hitler, was dismissed along with explicit anti-fascist notions such as those of Altiero Spinelli: European federal state with constitution. Altiero Spinelli, like Antonio Gramsci and other members of the Italian Communist Party, was among those imprisoned or exiled by Mussolini's fascist government in 1927 until its end in 1943. In his place of exile, the island of Ventotene, he wrote the "Ventotene Manifesto" in 1941 with fellow prisoners Ernesto Rossi and Eugenio Colorni.

They wanted a European federation, a federal state with a supranational military and supranational organs for the soon-to-be-founded post-war Europe: These were intended to disempower the forces from the corporate world that had repeatedly promoted totalitarian regimes in various states, such as those of Mussolini, Franco, Salazar, Hitler, Piłsudski and Pétain. "The European revolution must be socialist to meet our needs; it must work for the emancipation of the working class and the creation of more humane living conditions." This would have to be achieved through the direct participation of Europe's citizens and through a constitutional act.[88]

This and all other democratic, anti-fascist, socialist concepts for the reorganization of Europe were suppressed, stifled.

The Bank for International Settlements (BIS) in Basel had played an important role in financing Hitler Germany's war. It had been set up by

Wall Street in 1930 to maintain the national debt and repayment obligations of the German Reich, resulting from the Treaty of Versailles, for an initial 55 more years, until 1986, after the Reich governments stopped repayments. All the major warring parties were represented in the BIS until the end of the war, across the military lines of conflict - Germany, Italy, Japan, France, Belgium, Great Britain, Sweden, the United States, etc. It practiced money laundering for the benefit of Hitler's Germany and facilitated much of the war financing: Under the leadership of Wall Street banker Thomas McKittrick, representatives of militarily hostile states cooperated here. Like other Swiss banks, BIS converted Nazi looted gold and looted shares for the benefit of the German Reich into foreign currencies important to the war effort, such as US dollars, Swedish kronor, Swiss francs and Portuguese escudos.[89]

European economic integration under German leadership: a failure
German corporations in particular had been developing pro-capitalist concepts of Europe since the 1930s. For example, Carl Duisberg, chairman of the Reichsverband der Deutschen Industrie (RDI) and chairman of the supervisory board of the chemical monopolist IG Farben, declared in 1931, with reference to even older plans of German industrialists: "Only a united economic bloc from Bordeaux to Odessa will give Europe the economic backbone it needs to assert its importance in the world."[90] In 1936, the NSDAP Reich Commissioner for Economic Policy, Werner Daitz, declared that "Germany in the center of Europe" must build "a continental European large-scale economy."[91]

With the occupation of Western Europe, Nazi Germany achieved the so-called "European economic integration". It consisted, for example, of German corporations awarding paid contracts to French car, chemical, and steel companies such as Renault and Citroën for the production of military vehicles for the Russia campaign, for barbed wire and poison gas in German concentration camps, and the like.[92] The appropriate raw materials, machinery, agricultural products, and labor were extracted from other occupied countries and distributed throughout Europe. In addition, associated "neutral" states such as Sweden, Switzerland, Spain and Portugal also supplied raw materials, products and financial resources essential to the war effort. German banks coordinated the acquisition of company shares throughout Europe - either through regular share purchases or through Aryanization.

USA as regulatory power I: Marshall Plan

After the Second World War, the USA was the new Western superpower. Not only Germany was substantially weakened, but also the other imperialist states of Europe, especially Great Britain and France, but also the smaller ones like Italy, Belgium, Portugal and the Netherlands. Great Britain, in particular, was deeply in debt to the United States and politically dependent on it.

The reorganization of (Western) Europe organized by the USA did not bring peace: neither peace and security for the dependent workers, their organizations and their culture, nor peace and security between the peoples. There was no peace treaty, neither between capital and labor nor between East and West. The potential for the liberation of labor, strengthened in the anti-fascist struggle, was largely contained, partially destroyed: There were only pacifying concessions for a time - from 1990 onwards this period gradually came to an end, with the EU now also playing a more active role.

The economic boom of the Second World War, the biggest the USA had experienced up to that time, was to be continued after the war. The Marshall Plan (1947) was launched for this purpose. The aim was to gain access to a large area that was as uniformly organized as possible for US needs - exports, currency simplification, investments - with supranational, authoritarian decision-making bodies.[93]

Marshall-Plan: (Western) Europe in the US global market strategy
The Foreign Assistance Act of 1948 included, in addition to the Marshall Plan, war and military aid to Greece, Turkey, and the fascistoid General Chiang Kai-shek on the Chinese island of Taiwan (Formosa) that he had annexed since the 1920s.

The Marshall Plan was a partial instrument for the military-civilian domination of Europe. This is also reflected in the functions of its eponym: General George Marshall was the supreme commander of US forces in Europe and Asia during the war, in 1947 he championed the Marshall Plan as head of the State Department, in 1949 he became president of the American Red Cross, always very important to US civilian (post-)war management, in 1950 he was US Secretary of Defense and, in practical terms, head of NATO.

A precursor of the European Union

The driving motive of the Marshall Plan - 1948 to 1952 - was not the much-vaunted "aid" for destroyed Europe, because, for one thing, only capitalist Western Europe was meant, not the Soviet Union which had suffered the most destruction. Above all, (Western) Europe was to be molded as a prosperous sales market for US products. This included the following objectives, which were to be implemented in all 16 beneficiary states in as similar a manner as possible, and which proved to be an important model for the European Union:

1. Single currency area and currency stabilization, with reliable exchange rates in relation to the dollar (payment and monetary union);
2. Uniform trade provisions (single market, customs union),
3. Uniform regulations for lending and investment,
4. Safeguarding of capitalist private property: no nationalization!

The BIS, headed by Wall Street banker McKittrick during the war, now took over the monetary and financial responsibilities of the Marshall Plan.[94] For example, in order to protect US corporations, oil processing in the recipient countries was stopped and taken over by US corporate subsidiaries. US shipping companies had to be given preference for the maritime transatlantic transport of goods. The focus was on the production and export of goods of which the USA had a shortage. In particular, export-geared companies were promoted. The Marshall Plan authorities - from their headquarters in Paris - used quotas to control exports and imports among the recipient countries and also in relation to the United States. As a result, imports and exports between the US and the European recipient countries rose sharply. The colonies of the Western Europeans at that time were also included. For example, chrome mining in the British colony of Rhodesia (Africa) and uranium mining in the Belgian Congo were promoted.[95]

Exclusion of socialist parties and states

To receive Marshall aid, recipients also had to perform an anti-communist cleansing of the political, party and trade union systems. No communist - and not even the bourgeois Charles de Gaulle - was allowed to become a member of the government. Socialists and social democrats were allowed to participate in government only if they were also anti-communist. This was often achieved through CIA infiltration and bribery.

Socialist or people's democratic states neither wanted nor were able to join the Marshall set-up. The USA had planned this from the outset. It excluded the Soviet Union as early as 1944 when the International Monetary Fund (IMF) and the World Bank were founded.

Opening for the Marshall Plan: US war in Greece
When deemed necessary, the US instrumentalized and intensified civil wars, not only in Asia, such as in China, Vietnam and Korea. These then turned out differently than would have been the case given the balance of power in the country itself. 300 agents of the then US Secret Service (OSS), 450 US military advisors, and 1,200 US economic advisors were brought together in 1947 as the American Mission for Aid to Greece (A-MAG). They supported nationalist and monarchist militaries in Greece (some of which had cooperated with the Nazi occupiers) with money, dive bombers, and napalm bombs. Wealthy Greek business families, including shipowners like Aristotle Onassis, were given US ships cheaply and a-warded transportation contracts. The colonial power Great Britain, unable to defeat the anti-fascist resistance, ceded the field to the new super-power.96

Thus, in the middle of "peacetime", the anti-fascist liberation movement of Greece was destroyed economically, militarily and in intelligence terms. The USA waged the "Cold War" as a hot war if necessary, even in the middle of Europe. The US consolidated the monarchy in Greece, discredited by its Nazi complicity, and installed a puppet government under Prime Minister Alexandros Patagos, a nationalist civil war general. Between 1948 and 1952, tens of thousands of communists and leftists were imprisoned, and over 1,500 executed.[97] Then the Marshall Plan money started flowing as well.

Location Benelux: On the road to the EU
The Marshall Plan focused on four groups of countries. 1. The UK and France received the most. 2. Then came the FRG and Italy. 3. Turkey and Greece. Under the Truman Doctrine of March 12, 1947, Turkey and Greece were seen as being threatened by the Soviet Union. 4. The largest per capita share of aid went to the small monarchical states of Luxembourg, the Netherlands and Belgium (Benelux). They were small, power-

less, only half democracies, suitable as courteous vassals. They had offered no military resistance to the German army – despite or rather because of this, Belgium and the Netherlands were upgraded to occupying powers in post-war Germany for the benefit of the USA and were allowed to let their troops sit around pointlessly in a united Germany until the 2000s.

The first Western European institutions were established in Luxembourg and Belgium (European Coal and Steel Community - ECSC, European Atomic Energy Community, European Commission, European Parliament, Courts of Justice), plus later the US-led international financial institutions such as Clearstream (transnational financial transfers between banks and companies) and SWIFT (transnational cash payments), and last but not least NATO. This has remained the case to this day.

Surge in US investment

The Marshall Plan triggered a wave of US investment far beyond the scope of the planned aid: While US investment between 1950 and 1970 increased threefold in Latin America, fivefold in Asia (including Japan), and sixfold in the traditional neighboring market of Canada, it increased fourteenfold in Western Europe.[98]

In the EEC Treaty (1957, Article 70), it was then stated: "For the movement of capital between the Member States and third countries... the highest degree of liberalization" shall be aimed at. Customs duties were abolished even more rapidly, and the cross-border movement of services, people and capital was simplified.

As a result, US investors shifted their previous focus away from the UK, which was not part of the EEC, to the EEC founding states. Thus, the US became the most important foreign owner of companies in the Federal Republic as well, in the areas where the US led anyway: automobiles, petroleum, electronics, agricultural and office machinery, pharmaceuticals, and food.

US corporations mostly invested in several EEC countries simultaneously: General Motors, Ford, DuPont, Esso, Mobil Oil and Standard Oil, Caterpillar, 3M (industrial holding company in health, safety, food), Goodyear, General Electric, Standard Electric, National Cash Register, IBM, Hewlett Packard, Monsanto, Texaco, National Carbide, John Deere and International Harvester, Kodak, Woolworth, Maizena, Singer, Libby,

ITT, Firestone.[99] The Wall Street banks now also arrived, first and foremost Rockefeller's Chase Manhattan, Morgan Guaranty Trust, Citibank and JPMorgan.[100] This represented a doubling of the pre-war level.

Focus on the Benelux countries

In per capita terms, however, the Benelux countries were streets ahead, and among the three states, Luxembourg in turn was way out front.

After the war, the *Netherlands* offered particularly low wages and an extremely favorable location for raw material procurement by sea and onward transportation. Dutch cities and municipalities granted US companies hefty tax perks.[101]

In *Belgium* the government set up an office to attract investors from the USA. Caterpillar, General Motors, Ford, Monsanto, Texaco, Philipps Petroleum, National Distillers und Union Carbide came. Investment was concentrated in Flanders because unions there were "more conservative" than in French-speaking Wallonia, where there was more strike activity - something "American investors were particularly sensitive about."[102] Thus, the domestic government and US companies reinforced the division of the Belgian regions.

The 51st US State: Grand Duchy of Luxembourg

In *Luxembourg*, the ratio of US investment per capita was 10 times the EEC average. Several factors came together here: Since the end of the First World War, the Grand Duchy had developed its location as a financial oasis; here, following the example of Switzerland and the Principality of Liechtenstein, foreign companies could set up shell companies.

Goodyear, DuPont, Monsanto and Continental Fertilizer were granted favorable terms for investment.[103] Bankers Trust settled in Luxembourg. Covert financial operations of the Marshall Plan - in addition to the BIS in Basel - were handled through Luxembourg. No head of state visited a Western European country as often as Dwight Eisenhower, US president from 1953 to 1961, was in Luxembourg. Later, leading US Republicans such as Henry Kissinger, Caspar Weinberger, and George Bush Sr. all visited the country.[104]

Springboard for US banks

US banks such as Wells Fargo, Bank of America, Bank of Boston and Overseas Development Bank established branches in the small Grand

Duchy. In 1970, Wall Street founded the clearing institution Cedel (Centrale de Livraison des Valeurs Mobilières – clearing house for securities) here: This was the first center for timely transnational stock and securities transactions.

All the major banks and corporations in the US sphere of influence were involved in Cedel, including those from Switzerland, London, and the Federal Republic of Germany. Branch offices were gradually established in London, Tokyo, Hong Kong, Dubai, Frankfurt and Sao Paulo. Secret to illegal business was also conducted here, bribes for major projects, party donations for the German FDP, for example, funds from the Vatican and the fascist Italian Lodge P2. Most significant financially and politically, however, were US defense contractors such as Lockheed, Raytheon, and Northrop, which sought representation in Luxembourg for their sales to Gulf sheikdoms and other less prestigious US allies. In 1981 US President Ronald Reagan organized the ransom for US hostages in Iran through Cedel. Cedel was renamed Clearstream in 1999 and is now owned by Deutsche Börse and thus BlackRock & Co. The largest US management consultants, such as Arthur Andersen, set up large branches here; later, PwC and others did the same - leading to the "Luxembourg Leaks"[2] in 2014.[105]

Jean-Claude Juncker, later Luxembourg's finance minister and prime minister from the Christian Social People's Party, i.e. the representative of a tautologous populism, subsequently became president of the European Commission. He thus finally elevated Luxembourg's toadyism toward the US to the pan-European level. For instance, he refused to have the tax evasion of corporations organized by PwC via Luxembourg at the expense of the EU states investigated or, banish the thought, banned; in 2019, he concluded an agreement with US President Trump on the increased purchase of US liquefied natural gas, which was not only designed against strategic European interests, but was also environmentally harmful on several counts. Hence, since 1949, the small, secretive Grand Duchy of

---

[2] With its branch in Luxembourg, the 'auditing' group Pricewaterhouse Coopers, preferred advisor of the European Commission, had helped 300 companies, mainly from the USA, notch up "tax deals" up to zero tax. The two whistleblowers who uncovered this were convicted in Luxembourg.

Luxembourg, the central founding state of the EU, has been considered the 51st state of the United States.[106]

Single market and competition between states
Thus, US investors took advantage of the unification of the market that began with the EEC. But the EEC conferred only minor sovereign rights to the European Commission – under pressure from the USA.[107]

The Benelux countries granted the highest tax perks and other subsidies. The exact extent of the benefits could not be determined at the time because the EEC did not record them and the US attached importance to non-transparency: they preferred bilateral double taxation agreements that were not submitted to the respective parliaments.[108]

Some US company management boards complied with European labor and union laws, some did not. As a result, disputes over layoffs (for example, in the case of restructuring after company acquisitions), cuts in wages, social benefits and work breaks were much more frequent than in purely European corporations at the time.[109]

EC and EU: The extended "globalization"
The US and the capitalists in core Europe it protected bided their time. They gradually shored up their power, let Nazi collaboration be forgotten. It was not until the early 1970s that new members were admitted to the EEC - subsequently renamed the European Community (EC), and ultimately the European Union (EU): Denmark and the UK in 1973, the poorer southern European states of Greece, Spain and Portugal in the 1980s, then Finland, Austria and Sweden in the mid-1990s.

The three Baltic states and Poland, Slovakia, Slovenia, the Czech Republic and the meanwhile important financial havens Malta and Cyprus did not follow until 2004, then the poorest states Romania and Bulgaria, and finally Croatia (2014). At the same time, loose forms of association were developed, on the one hand to sweeten up new aspirant states, to discipline them, even to exploit them and, for example, to siphon off migrant workers, but not least to instrumentalize them militarily. This applies to varying degrees to Serbia, Bosnia and Herzegovina, Ukraine, Kosovo, North Macedonia, Albania and Montenegro.

1980s: European companies step up investment in the US
Starting in the 1980s, companies from Western Europe stepped up investment in the United States. The superpower was considered "economically" successful even though, or rather because, the working poor had established themselves as a permanent systemic phenomenon during this period: A growing share of the dependent workforce, and not only the black but also the white population, remained poor despite work: Wages and social security had been lowered, and trade unions were already severely weakened, unlike in Western Europe.[110] In particular, all European - as well as Japanese - car companies, and also the pharmaceutical companies set up production plants. All major banks in Western Europe established branches in New York.

This was repeated after the financial crisis of 2007. Western European companies again accelerated their investments in the USA. Pharmaceutical groups such as Novartis, Bayer and BASF, automotive groups such as BMW, VW and Daimler, the technology groups Siemens and ThyssenKrupp, automotive suppliers such as Continental, Deutsche Telekom and now 3,500 German SMEs are in some cases notching up higher sales and profits in the USA than in Germany itself. In the US, they also donate to the two pro-capitalist parties that take turns in government. But in 2016, while the high and mighty in the EU along with the German government were still sticking to the Democrats and their presidential candidate Hillary Clinton, German, English and Swiss corporations swung their campaign donations to the nationalist class warrior, the oaf Donald Trump.[111]

Increased US dominance, Americanization of labor conditions
Despite increased investment by Western European corporations in the US, US dominance in the EU has not only been maintained, but has been expanded further since the beginning of the 21st century.

Wall Street investment banks such as JPMorgan and Goldman Sachs, partly brokered via the European Commission, were used from the mid-1980s onward for the privatization of major state-owned enterprises such as the postal service, railroads, media, and their IPOs, first in Great Britain by the Tory governments from Thatcher to Major, then also in Spain and Italy, for example, and by the German government led by Chancellor

Kohl. In 1990, Kohl brought them into the Treuhandanstalt as key advisors to sell the ex-GDR's businesses to Western investors.[112]

At the beginning of the 21st century, with the program "Unbundling of Deutschland AG", the German government of SPD and Greens under Chancellor Gerhard Schröder promoted the purchase of German medium-sized companies and public housing stocks by private equity investors ("locusts") such as Blackstone, KKR, Carlyle, Texas Pacific Group, Fortress, Cerberus. By 2019, they had bought and disposed of around 10,000 well-performing, unlisted SMEs in Germany alone. After the incursion in Germany, a similar process was also seen in the other EU countries.

With the financial and economic crisis of 2007, the bigger capital organizers of the premier league then joined in: BlackRock, State Street, Vanguard & Co. They are now the major shareholders of the most important 500 or so stock corporations in Germany - including the largest five new housing groups. To a lesser extent, this is now also the case in France, Italy, Spain and also Switzerland.

With the new investors, who now also own the formerly powerful banks, the "civilian private army of transatlantic capital" - from the US the rating and PR agencies, management consultants, business law firms, 'auditors', union busters - has also established itself in the EU, in Brussels and in the capitals of the important EU Member States as a permanent assistant to the governments.[113]

This has also served to "Americanize" working conditions in the EU: The regulated full-time and lifelong workplace is being replaced by the highly flexible US-style "job". (see page 184ff.)

United States as Regulatory Power II: NATO
What was later called the "Cold War", already began during World War II: The Soviet Union (again) went from being a military ally to an enemy of the system. One trigger was the unforeseen victory of the Red Army over the Wehrmacht in the decisive Battle of Stalingrad in 1943.

NATO: The founding lie
In the run-up to NATO's formation, US leaders knew: the Soviet Union posed no military threat. Even if it wanted to, the weakened power could not sustain an attack on Western Europe: The Soviet Union's economy is too weak; its transportation system too primitive; its underdeveloped oil

industry far too easy to attack. The men in the Kremlin were clever tyrants, judged the chief planner in the State Department, George Kennan, who would not risk their domestic power with military adventures abroad. "They want to win the battle for Germany and Europe, but not through military action." From 1948 onward, Kennan recorded all this repeatedly in various memoranda for Secretary of State Marshall, for President Truman, and for US ambassadors.[114]

USA: Push 'defense' line forward to Europe
In March 1943 Walter Lippmann, the father of neoliberalism, wrote: Having conquered North America, Central America, the Caribbean, the Philippines, and several islands in the Pacific (Wake Islands, Guam, Hawaii, Japanese mandate islands), the US has so far been forced to "defend two-thirds of the earth's surface from our continental base in North America". Now, however, with the foreseeable defeat of the Axis powers Germany, Japan, Italy and their allies and collaborators, much more intensive access from new locations was opening up.

The US can no longer "defend" its conquered territories from its North American territory and scattered islands in the Pacific alone, according to the geostrategist. From Europe, the US could move to "active defense" of its national interests.[115]

Thus, the intensified military expansion was now being passed off as "defense". From 1776, since its founding, the US literally had a War Department: Through wars - if necessary with genocide - the North American continent, Central America, the Caribbean, Cuba, the Philippines, Puerto Rico, Hawaii, etc. were conquered. But precisely at the peak of its military expansion to date, the War Department was renamed Defense Department in 1947.

NATO: Twin of the Marshall Plan
From 1947, all subsequent founding members of NATO received aid from the Marshall Plan: Even Turkey, which suffered no war destruction at all. In some cases, Marshall Plan aid was reallocated for military purposes.[116] On April 4, 1949 - a few weeks before the founding of the Federal Republic of Germany - the military alliance North Atlantic Treaty Organization, NATO, was founded in Washington. It was passed off as a "defense" alliance, in line with US language protocol. All other members were dependent on the US, not only through the Marshall Plan, but also through addi-

tional loans, military aid, and investments. Until 1952, NATO's headquarters were in Washington.

NATO was the twin of the Marshall Plan. The military-civilian dual character was embodied, as already mentioned, by George Marshall: first foreign minister, then 'defense' minister and de facto NATO chief. In 1950, he organized brutal interventions, including napalm bombings, against liberation movements around the globe, in Korea as well as in Greece.

War against liberation movements in the European colonies
NATO's founding members were majority Christian-racist colonial powers, much as the US itself, but the latter embodying the more modern variety. It supported the wars waged by the European colonial powers against the liberation movements in the colonies, which had gained strength after World War II. The colonial powers there promoted the exploitation of the local workers to the point of slave-like conditions.

United Kingdom
The US took over the military suppression in Greece from the British. At the same time, they financed three-quarters of the cost of the British occupation forces in West Germany, so that - like France - Britain could also appear as a seemingly powerful occupying power.[117]

During the war, Great Britain had ceded several military bases in the Commonwealth to the United States. At the time of NATO's formation, the Labour-led government was also fighting the liberation movement in Ghana in the African colonies, calling the leader of the Convention People's Party, Kwane Nkrumah, a "little local Hitler" and putting him in prison in 1950. It was not until 1957 that Ghana was able to become independent with Nkrumah, but he was overthrown in 1966 with the help of the CIA.[118]

France, Belgium, Netherlands
The World Bank under Wall Street lawyer John McCloy granted a loan to France even before the Marshall Plan, on the condition: De Gaulle and the Communists must not switch from the provisional government to the regular government! US Secretary of State Byrnes, Marshall's predecessor, promised a 650 million loan and the additional supply of 500,000 tons of coal.[119] The US rearmed three French divisions in 1948 so that France

could act as a serious occupying power in its occupied territory in West Germany.[120]

From May 1945 until independence in 1962, the French military killed hundreds of thousands of independence fighters and civilians in the annexed colony of Algeria. A racist apartheid system prevailed there. But Algeria immediately became NATO-covered territory. At the same time, the French government demanded military aid against "communism" for its colony Indochina: The Democratic Republic of Vietnam proclaimed in September 1945 by the Viet Minh independence movement under Ho Chi Minh was to be destroyed - the US helped with military advisors, food and arms.[121] McCloy, as president of the World Bank, also approved a loan for this purpose in 1949, the year NATO was founded.[122]

Similar things happened in the colonies of Belgium (Congo) and the Netherlands (Indonesia). Hundreds of thousands of natives were murdered.[123]

Denmark

In Denmark, after the Nazi period, a government was formed that included the Communist Party. With the help of social democracy and the Marshall Plan, the original plan for non-alignment was banished. The Danish colony of Greenland, where the US had established military bases as early as 1941, was declared a NATO defense area in 1951. The US military base at Thule was, and has been ever since, expanded to explore the Arctic and spy on the Soviet Union and then Russia. Although Greenland is now "independent", its foreign and security policy remains under the wing of the particularly loyal NATO member Denmark. For this reason, the Danish government, due not least to US intervention, has prevented the Greenlandic government, from developing economically with the help of China (substituting for the declining importance of fishing).[124]

Norway

In Norway, the Social Democratic government, which had an absolute majority, wanted to remain non-aligned after the German occupation. But with the help of the Marshall Plan and additional rearmament aid, the US maneuvered Norway, like Denmark, into NATO.

Federal Republic of Germany
In 1950, shortly after the founding of the separate state of the Federal
Republic of Germany (FRG), its chancellor Adenauer promised the USA
rearmament (secretly). As early as 1950, the US was already promoting
FRG arms production for the needs of the war against the People's Liberation Movement in Korea. The majority of West German arms industrialists were in favor of NATO. In September 1950, NATO included the FRG
in the NATO defense area - five years before the Bundestag formally decided to join NATO.[125]

Spain and Portugal
Franco's fascist dictatorship was a good premise to include Spain in the
anti-communist 'defense' alliance. Although formal NATO membership
was initially postponed for cosmetic reasons, the United States provided
economic support and expanded military bases. Spain and Portugal
formed a "special bulwark" for the United States in postwar Europe, according to the US ambassador who resided in Madrid until 1945.[126]

The US returned the Asian colonies of Timor and Macau, which had
been occupied by Japan, to the colonial power Portugal.[127] The US and
NATO could now use Portugal's Atlantic islands, the Azores, as military
bases.

US economic incursion in the European colonies
Not only militarily and in terms of intelligence, but also economically, the
USA infiltrated the colonies of the Europeans. The Marshall Plan headquarters in Paris maintained the "Strategic Commodities" division. It re-
connoitered and inventoried in the colonies of the European colonial powers, for example, manganese and graphite in Madagascar; lead, cobalt, and
manganese in Morocco; cobalt, uranium, and cadmium in the Congo; tin
in Cameroon; chromium and nickel in New Caledonia; rubber in Indochina; oil in Indonesia;[128] besides industrial diamonds, asbestos, beryllium,
tantalite, and columbite.[129]

1990: No peace treaty for Europe
The victory over socialism was only an intermediate step towards the
aspired position of the USA as the "sole world power" (according to the

US strategist and geopolitician Zbigniew Brzeziński).[3] The goal was not only the domination of Western Europe from Lisbon to Berlin with the help of the EU, but the domination of all of Eurasia from Lisbon to Vladivostok. The Eurasian landmass, its strategic position and resources, proved to be an even more urgent object of capitalist desire for the US since the People's Republic of China emerged as the most successful economy and increasingly cooperated with Russia.

That is why the USA and the obedient EU refused to sign a peace treaty for Europe even after 1990. The war guilt and the war debts of Nazi Germany remained unpunished and forgotten as well as the collaboration of the German and Western European industrial and financial elite and of US corporations with Nazi Germany.

Thus, Germany was spared the regulations covering war reparations, which had been repeatedly postponed for 45 years with reference to a peace treaty yet to come. In the 2+4 treaty between the FRG and the already dying GDR on the one hand and the four military powers USA, France, Great Britain and the also already dying Soviet Union on the other hand, neither international law nor universal human rights were installed in 1990.

The 2+4 Treaty was an international treaty and was called the "Treaty on the Final Settlement with Respect to Germany". It authorized the reunification of Germany. All previous restrictions on Berlin and Germany by the four occupying powers were lifted. Germany was finally to be a sovereign state.

The treaty was not referred to as a "peace treaty" in the text of the treaty itself, but was nevertheless portrayed as such in the populist presentation, although it isn't. This is shown, for example, by the fact that only "East Germany", i.e. the former GDR, was defined as a nuclear-weapon-free zone. So West Germany was not supposed to be a nuclear-free zone. Why, actually? Because the treaty said: Germany renounces nuclear, biological and chemical weapons finally and forever! So where do the nucle-

---

[3] The Polish-born Brzeziński advised US presidents from Nixon to Reagan to George Bush on Eastern European policy. German Foreign Minister Hans-Dietrich Genscher wrote an extremely laudatory foreword to Brzeziński's German edition: Die einzige Weltmacht. Amerikas Strategie der Vorherrschaft, Weinheim 1997.

ar weapons come from, which nevertheless continue to be stationed in West Germany?

Forced labor – was that a thing?
Universal human rights do not apply either. They prohibit forced labor. The millionfold forced labor practiced in occupied Europe and especially in Germany by German and US companies was not even mentioned in the 2+4 Treaty, let alone compensated or punished or banned for the future. The Coal and Steel Community, the EEC and the EU never addressed the various forms of forced labor either, including that of Jewish concentration camp prisoners.

The UN Social Covenant from the 1960s with labor and social rights, which had been ratified by France and Great Britain and the Federal Republic, was also not included. The 2+4 Treaty made peace with the capitalists, but not with the dependent workers, neither for the past nor for the future.

In convoy: Eastern Enlargement of EU and NATO
NATO was and is an alliance that, under US leadership, from the start violates the UN Charter, Article 1 "Self-Determination of Nations", in principle and permanently.[130]

Today, the EU is obediently following the call imposed under President Barack Obama to increase the 'defense' spending of its Member States to two percent of economic output. Even the boorishness of Obama's successor Donald Trump, repeatedly criticized by EU representatives, did not prevent the governments of the EU states from fulfilling this call.

The "greater independence" from the USA demanded by the French and German heads of government Macron and Merkel is not accompanied by a peace policy in conformity with international law, but by increased claims to their own world power status: The former German 'defense' minister von der Leyen, who was boxed through as the new president of the European Commission in 2019, stands out prominently here. The increased military spending of the European NATO countries merely serves to take pressure off the USA, which since Obama has been pivoting towards Asia, against the new enemy number one, China.

"More European independence"?
The US continues to maintain its own military bases in numerous EU and NATO countries, including the Baltic States, Italy, Denmark, Spain, Belgium, the Netherlands, Bulgaria, Poland, Bosnia-Herzegovina, and above all in the most powerful state, Germany. And the US is building new military bases like the one in Ulm (for the deployment against Russia) and expanding them technologically. From here, in contravention of the German Basic Law and international law, worldwide military operations and drone assassinations continue to be carried out, for example from Ramstein/Rhineland-Palatinate and from AFRICOM/Stuttgart. The German Parliament's Academic Service has identified about two dozen US military bases in Germany, but admits that the exact number cannot be determined because the US side does not respond to questions.[131]

The EU concurs with the expanded deployments, maneuvers, and stationing of US military, particularly in the Baltics, Poland, and Ukraine. The EU raises no objection to the establishment of an "Eastern NATO" undermining EU unity, with reactionary and nationalist anti-Russian Poland at its core. The Eurasian region including the Arctic is finally to be conquered and economically developed - if necessary again with war, and this time also (again) with nuclear bombs.[132]

Global political conspiracy theory
Nor does the new "European Defense Union" (PESCO, Permanent Structured Cooperation) - a new edition of a concept developed as early as the 1950s - represent any competition to NATO.[133]

In the declaration on the 70th founding year of NATO in December 2019, Trump, Macron, Merkel, von der Leyen, etc. agreed that, in addition to terrorism and Russia, China is now part of the new threat. On the great global political conspiracy theory, there is agreement.

Conquer Russia at last
In Kosovo, the US maintains Camp Bondsteel - named after a highly decorated Vietnam veteran - its second-largest military base outside its own territory, after Ramstein/Pfalz. The region had been seceded from Serbia by the USA together with the EU in violation of international law. The fact that the government is corrupt, that its president is accused of the most serious war crimes before the special international tribunal on Kosovo in The Hague, and that the majority of the population is poor does not

bother them. Russia is to be conquered, regardless of whether it is run communistically or capitalistically with Putin - that has been the core of NATO from the beginning.

The NATO edifice of lies, nurtured for decades, is more fragile than ever. Today's Russia is militarily incomparably weaker - at least in terms of offensive potential, not in terms of defensive capability - than the former Soviet Union and compared with today's even more highly upgraded NATO. All the more intense is the fake fabrication about the alleged "Russian danger" and the "evil Putin".

Poor EU states with the highest military spending
When it comes to military spending, the poorest EU states are at the forefront.

State	Military spending as percent of GDP:
USA	3.42 percent
Greece	2.24
Estonia	2.13
UK	2.13
Romania	2.04
Latvia	2.01
Poland	2.01
Lithuania	1.98[134]

US harms its EU vassals
The IMF under Christine Lagarde granted loans to over-indebted Ukraine that, measured against the same criteria, were denied to Greece.[135]

The US-imposed boycott of Russia is harming the German economy, for example through the loss of 60,000 jobs at German companies and suppliers in Ukraine. German companies initially protested, but then backed down. The German vassal accepts the damage - albeit not so much at the expense of shareholders, but of dependent employees, both in Ukraine and in Germany.[136]

Nationalism, ethno-politics
The USA and NATO not only waged a military war against Yugoslavia. They promoted nationalist, ethnic and religious fundamentalist, right-wing

and post-fascist movements, individuals and parties in this previously multi-ethnic state. In Poland and Croatia, this also includes the Catholic Church. In doing so, the US-led West, beginning in 1990, also drew on traditions of anti-Semitic, monarchist, and nationalist forces that had co-operated with the Nazi Wehrmacht and the fascist occupation forces of Italy during World War II.[137] Anti-communist exiles, who had fled to the anti-communist West after their defeat in 1945, were brought back from the Federal Republic of Germany, USA, Canada, Australia.

This was professionally promoted with the help of Western PR agencies, especially from the USA, such as Hunton & Williams, Patton Boggs, Global Enterprises Group, Rudder Finn, Waterman Associates, White & Case, The Washington International Group, Burson Marsteller, Van Kloberg Associates, Herzfeld & Rubin:[138] Nationalism, racism, fake production on the highest professional level!

Thus, Yugoslavia was broken up into several small states, whose wars against each other were promoted with agitation, advice, weapons, and intelligence and Catholic Church assistance from the West. The symbolic figure of the Polish-born Pope Karl Woytyla stands for the old and new ecclesiastical connections - to no other state did he make so many official visits as to the small Catholic-nationalist and ethnically cleansed reborn state of Croatia. (see page 206).

The new nationalist mini-states continue their non-military conflicts and rivalries under the umbrella of the EU and NATO, which can thus exercise their supremacy all the more easily. The "globalizers" and propagandists of a "united Europe" prefer and rule best with the help of nationalist mini-states.

3.
The seeds of the EU:
Coal and Steel Community, EEC, Euratom

The EU was primed over many years within the narrow framework of six founding states. Economically, the Federal Republic, the detached state founded by the US, and France, weakened in the war and amenable to US aid, dominated; politically, the Benelux countries played the leading role. It began in 1951 with the European Coal and Steel Community (ECSC).

Before and during the Second World War: Western European cartels
The Western European coal and steel industry had already begun to form cartels in 1926, regulating trade with quotas and prices. Ruhr companies acquired shares in companies in Luxembourg and France, for example, and vice versa. The Luxembourg steel group ARBED had subsidiaries in the Ruhr area, and the Dutch industrialist Fentener von Vlissingen had shares in the largest German steel group, Vereinigte Stahlwerke.

Western European cartel builds the Maginot Line
A highly symbolic cartel project - beyond political-national borders and enmities - was the 1,000 kilometers of France's elaborate Maginot defense line with bunkers, rail systems and guns: This was a joint production of the cartel. Construction had begun in 1930, continued during Hitler's regime after 1933, until 1940. The corporations were already demonstrating that they could work for friend and foe at the same time.

European economic integration under German occupation
During the German occupation of Western Europe, the state *"Reichsgruppen"* of German industry, organized by sector, took over the Europe-wide coordination of, for example, coal mining and steel production.[139] The *Reichsgruppen* and German companies from other sectors were part of the military administration in Paris, Brussels, Luxembourg, Amsterdam, Oslo etc. They turned the companies of the occupied states into junior partners, awarded them contracts, acquired additional shares. During the war, for example, Vereinigte Stahlwerke acquired a majority stake in Vlissingen's Dutch steel group Hoogovens. Rheinmetall acquired shares in the Dutch train equipment manufacturer Werkspoor.[140]

German companies placed orders according to the needs of German war production: Renault and Citroën, for example, produced tank plates and aircraft parts for the Wehrmacht. The German steel trading group Otto Wolff placed orders with a French steel company to supply barbed wire for the Dachau concentration camp.[141] The companies in the occupied states were paid market rates for this and were also able to make additional profits through Aryanization. Wage freezes were agreed, tariffs were lifted. The French collaborationist government in Vichy under Marshal Pétain supplied forced laborers to Germany and deported Jews to extermination camps.[142]

The Nazi program was called "European Economic Integration" or "New Order in Europe". For this purpose, the Ministry of Economics had a "New Order" planning division, similarly Göring's Four-Year Plan. In 1942, the Minister of Economics and Labor of the Vichy government, Jean Bichelonne, described the German *Reichsgruppen* as exemplary for the new, state-organized capitalism, now also on the European level.[143]

Transatlantic economic integration before and during the war

"European economic integration" also already had a transatlantic dimension. With the international market division, for example, in the IG Farben cartel with DuPont and Standard Oil and, since 1931, with the simultaneous share ownership in the Cologne Ford branch, divided between IG Farben and Ford headquarters in Detroit - even during the war - US corporations were involved.

Thus, at Ford Cologne truck production for the Wehrmacht peaked between 1939 and 1944. Edsel Ford remained a member of the Supervisory Board until his death in 1943. US ownership was retained, and profits were paid out to the US after the war. From Cologne, the Ford board-controlled production at Ford's European sites for the Wehrmacht in occupied France (Poissy), Amsterdam, Antwerp, and Copenhagen. Suppliers to the German Wehrmacht also included General Motors (owner of Opel: "Opel-Blitz" light trucks for the Russia campaign), General Electric, Standard Oil, Raytheon etc.[144]

European Coal and Steel Community

In the European Coal and Steel Community (ECSC), the prior (Western) European cooperation was continued and modernized after the war - now, however, superimposed by the victorious power, the USA.

Before the new institution became the object of political-state discussion, the corporations negotiated among themselves, under the supervision of Western intelligence agencies. At the military tribunal in Nuremberg (1946-49), the Nazi collaborators from France, Italy, the United States, and the Benelux countries were not indicted; as witnesses, they attested to the German corporations' "good behavior", for instance the representatives of the Belgian foundries in the trial of Flick manager Otto Steinbrinck, who was charged with "plundering the occupied territories".[145]

The Cologne banker Robert Pferdmenges of the Sal. Oppenheim bank was chairman of the supervisory board of Thyssen-Hütte. In 1947, he offered the French steel groups, represented by the industrialist Humbert de Wendel, a larger stake in the Ruhr corporations. As a CDU member of the Bundestag, Pferdmenges was in close contact with banks and corporations from the United States; he had them confirm the guiding principle: The shareholders' power of disposition must be safeguarded![146] General Manager Hermann Reusch of Gutehoffnungshütte also negotiated with the French steel syndicate, with the participation of Alois Meyer, head of ARBED in Luxembourg. Group delegations traveled back and forth between the countries.[147]

The US High Commissioner for the Federal Republic, the Wall Street banker John McCloy, gave the assurance: With the Coal and Steel Community, the owners of the Ruhr corporations will not be nationalized! They had been essential pillars of the Nazi system. This included a guarantee that they could keep their war profits and that public demands for trust busting, nationalization and punishment of owners and managers would be ignored. In this way, the newly founded and internationally still ostracized detached state FRG was also supposed to be able to return to the "community of nations".[148]

The French side hesitated. It had pushed through the establishment of an International Ruhr Authority so that the German groups would be controlled and downgraded. But the US forced France to give up its hoped-for privileges from the Allied victorious position. Secretary of State Dean

Acheson issued an ultimatum to the French government in 1950, and it buckled.[149] McCloy, simultaneously head of the Western High Commissioners, also brought his colleagues from Great Britain and France into line.[150]

US banker as "founding father of Europe": Jean Monnet

A banker without a ministerial post drew up the definitive plan for the new cartel: Jean Monnet. He was a "born behind-the-scenes string-puller" who used "indirect methods".[151] He is considered the "founding father of Europe", or the European Union, to this day.

Western European-American arms coordination

Monnet, born in 1888 in Cognac/France, initially sold Cognac all over the world as an entrepreneur with the Martell and Hennessy brands. On the Reparations Commission of the League of Nations, founded in 1919, and as its deputy secretary-general from 1920 to 1923, he befriended John F. Dulles, a Wall Street lawyer who was also active there and who was close to the government. This is how he found his start as an entrepreneur and banker in the USA. He made juicy profits here as an alcohol trader during Prohibition, which unintentionally promoted illegal trade between 1920 and 1933. His Hudson Bay Company also sold alcohol to Indians. With the profits, Monnet founded the bank Bancamerica in San Francisco in 1929.[152] At the same time he represented the US Federal Reserve at the Banque de France, France's central bank.

In the 1930s, together with the London-New York investment bank Lazard, he financed railroads for the feudal capitalist government of General Chiang Kaishek in China, who was also supported by the US government, Mussolini, and Hitler: In addition to generals from the US Army, Hitler's Wehrmacht - von Seeckt and von Falkenhausen - served as military and industrial advisors; IG Farben, Heinkel, Rheinmetall, Messerschmidt, and Krupp rearmed Tschiang's army just as US arms companies did.[153] In 1935, Monnet founded the Monnet Murnane bank with Dulles in New York: the whole world became Monnet's business territory.

He was a merciless opportunist. When he wanted to divorce his first, Catholic marriage and this was not possible in France, he let his second wife take Soviet citizenship - not without promising the hard-pressed Soviets economic connections in the USA - and married as a dyed-in-the-wool anti-communist under the atheistic law of the Soviet Union.[154]

In 1938, Monnet organized US loans so that France could buy US fighter planes and modernize its own aircraft industry. In 1939, he initiated a Franco-British commission to procure arms for the foreseeable war against Germany, primarily in the United States. On behalf of the British government under Winston Churchill, he coordinated British borrowing and arms purchases in the US from 1940 to 1943 in the Roosevelt administration.

Monnet: De Gaulle "must be destroyed!"

In 1943, as Roosevelt's high commissioner for the French colonies of North Africa - Algeria, Tunisia, Morocco - Monnet organized the integration of the French military stationed there, which had submitted to the collaborationist regime in Vichy, under the fascist and anti-Semitic General Henri Giraud, into the invading British and US military.[155]

Monnet needed this in public as proof of his anti-Hitler stance, but hated de Gaulle because of his concept of French national sovereignty. Moreover, Monnet's formal support of de Gaulle avoided upgrading the even stronger and more popular Résistance of the left. The future "founding father of Europe" showed his real attitude only covertly. From Algiers on May 6, 1943, he called on the US government: No understanding is possible with de Gaulle, he is an enemy of the "European construct" and "European reconstruction": he must therefore be "destroyed".[156]

With Roosevelt: Concept for European Economic Community

In 1943, when the victory of the Allies over Nazi Germany was foreseeable, Monnet conceived the "European Economic Community" on behalf of Roosevelt for the post-war period - in the context of the "Victory Program": US production, trade, and credit relations with Europe, developed during the war, were to be converted and expanded to peacetime terms and placed under US leadership. At the same time, the "United Europe" was to be only an economic community, i.e. not an independent *political* community. The core was to be formed by the Western European corporations in the coal, iron and steel sectors - including the German companies. The name: European Coal and Steel Community, ECSC.

Because of General de Gaulle's public reputation, the United States had to let him form a provisional government after the liberation of France in 1944, including ministers from the Resistance, among them Communists. But the US never recognized this government and prompted de

Gaulle's resignation as early as 1946. They placed Monnet in the new, "Christian"-led government as head of the newly created planning agency: He organized the "modernization" of the French economy, often with the help of US loans. Monnet retained this function until 1950, under changing governments.

Thus, Monnet became the most powerful man in France without holding a ministerial post. He was the liaison between the US government, Wall Street, the Marshall Plan authority in Paris, and the French government. He worked with the American Committee on United States of Europe (ACUE), founded in 1948 by future CIA chief Allen Dulles. In this role, which involved many links with US actors, Monnet had negotiated a USD 550 million loan with the United States for the modernization of the French steel industry even before the Marshall Plan. He was joined by Robert Nathan, the former head of planning for the Roosevelt administration's US War Production Board.[157]

Second "founding father of Europe": Robert Schuman
The German-Frenchman Robert Schuman, born in Luxembourg in 1886, was a member of the Catholic fraternity Unitas Salia as a student in Bonn - just like his Catholic German peer and friend Konrad Adenauer. Schuman also operated as a "Christian" politician throughout his life.

In 1913, for example, Schuman was the organizer of the German Catholic Day in Metz: the city had been turned into a Prussian administrative and fortress city after the conquest of Alsace-Lorraine in 1870/71. During the First World War Schuman served in the German Empire against France. A staunch Catholic, he became a minister in the pro-fascist collaborationist government of Vichy in 1940, but later put on airs as a resistance fighter.[158]

Like the other leading minds of the new Christian parties founded after World War II in Italy, Belgium, the Netherlands, Luxembourg and West Germany, Schuman was financed by the United States and supported by the Vatican. From 1946 to 1952, after de Gaulle's fall, the versatile chameleon was alternately finance and foreign minister and sometimes prime minister.

In 1950, he presented the "Schuman Plan" - of which he had not written a word himself - for the establishment of the ECSC. Lachrymosely, it said: The ECSC is the first step towards "a much broader and deeper community of peoples who have long suffered under bloody divisions".

However, the core of the ECSC was formed not by those who had suffered under the invoked "bloody divisions" but by those who had caused them: (West) German companies such as Thyssen-Hütte, Krupp, Mannesmann, Preussag, Salzgitter (= the former Hermann Göring factories), Klöckner, Hoesch, Saarstahl, Dillinger Hüttenwerke, Otto Wolff, Gutehoffnungshütte and diverse companies of the Flick corporation. From France, for example, the companies of the de Wendel and Schneider groups, such as Usinor and Sidelor, from Luxembourg ARBED, from the Netherlands Hoogovens, from Belgium Cockerill and Usines Gustave Boël were involved. In Italy, this industry was yet to be established. The scope also included the French colony of Algeria, which had been declared a NATO defense area shortly beforehand.

Super-bureaucracy with US fathers
Monnet became the first head of the Coal and Steel Community in 1952 as "High Commissioner". He was a personal friend of the US actors responsible for the reshaping of Europe. With Wall Street banker John McCloy, then High Commissioner to the Federal Republic and Treasurer of the ACUE, with banker and US Secretary of State Dean Acheson. He was in constant consultation with his former banker colleague and now US Secretary of State John Foster Dulles, and with the neoliberal chief ideologue and world's best-paid multi-talented journalist Walter Lippmann.[159] Thanks to his Wall Street connections, especially with the head of the investment bank Lazard, André Meyer, he was able to negotiate special loans for the ECSC, which were guaranteed by the US government.[160]

Adopted from the USA, the bureaucratic management structure under Monnet was called the High Authority. The job title "High Commissioner" was carried over from his position as High Commissioner to the US government in North Africa during the war. The terms encapsulate the authoritarian, anti-democratic self-perception.

Authoritarian structure, designed by US law firm
The High Authority and Monnet's position as High Commissioner did not come about through elections. Their immutable existence and structure were set in stone for 50 years. The governing officials were appointed for

six years, were paid more than the heads of government of the contracting states, enjoyed tax perks, exterritorial status, and were exempt from criminal investigation.

The founding treaty was not written by European politicians. Rather, it was drafted in outline by US banker Monnet, and the formulation was the responsibility of US law firm Cleary, Gottlieb, Friendly & Ball.[161] This was a commercial law firm that was close to the government as well as to banks and corporations. The co-owner was George W. Ball, a lawyer and banker, who from 1942 worked on the US lend lease program (supplying the Allies, especially Great Britain, with US goods), then became an advisor in the Marshall Plan, and finally Deputy US Secretary of State.

In 1949, it was the first US law firm to establish a branch in Europe after the war, in Paris to handle the Marshall Plan. With the growing importance of Brussels as the EU headquarters, the firm opened a branch there as well. Even today, the firm boasts that its founding partner Ball was "closely associated with Jean Monnet".[162]

Headquarters in the financial haven of Luxembourg

The authoritarian super-bureaucracy was based in the Grand Duchy of Luxembourg. The latter's ruling family had lived in North America during the war and had forged close ties with the Roosevelt administration. The mini-state, politically organized as a parliamentary monarchy, liberated by the US Army, which also laid the foundation for the private radio station Radio Luxembourg, which broadcasts throughout Europe, now continued to develop its function as a financial haven, which it had begun after the First World War.[163]

The ECSC was financed not only through Luxembourg, but through all the major financial havens of Western Europe at the time. The Coal and Steel Community received a USD 100 million loan from the federal US Export-Import Bank in 1954. It went to companies in the six participating countries. It was handled by the New York Wall Street banks Lazard and Kuhn Loeb and the Swiss bank Crédit Suisse through the enduring Bank for International Settlements in Basel (BIS).[164] Funds that did not go through the BIS went through Luxembourg.[165] The public was unaware of these covert channels.

In this manner, the companies were able to continue and expand, protected several times over by an unelected bureaucracy, by their headquar-

ters in a financial haven privileged by the Western powers, and by professional opacity on money flows. Former Nazi collaborators were given key
roles: Ivan Scribanovitz, for example. During the German occupation, he
was the finance minister of the Nazi collaboration government Vlassow in
Ukraine, now he became the chief financial officer of the European Coal
and Steel Community.[166]

Subsidy abuse and self-enrichment
In this milieu, corruption and state-sponsored cronyism could flourish: For
example, billions in subsidies awarded by the High Authority to modernize Belgian coal production seeped away for years without the publicly
declared effect: Expensively mined Belgian coal remained on the stock-
piles, and the leading coal producers in Germany and France continued to
dominate the market. Numerous fatal accidents in Belgium's dilapidated
coal mines remained the norm - after all, they mostly involved only the
"foreign workers" from Italy, Portugal and Greece procured by the ECSC.
The pampered Belgian entrepreneurs did not need to modernize their
plants; they were able to rake in extra profits. The Belgian government
served as an accomplice.[167]

One of the favored Belgian steel entrepreneurs, Baron René Boël, was
president of the Belgian-American Association as well as treasurer of the
ACUE-funded European Movement and its offshoot the European Youth
Campaign. Boël received monthly payments for this through a special
account, as did the ECSC propagandists Monnet, Schuman, and the top
Belgian politician Paul-Henri Spaak.[168]

Spaak was a member of the Socialist Party but militantly pro-capitalist
and pro-American. During World War II, as Belgian foreign minister, he
had organized the customs union of the three Benelux states of Belgium,
the Netherlands, and Luxembourg, which were occupied by and cooperated with the Wehrmacht. From Nazi orientation to US orientation - that
was an organic transition for him, too.

Producing for the Korean war
ECSC companies produced for the military buildup in Western Europe as
well as for the US war in Korea, and contributed to the economic integration of Western Europe through arms production.[169]

For the exports of the companies represented in the Coal and Steel
Community, the ECSC organized nearly three dozen cartels by 1964

alone, even though this was in breach of its own anti-cartel Article 65.[170] This (apparent) contradictory behavior is a hallmark of the EU to this day.

Monnet seeks compliant trade unionists

In the run-up to the founding of the ECSC, Monnet, supported by the CIA, invited "free and Christian trade unions" of the six participating states to Luxembourg. He promised them a role in the Coal and Steel Community, an expansion of production and an increase in wages. Moreover, the Coal and Steel Community would have an impact on all other economic sectors. The trade unionists were goaded that peaceful action was preferable to violent revolution - which was how Monnet dramatized the call for nationalization.

Monnet found a particularly close friend in Walter Freitag, who had represented IG Metall on the board of the DGB since 1950, had been an SPD member of parliament since 1949, and was also vice president of the International Confederation of Free Trade Unions (ICFTU). Freitag distanced himself from his own party, the SPD, which had declared its opposition to the ECSC.[171] Freitag became a member of the ECSC Advisory Committee, dislodged the previous DGB chairman and ECSC opponent Christian Fette with the help of the CIA in 1952, and began cooperation with the Christian trade unions. (on the CIA see page 46, 78, 166ff., 176ff, 211ff. and 222)

The fact that Monnet and the head of the West German government, Adenauer, were able to pull the DGB over to the ECSC was of major political significance. Because this decisively weakened the criticism of the SPD. SPD chairman Schumacher had categorically rejected the Coal and Steel Community, thundering that it was a "conservative-clerical-capitalist-cartelist" attempt to unify Europe.[172] Such a characterization, however, is, when necessary, part of the demagogic tools of trade of right-wing social democrats - it was clear to buffs like Monnet and Adenauer that agreement to the opposite was not far off.

In the years when the ECSC was decided, the trade unions in the Federal Republic were fighting for co-determination. But the Adenauer government limited it to the 140 or so companies in the coal and steel industry. Under the Coal, Iron and Steel Codetermination Act of 1951, trade unions were only allowed to appoint half the members of the supervisory board in this tiny minority of companies, as well as a labor director who was part of the management board.[173] Behind the scenes, the DGB chairman Freitag had long since given the nod to this solution.

In 1954 Monnet announced his departure from the High Authority. He wanted to drive European economic integration ahead more forcefully. A German trade union delegation visited him for this purpose. It consisted of the DGB chairman Freitag, the IG Metall representative Heinrich Sträter and the IG-Bergbau representative Heinrich Imig. Sträter had also been an SPD member of the state parliament in North Rhine-Westphalia since 1947, while Imig had been an SPD member of the Bundestag since 1949. They met secretly in the Hotel Kons at the Luxembourg train station. Freitag & colleagues again assured that, contrary to the SPD, they would also support Monnet's new Action Committee for the United States of Europe. "I have never encountered firmer and more loyal support than this," Monnet enthused, hoping that in this way the SPD's stance would also change.[174]

Pan-European management of cheap migrant labor

The High Authority, in consultation with the governments of the participating states, coordinated the cross-border procurement of labor. This was regulated by Articles 68 and 69 of the ECSC Act. Skilled workers should be able to move freely across borders, and their skilled worker qualifications should be harmonized. To speed up migration of the low-skilled, national governments should revamp immigration laws.

Thus, the Coal and Steel Community brought cheap migrant workers from the poor regions of non-member states, initially with short-term work permits, especially to France, Belgium, Luxembourg and the Ruhr region. The Coal and Steel Community was able to draw on the prior practices of Member States: Luxembourg had already started in 1948, France followed in 1951. From 1955, the Federal Republic also concluded such agreements, in particular with Italy, Greece, Portugal, Spain, and then also with Turkey, Morocco, South Korea, Tunisia, and finally Yugoslavia. The High Authority of the ECSC undertook the coordination.

Labor migration and military policy

Foreign and military policy considerations also played a role. Workers were also brought to the Federal Republic of Germany when unemployment prevailed and when millions of East German refugees had to be integrated. Thus, the immigration law with Spain also came about because dictator Franco was being courted for membership in NATO and wanted to get rid of workers suspected of sedition. Turkey was to be relieved with the admission of labor from poor rural regions and from Kurdish areas, and its position as an advanced NATO outpost against socialism safe-guarded.

Faraway South Korea was important because of the war and the expansion of the US presence there; manpower was also drawn from there. Likewise, NATO founding member Portugal was rewarded - dictator Salazar wanted to get rid of his poor and "communism"-prone young men, at least temporarily. In the case of Yugoslavia, one witnessed Western attempts to wrench the state out of the association of socialist states and open it up, including through labor migration.[175]

Time limits for menial work
Starting with the sometimes still very dangerous, difficult work in the coal mines and steel mills of the ECSC, the "guest" or "foreign" workers were then also placed in other tough, menial, "dirty" jobs. For most of these workers, this was an improvement and seemed bearable because the work was (initially) limited in time - both in terms of state planning and, in most cases, in terms of individual life planning.

Under Article 68, the High Authority was supposed to intervene in the case of labor wages that it deemed too low by comparison. However, this only applied if such low wages pushed down the prices for the sale of coal and steel, thus distorting competition between Member States. But if all guest and foreign workers from the poor states were paid equally poorly, then there was no price dumping. There were no plans for broad action against low wages and poor working conditions.

This contributed to the social and financial improvement of a large part of the indigenous labor force in the ECSC states: In the Federal Republic, 2.3 million workers rose to salaried positions between 1960 and 1970. Thus, labor migration managed by the Coal and Steel Community also helped local workers earn more, work shorter hours, and get more vacation time.[176] The fragmentation of the working class through poverty-labor migration had begun (again).

Summary: The ECSC as the nucleus of the EU
The ECSC became the nucleus of the European Union in many respects:
- The "High Authority" with privileged officials, which was not subject to parliamentary control, became the COM.
- The "Consultative Assembly" became the European Parliament, which to this day also has only an advisory function that has been only slightly spruced up.
- The Coal and Steel Community institutionalized the division of Europe by rendering full legal and economic cooperation with the Soviet Union and the socialist states impossible.
- The subordinate role of dependent workers and their organizations was accepted and perpetuated with the help of privileged, social-democrat-affiliated and CIA-directed leading unionists.
- The management and use of cheap and, in legal terms, second-class migrant workers is becoming more and more widespread in the EU and more and more legally and extra-legally refined or brutalized (topical examples: Seasonal and contract workers in the agricultural, construction, health, brothel and meat industries).

The cliché of "right and left-wing nationalism"
Founding father Monnet described the rejection of the ECSC by communist, social democratic as well as conservative parties (de Gaulle) at the time as "right-wing and left-wing nationalism united".[177]

The "founding father of Europe" thus coined the populist demagogy that is repeated by the capitalist lobbyists to this day: Anyone who criticizes the EU and the COM is considered a right-wing or, optionally, left-wing nationalist. In this context, these two positions are seen as basically the same and outside the democratic spectrum, even though the positions described as "right-wing" are close to the capitalist lobbyists and in many cases even identical with them.

No democracy, cooperation with dictatorships
The ECSC was an anti-democratic project. The rights and interests of private capital owners were the guiding principle. Universal human rights, ILO labor rights and international law, as decided by the UN after the Second World War, were ignored.

This was also true in the states that had been members of the UN and the ECSC from the beginning, such as France, Belgium, Luxembourg and the Netherlands, and from 1955 also Italy. Dictatorships such as Spain, Portugal and Turkey were natural cooperation partners.

Breach of the promise of prosperity
The ECSC also laid the foundation for breaking the founding promise to increase general prosperity. The management of labor migration begun in the ECSC was expanded further, with the consequence of growing impoverishment of large sections of the dependent workforce, in the rich Western founding states themselves as well as in the peripheral states newly admitted to the EU or having candidate status. "Free movement of labor" is the slogan: labor needs and working conditions are defined by corporations and legalized and coordinated by the EU.

Thus, a diverse socially, ethnically and religiously divided workforce emerged. The indigenous dependent employees gained advantages - at least some of them - intentionally or unintentionally, but there was also something in it for the foreign workers and their families. This complex constellation has undergone many changes up to the present day.

At the same time, with the ECSC and around its head Monnet, who was active until 1954, in the shielded little Grand Duchy of Luxembourg, there emerged on the other side "an elite of high European functionaries whose role was to unfold further with the Treaty of Rome in 1957".[178]

European Communities
The ECSC was established for half a century. It was dissolved in 2002, but its tasks and regulations were transferred to the European Treaties, most recently the Treaty of Lisbon (2009).

High Commissioner Monnet retired from the High Authority in 1954. The publicity-shy backroom player, who never held a political office in the classical sense, continued to drive developments.

Action Committee for the United States of Europe
In 1955 Monnet launched the *Action Committee for the United States of Europe*. This was a double of the *American Committee on United States of Europe*. Instead of ACUE the abbreviation was now ACUSE. Monnet brought in Max Kohnstamm as Secretary General: the Dutchman had studied in the USA before the war, was private secretary to Queen Wil-

helmina after the war, then responsible for the Marshall Plan in the Foreign Ministry, then Secretary of the Coal and Steel Community from 1952.

ACUE continued with the Americanization of life in (Western) Europe, also funded ACUSE. The "progress" was that Monnet now brought in (Western) European personnel. Now not only mainly "Christian" politicians joined in, but also squeaky-clean "liberal" ones, and even more "socialist" and "social democratic" ones. From the Federal Republic, for example, Herbert Wehner and the Berlin SPD leader Willy Brandt became involved in the committee, as did Walter Scheel of the FDP. The socialists from Italy, France and the Benelux vassals worked on by ACUE were now also present in large numbers.

ACUSE acted as lobby and think tank for two decades. It presented concrete projects to politicians.[179] The two most important were

- the European Economic Community (EEC) with the goal of the "Common Market",
- the European Atomic Energy Community (EURATOM).

To prepare both projects, Monnet set up a commission under the Belgian socialist Paul-Henri Spaak (Spaak Commission). Walter Hallstein, one of the closest confidants of German Chancellor Adenauer, was also a member. In 1957, the heads of government of the six states of the Coal and Steel Community signed the two "Treaties of Rome" in Rome: on the EEC and on EURATOM.

The European Atomic Energy Community (EURATOM)

The two superpowers, the USA and the Soviet Union, had at their disposal the war-born new energy source, nuclear power, which had been researched in Europe, especially in Germany. In France and the Federal Republic in particular, energy companies and politicians also demanded access after the war. In the Federal Republic it was the government with Adenauer and defense and minister for nuclear energy Strauß (CSU) who, in their Christian altruism, now demanded atomic energy also for "Germany", and not only for civilian but also for military purposes. They also wanted the atomic bomb for the Bundeswehr.

No nuclear bomb for the European friends!
But the USA, when it came to real power, wanted to keep the Europeans away from the atomic bomb. Monnet had to see to that. That is why he set up EURATOM. It was to ensure that the uranium 235 supplied from the USA was only used for civilian purposes. All other trade in nuclear materials with third countries was also to be controlled by the new High Authority EURATOM.

For the negotiations, Monnet brought in Hans Furler, a CDU member of the Bundestag, from Germany: the SA and NSDAP member and, from 1941-1944, member of the civil administration in German-occupied Alsace was already sworn in as a member of the ECSC Common Assembly and as chairman of the Bundestag's "Common Market/EURATOM" committee. He was then Vice-President of the European Parliament until 1973.

Monnet also brought in Social Democrats, SPD party chairman Erich Ollenhauer and parliamentary group leader Wehner. The trade unionists were represented by the DGB chairman Freitag, who continued to be monitored by the CIA[180] and was also vice president of the ICFTU. He had already served as the workers' figurehead in the Coal and Steel Community.

Personnel coordinated with US State Department
EURATOM was also given the same structure as the Coal and Steel Community: High Authority, led by a High Commissioner, legally and fiscally privileged staff, extreme lack of transparency.

Monnet discussed the appointment of the management staff with US Secretary of State Dulles. The first High Commissioner, Louis Armand, coming from the Resistance, was a concession to the French to make them agree to the creation of EURATOM. But with this background, he proved unreliable for the USA. Therefore, Monnet zealously looked for a successor: Etienne Hirsch. He had worked with Monnet in the US mission in North Africa from 1943 and in the French government's planning agency from 1946. Monnet telegraphed Dulles on October 3, 1958: "I am sure you will like Hirsch. I regret the late decision, but I assure you it was only due to internal problems here."[181]

Advisor: Cleary Gottlieb again
As with the ECSC, the US envoy brought in the US law firm Cleary
Gottlieb Friendly & Ball. It still boasts of this assignment today as well.[182]
Today, unknown to the public, the firm still plays an important role in the
EU. In 1960 it had established its branch in Brussels.

If, even in the 21st century, the German government does not dare to
ask German or European lawyers, for example, whether it would have to
extradite US citizen Edward Snowden should he be in Germany: then they
turn to Cleary Gottlieb. Similarly, Commerzbank, for example, whose largest shareholder is the German government, when it "must" bend German
labor law in the face of US sanctions.[183]

France: Lured with agricultural subsidies
EURATOM's task was to control the nuclear energy of the European
allies. A second reason was to thwart France's already announced intention to become a military nuclear power as well.

Powerbroker Monnet had lured the therefore hesitant French government with lavish agricultural subsidies for French farmers - and won. The
French consequently agreed to the EURATOM Treaty - which, however,
did not prevent them from pursuing their intentions further, especially
from 1958 under de Gaulle. But this way, at least the most important vassal, the Federal Republic, was restrained.

European Economic Community (EEC)
Monnet was simultaneously preparing the European Economic Communi-
ty (EEC) with ACUSE, supported by its US finances and US networks.
The goals defined by the Marshall Plan continued to set the agenda.

Advisor: Cleary Gottlieb again
The "united Europe" was now to be extended to all economic areas and to
other states. Article 70 of the EEC Treaty stated that "the movement of
capital between Member States and third countries ... shall be liberalized
to the maximum extent possible". Tariffs were dismantled even faster,
rules for the cross-border movement of services, people and capital were
developed. The EEC was once again a "High Authority". Parliamentarians
of the Member States were again present only in an advisory capacity;
they had no right of initiative or decision.

Walter Hallstein is considered the author of the EEC Treaty. But the EEC Treaty was also drafted with the help of Cleary Gottlieb Friendly & Ball. Again, without being explicitly mentioned, US interests were thus legally secured.[184] That was not publicly known in this case either - and still is not.

First EEC president Walter Hallstein: Chosen by Monnet
In 1958, the foreign ministers of the six states of the Coal and Steel Community and EURATOM appointed the West German CDU politician Walter Hallstein as the first President of the EEC Commission. He had been appointed head of the West German delegation to the ECSC by Adenauer in 1950, became State Secretary under Hans Globke in the Chancellery that same year, and then, with the approval of US High Commissioner McCloy, became State Secretary in the Foreign Office in 1951, which was then headed by Adenauer himself in parallel.

Hallstein remained EEC Commission President until 1967. He had, of course, been chosen by Monnet. Adenauer had first sent an industrialist friend to Monnet's private dinner at his Houjarray estate near Paris. Monnet was to examine the candidate. Monnet was dissatisfied, and his wife did not have a good impression either. Monnet therefore sent the candidate back and told Adenauer: He is no good, send me someone else. Adenauer sent Hallstein. Monnet and Hallstein hit it off immediately.[185]

This can be explained by the - until today suppressed - prehistory. Hallstein, too, had close ties to the USA and shared with Monnet the idea of an economically united "Europe" under direct capital and US domination.

Hallstein with Mussolini and Hitler: "The new Europe"
Hallstein was a leading international law expert of the Nazi regime. From 1941 he was professor of international business law and labor law at the University of Frankfurt/Main, which was central to the Nazis.[186] He was a member of the National Socialist Lawyers' Association and Lecturers' League. In 1942, he was drafted into the Wehrmacht and, like his later cabinet colleague under Adenauer, Franz-Josef Strauß, acted as a National Socialist command officer: As political commissar, his role was to motivate the soldiers in northern France to persevere.[187]

In May 1938, he had been part of Hitler's delegation, which was feted by Mussolini and King Victor Emmanuel III at a German-Italian conference in Rome with a gala dinner and Verdi opera. At the time, Hallstein praised "the incomparable legislative genius of Mussolini and Hitler" and extolled the Nazi vision of the "new Europe".[188] For the labor lawyer, the vision had also included the cross-border management of cheap labor - with many gradations from paid and socially insured workers from France down to the disenfranchised concentration camp prisoners from the East who were exterminated in the work columns.[189]

Reshape the map of Europe with "Greater Germany"!
In 1939, at a conference he organized in Rostock - where he had received his first professorship - Hallstein declared, "The creation of Greater Germany is an act of the Führer with universal scope, reshaping the map of Europe and responding to an ancient longing of the peoples ... We must not only renovate the dilapidated house, but build a new structure for an expanding family."[190]

Hallstein was captured by US troops in France in 1944. "At the Como POW camp in the US state of Mississippi, Hallstein helped establish a camp university for further education," according to the fake medium Wikipedia.[191] Quarter-truths - the most important thing is missing. After all, how did he get to the US, Camp Como, Fort Getty? US intelligence agents immediately and single-mindedly sought out among the prisoners, especially the officers, individuals who would be useful to the postwar order. Hallstein was interned here with other useful people and was groomed for the future - for one year. For this, the well-known Nazi professor Hallstein was also allowed to prepare the others in the "camp university". He did not need to hide his brown past, on the contrary: it qualified him for the US concept of "united Europe".

Again: US investments in the Benelux countries
The opening was aimed primarily at the USA. Shortly beforehand, David Rockefeller of the leading Wall Street bank Chase Manhattan, to which US High Commissioner McCloy had since returned, had co-founded the Bilderberg Conference with the figurehead of Prince Bernhard in the Netherlands.[192] He organized conferences in Paris, Brussels, and London: He touted to governments the benefits of US investment in the EEC.[193]

For this reason, US investors shifted their preferred focus since 1945, Great Britain, which was not part of the EEC, to the EEC founding states.

This thus affected France, Italy, the Federal Republic of Germany and the three Benelux countries.

US corporations mostly invested in several EEC countries simultaneously: General Motors, Ford, DuPont, Monsanto and National Carbide, Esso, Mobil Oil, Texaco and Standard Oil, 3M, Goodyear, General Electric, Standard Electric and National Cash Register, IBM and Hewlett Packard, Caterpillar, Singer, John Deere and International Harvester, Kodak, Woolworth, Maizena and Libby.[194] Likewise, the Wall Street banks also arrived, first and foremost Rockefeller's Chase Manhattan, Morgan Guaranty Trust, Citibank and JPMorgan.[195]

In 1965, 489 US companies were operating in the Federal Republic. This was roughly double the number during the Nazi era. In France, the number of US companies was even higher, at 616. In Italy, there were 432 US companies with a focus on the petrochemical industry.

However, on a per capita basis, the Benelux countries initially formed the absolute center of gravity, and among the three countries, Luxembourg was well out front.

The *Netherlands* again offered particularly low wages as well as the favorable location for raw material procurement by sea and onward transportation. Dutch cities and municipalities granted US companies juicy tax benefits.[196]

In *Belgium*, the government set up its own office to attract investors from the USA. Caterpillar, General Motors, Ford, Monsanto, Texaco, Philipps Petroleum, National Distillers and Union Carbide came. Investments were concentrated in Flanders because the unions there were more "conservative" than in French-speaking Wallonia, where there were more strikes.[197] Hence, US corporations reinforced the political right-wing development in Flanders and the already prevailing division between the Belgian regions.

Again: Luxemburg as 51st US state

In *Luxembourg*, the ratio of US investment per capita was 10 times the EEC average. Several factors played a role here.

Since the end of the First World War, the Grand Duchy had developed the location as a financial haven; here, following the example of Switzerland and the Principality of Liechtenstein, foreign companies could establish letterbox companies. In 1927, banks from Germany and France founded the Luxembourg Stock Exchange.

The mother of US President Roosevelt, who was in office until 1945, came from a Luxembourg family. Close ties had developed with the Grand Ducal family of Luxembourg, which was in American exile during the war. Goodyear, DuPont, Monsanto and Continental Fertilizer were granted favorable investment terms.[198] US banks such as Wells Fargo, Bank of America and Bankers Trust set up branches in the mini-state. In 1970, they founded the clearing institution Cedel (Centrale de Livraison des Valeurs Mobilières) here: This was the first multinational center for timely, cross-border stock and securities sales. Cedel became the back office of the financial global village.

Covert financial operations of the Marshall Plan were handled through Luxembourg - in addition to the BIS in Basel. No head of state was in Luxembourg as often as Dwight Eisenhower, US President from 1953 to 1961. Later, leading US Republicans such as Henry Kissinger, Caspar Weinberger and George Bush Sr. came and went endlessly - all without fuss, discreetly.[199]

All the major banks and corporations in the US sphere of influence were involved in Cedel, including those from Switzerland, London and the Federal Republic of Germany. Branch offices were gradually established in London, Tokyo, Hong Kong, Dubai, Frankfurt and Sao Paulo. Most important financially and politically were US defense contractors such as Lockheed, Raytheon, and Northrop, which were represented here for their sales to Gulf sheikdoms and other less prestigious US allies. US President Ronald Reagan organized the ransom for US hostages in Iran through Cedel in 1981. Cedel was renamed Clearstream in 1999 and is now owned by Deutsche Börse and thus BlackRock & Co.

Tens of thousands of Luxembourgers benefit as well: The small state has by far the highest per capita income of all EU Member States, averaging EUR 96,700, despite an army of low-wage workers for menial services: In the Federal Republic of Germany, usually referred to as the richest EU state, the per capita income of EUR 40,800 is less than half, and in the poorest EU state Bulgaria it is only one-twelfth, namely EUR 7,800.[200]

Jean-Claude Juncker, who later became Luxembourg's finance minister and prime minister from the "Christian Social People's Party", i.e. the representative of a tautologous populism, subsequently became president of the COM. The EU, with the approval of German Chancellor Merkel, thus finally elevated Luxembourg's toadyism toward the US to the pan-European level.[201]

For US investment: Subsidies and freedoms
Thus, following the Marshall Plan boost, US investors took advantage of the continued drive toward market unification with the EEC. On the other hand, the EEC Treaty conferred only minor sovereign rights on the European Commission - under pressure from the USA.[202]

"Liberalization" did not simply mean "opening up", but also as many public subsidies as possible. Thus, especially the wooed US corporations, which invested simultaneously in at least two EEC states, took advantage of the ongoing competition between these states, especially in investment subsidies and tax perks. The EEC states developed an extensive, opaque web of national, regional and local subsidies.[203]

The Benelux countries granted the highest subsidies. The exact extent could not be determined at the time because the EEC did not record them and the US attached importance to non-transparency: they preferred bilateral double taxation agreements that were not submitted to the parliaments.[204]

US corporations: Pioneers of labor injustice
In part, US corporations complied with European labor and union laws, in part they behaved as they did in the United States. Thus, disputes over layoffs, for example in the case of restructuring after company acquisitions, and wage cuts, social benefits and work breaks, were much more frequent than in exclusively European corporations at the time.[205]

For example, the fast-food company McDonald's, as a fundamental enemy of trade unions, systematically built its Europe-wide chain of stores with temporary part-time jobs, much like United Parcel Service (UPS): pioneers of low-wage work. After 1990 and in the 21st century, US players were the pioneers of union busting in the EU.[206]

Imbalance EEC – USA
Although the US emphasized equality between the two sides, and European investment in the US was welcomed, the real-world imbalance remained and was reinforced in favor of the USA. In addition, US compa-

nies and consultants such as McKinsey brought their management methods with them, which were faithfully adopted in the EEC.

In terms of investments in the US from Europe, the non-EEC countries, namely Great Britain, Switzerland and Sweden, initially led the way. And from the EEC countries, most direct investment in the US came not from France, the Federal Republic and Italy, but by a long way from the Netherlands (Shell, Unilever, Philips, AKU). Here, too, the Benelux countries dominated, at the same time hosting proportionately the most US investment. "The Benelux countries accounted for 78 percent of EEC direct investment in the United States."[207]

This only changed in the course of the expansion of the EEC into the EU, from the end of the 1990s and then definitely after the financial and economic crisis of 2007: "In favor" especially of Germany, France, Switzerland and, again, the UK.

Awarded: Charlemagne Prize for Monnet and Hallstein
Monnet and Hallstein, the "founding fathers of Europe", received many awards. Their biographies are faked to this day.

The Charlemagne prize
The highest prize awarded by the EU is the Charlemagne Prize. It refers to "Charlemagne", who reinforced the feudal exploitation of peasants throughout Europe in the 8th and 9th centuries. The holy warrior waged a Thirty Years War, with gruesome punitive expeditions. He also gained the honorary title of "Saxon Butcher": mass killings and mass forced baptisms in the name of Christianity for a united Europe. In the year 800, the Pope crowned him emperor in St. Peter's Basilica. The prize is awarded annually in Emperor Karl's former residence, the Royal Palace in Aachen, in the presence of EU VIPs.

The initiator of the award was Kurt Pfeiffer, a member of the NSDAP since 1933 as well as of five other Nazi organizations, and after 1945 co-founder of the CDU in Aachen.[208]

Jean Monnet: Guarantor of US supremacy

Monnet received not only the Order of St. Pius of the Vatican in 1956, but also the Charlemagne Prize in 1958. In 1963, he received with special distinction the US Medal of Freedom for services to the "unification of Europe" and transatlantic cooperation. US President Kennedy was full of praise: "Dear Mr. Monnet: For centuries, emperors, kings, and dictators have tried to unify Europe by force; they failed. But under your inspiration, Europe has found more unity in less than 20 years than in a thousand years ... Since the war, the reconstruction and unification of Europe have always been the goals of US policy." The atomic war being prepared by the USA in Europe as possible – not a word from golden-boy Kennedy or the recipient of the praise.

With McCloy und Meany

Monnet was also honored in the US, along with his friend John McCloy and CIA agent George Meany.[1] The latter had been awarded the Federal Cross of Merit by Adenauer a few years earlier. Even after his High Commissioner role, Monnet had ensured with his think tank ACUSE that US supremacy was safeguarded. Thus, the 1963 friendship treaty between the Federal Republic of Germany and France, negotiated between de Gaulle and Adenauer ("Élysée Treaty"), went too far for Monnet. This would endanger not only the integration of Europe, but also the cohesion of NATO and the leadership of the USA. For this reason, Monnet managed to have the close ties with the US mentioned as an overriding relationship in a subsequent preamble. The preamble was quickly and as if by magic added to the friendship treaty before the Bundestag and the Assemblée Nationale ratified it.[209]

Walter Hallstein:
From "Greater Germany" to "united Europe"
Monnet's pupil Hallstein, Nazi propagandist of the "New Europe" according to the visions of Mussolini and Hitler, was awarded the Order of the Republic of Cuba in 1957 in addition to the early Federal Cross of Merit: The dictatorship there under Fulgencio Batista was a preferred location for corporations, mafia and brothel operators from the USA. *This* Cuba also appealed to Adenauer and his then Secretary of State in the Foreign Ministry, Hallstein. In 1961 and 1962, the latter received the Charlemagne Prize and admission to the American Academy of Sciences, the same honors as his master.

Merkel and EU parliament extol Hallstein
On Nov. 13, 2018, Chancellor Merkel effusively reaffirmed Hallstein's services to a united Europe before the European Parliament, saying he had led it to security, prosperity and peace with "unprecedented courage".[210]

In the United States the Hallstein file is still largely under wraps.

4.
Expansion to (almost) all of Europe

The "united Europe" was also a counter-project against the UNO:
- against the new international law created with the help of the Soviet Union (non-intervention in other states, Security Council decides on peacekeeping operations),
- against Universal Human Rights, which went beyond previous civil rights with social and labor rights.

Single Market, EURO, Eastern Enlargement
The principles and practices consolidated over two decades in the Coal and Steel Community, EURATOM, and the EEC were gradually and increasingly rapidly extended to new countries and state functions beginning in the 1980s.

1973: First enlargement:

UK, Irish Republic, Denmark, Greece
Under pressure from the USA, new members were admitted to the "united Europe":
- The UK had so far refused membership because of its illusory Commonwealth claims, which the elites continued to dream of, and because of its coddled special relationship with the United States. But the US considered a strengthening of the EEC by the economically and strategically important country necessary and pushed through membership even against the resistance of France;
- Ireland was still suffering from the consequences of British colonization, which only formally ended in 1949: emigration, high unemployment, poverty. The EU promised massive subsidies to develop Ireland into an additional financial haven and a low-wage zone; both have since been used primarily by US companies;
- Denmark hosted in its colony of Greenland the military base of Thule, occupied by the United States in 1940, which had become even more important at the height of the "Cold War";

- Greece was the next state to join in 1981, on the one hand because of the country's high symbolic importance for European educated elites. On the other, the NATO state became more important as an outpost towards the Middle East, because of the increasing importance of Israel for US foreign policy, then because of the border conflict between Greece and Turkey on Cyprus (the British military base there was endangered), finally because of the potentially still strong NATO-critical opposition in Greece, which "threatened" to win the election in 1968 if the CIA-backed coup had not prevented this.

1985: Abolition of checks on persons at internal borders ("Schengen")
The "Schengen Treaty" was adopted in Schengen/Luxembourg: Abolition of checks on persons at internal borders. Since then, this has been touted to the populations of the Member States as a special "freedom", so that they no longer have to show their passports when going on cross-border vacation, for example. With the influx of refugees - starting a few years later after the demolition of Yugoslavia - the snag became apparent: the states to the east and south were left high and dry by the rich founding states. The Schengen Treaty proved to be the basis for the inhumane "Fortress Europe".

1986: Single European Act
The Single European Act, adopted in Luxembourg in 1986, aimed to "complete" the European Single Market and to establish common product standards. The four civil "freedoms" were reaffirmed: Free movement of goods, free movement of capital and payments, freedom to provide services, free movement of persons. Public contracts were now to be put out to tender throughout Europe. In the same year, Spain and Portugal were admitted, the two dictators Franco and Salazar had died, and EEC- and NATO-friendly, social-democratic governments had been established.

1992: European Community (EC), "Maastricht Treaty"
In the Maastricht Treaty, the three European Communities - the Coal and Steel Community, EURATOM and the EEC - were renamed the European Community (EC). A common foreign and military policy was agreed upon, as well as cooperation in the areas of justice, police, home affairs and culture. The core of the common economic policy was to be monetary union with a single currency. Government budgets were also targeted: The

"Maastricht criteria" have since limited permissible government debt - a maximum of 60% in relation to gross domestic product, and a maximum of 3% new annual debt. This is an incentive or compulsion to privatize. In 1995, additional members were admitted: Finland, Sweden and Austria.

1998: Euro Group
The Euro Group was established in 1998. It comprises those 19 EU Member States that have adopted the single currency and monitors their budgetary and fiscal policies (compliance with the Maastricht criteria). The first chairman was Jean-Claude Juncker, Prime Minister of Luxembourg, the largest financial haven in the EU. His mandate was extended several times until 2013 in contravention of the statutes, supported in particular by the French Finance Minister Christine Lagarde, the future head of the ECB. After Juncker, the ECB was chaired by Jeroen Dijsselbloem, finance minister of the Netherlands, the EU's second-largest financial haven.

The "Maastricht criteria" were repeatedly violated, including by Germany and France, but - in contrast to small EU states - this remained without sanctions. In the meantime, most investments in the EU, including those by the large US digital groups, go via Luxembourg and the Netherlands, which thus contribute to bloating the national debt of the other EU states further. With the "corona" rescue program, the "strict" Maastricht criteria were declared invalid without further ado.

1999: European Central Bank (ECB) and Euro
The ECB is provided for in the Maastricht Treaty and came into operation in 1998, in the run-up to the introduction of the euro. With the takeover of the GDR finally making the Federal Republic the most powerful EU state, the ECB was located in Frankfurt/Main.

The ECB is the guardian the euro currency, it is said. The new central bank had been prepared in the US-controlled BIS, under the direction of ex-Goldman Sachs banker Mario Draghi. It has since replaced the previous national central banks, and has now also taken over banking supervision and determines which banks are considered "systemically relevant", meaning they must be bailed out by EU citizens in the event of insolvency, in breach of market norms.

However, the "common" currency is only valid in 19 of the 27 EU Member States after the completion of Brexit. On the other hand, the euro

is also valid in six micro and small states that have only limited state quality and are suitable, for example, for money laundering and as US military
bases: Andorra, Monaco, San Marino, Vatican City, Montenegro, and
Kosovo. Some states, such as Croatia, have pegged their currency to the
euro.

The euro favors countries that are already strong financially and economically. The financial havens Luxembourg and the Netherlands have
the greatest advantage, followed by Germany as the largest exporting
country, and then France. The countries that are weaker anyway are doing
particularly badly. By contrast, countries without the euro, whether EU
members or not, tend to fare much better, such as Switzerland, Denmark,
Sweden and Norway - and especially Russia, which has by far the lowest
national debt.

From 2004 Eastern enlargement: Capitalist-military pincer grip
In 2004, the first Eastern European states were admitted, again in concert
with NATO. Some states should not have been admitted according to the
Maastricht criteria and other EU 'values' (anti-corruption, rule of law),
such as the Baltic states and Kosovo, but were admitted because they are
important above all for NATO and have nationalist, anti-Russian governing parties.

Thus, on May 1, 2004, the following were admitted on the same day:
Poland, the Czech Republic, Slovakia, Hungary, from former Yugoslavia
only Slovenia, the three Baltic states Estonia, Latvia, Lithuania and the
small financial haven Malta. Latecomers were Bulgaria and Romania in
2007, and Croatia in 2014, the last country to join so far. However, the
referendums showed only low approval. It was around a quarter to a third
of those eligible to vote. In Hungary, 45 percent participated in the election, of whom 83 percent voted in favor. In the Czech Republic, 55 percent participated, of whom 77 percent voted in favor. In the last vote in
Croatia, the result was the worst: 43 percent took part, of which 66 percent voted in favor.

In these states, the EU and the US, with differences, promoted domestic oligarchs and anti-communist to criminal groups well before formal
membership. Opinion-making with emotionally charged, shallow mass
entertainment and overt or subcutaneous neoliberalism is dominated by
the oligarchs and Western media corporations. Since accession, the EU

has dutifully urged the fight against corruption repeatedly, but is perfectly happy with the lack of success.

Eastward enlargement, that means: public property has been privatized, trade unions are marginalized, labor income and social benefits are particularly low, unemployment is high, one third of those able to work have emigrated. It is not "capitalism" and "democracy" that have been spread, but the hegemony of Western capitalists, promoted by right-wing to fascistoid politicians. NATO membership is an organic component.

2009: Claim as third world power: Treaty of Lisbon

Actually, the EC was supposed to be terminated and the European Union to be founded, with the help of a constitution: EU Reform Treaty. Due to negative referendums in France, Ireland and the Netherlands, the treaty did not come into being and is therefore not a constitution. The replacement is the Treaty of Lisbon (TFEU), which includes further authorizations for the EU. The EU is to become the "most competitive region" on earth. Above all, the EU has since been explicitly a military alliance and has a newly created External Action Service and a Foreign Affairs Commissioner. For this claim as a new world power, some populist sweeteners were handed out, such as the European Citizens' Initiative: If one million signatures from at least seven states are submitted, the request is to be "heard" in the European Parliament.

The EU Charter of Fundamental Rights was also adopted in Lisbon. It speaks of "dignified working conditions" - vague and non-binding. (see page 117ff.)

2011: ESFS, ESM, Fiscal Compact, European Semester

Since its inception, the COM has been gradually intervening more deeply in the decisions of EU Member States. In addition to the Troika, they and the EU heads of government initially decided on the European Stabilization and Financing Facility (ESFS) to "rescue" over-indebted EU states. It was replaced by the European Stability Mechanism (ESM). The Fiscal Compact is intended to centralize the COM's control of national and federal state budgets, and meanwhile also of municipalities and social security funds in EU Member States (European Semester).

Since 2011, this has meant that the revenues and expenditures of the nation states need Brussels' approval and are linked to "structural adjustment measures", based on the practices of the IMF: reduction of labor rights and labor income, social benefits and pensions, later retirement age, privatizations, budget cuts, "streamlining" of public services, commercialization of social and cultural tasks.

This constitutes a kind of permanent emergency constitution and undermines existing trade union and labor rights.[211]

2012: EU – a political union?

When criticism of the undemocratic measures taken by the EU and the Troika to bail out the banks erupted, German Chancellor Merkel and the particularly anti-social Finance Minister Schäuble suddenly proposed: The EU must finally become a *political* union.[212] To this end, an EU president should be directly elected throughout Europe. But even this tenuous attempt at a political union came to nothing. The EU remains a modern capitalist bureaucracy, with osmotic links to the equally unelected military bureaucracy of NATO.

2015: Fortress EU –
Sealing off the Mediterranean, deployment against Russia

With its attempted ascent to the status of a military world power as well and its growing participation in military interventions - albeit in the retinue of the USA and NATO - the EU is increasingly causing the exodus of war victims. It began in devastated Yugoslavia and continued through Afghanistan, Iraq, Libya, Syria, and, due to EU-induced underdevelopment, in Africa.

Since 2015, the EU has been increasingly expanding Fortress EU, with the cooperation of police, military and intelligence services. They operate around the Mediterranean and penetrate deep into neighboring states like Libya. The longer-standing units such as EUROPOL and the border and coast guard FRONTEX work together with the new naval unit European Naval Force - Mediterranean (EUNAVFOR MED). The EU does not fight the causes of conflict and war, but the refugees and the traffickers. It is thus responsible for the mass drowning in the Mediterranean and systematically violates the elementary human right to be rescued from distress at sea.

At the same time, the EU is pooling its military and arms production - a long-held desire since the European Defense Community failed due to opposition from the French National Assembly in 1954. The EU is organizing the buildup against Russia under US leadership, coordinated with

NATO, and also officially agreed in 2019 to expand NATO's list of bogeymen to include the People's Republic of China (NATO 70th Anniversary Declaration in London).

Legal gray area with systemic crime

The EU has no valid constitution and is not a parliamentary democracy.
The main bodies - COM, Council, Parliament - are subject to opaque private influences. At its core, the EU cannot protect its citizens, companies
and administrations against spying by US digital corporations and US
intelligence agencies. It cannot enforce the taxation of large corporations
at the place where profits are generated, but rather contributes itself to
global tax evasion by corporations, banks and investors operating on its
territory.[213] With its free trade agreements, the EU places Member States
at the mercy of private tribunals.

Ongoing breach of the constitution I

The EU violates its own treaty basis. According to Articles 153, 157 and
158, elementary labor and trade union rights are excluded from the EU's
grasp, such as pay, the right to strike and freedom of association. Nevertheless, the EU is intervening more and more in these areas, on the one
hand indirectly, for example through privatization and subsidies. On the
other hand, it intervenes directly through directives, rulings by the European Court of Justice (ECJ), the dozen agencies dealing with labor issues,
and labor market policy instruments.

According to its treaty basis, the EU is financed by contributions from
Member States. But in the "corona crisis" it is taking out loans for its
EUR 750 billion reconstruction program.

The ECJ and the European Court of Human Rights (ECHR) often issue
rulings that are not respected by the COM or by the governments and
judiciary of the Member States. For instance, the ECJ ruled in 2017 on the
free trade agreement between the EU and Singapore: Ratification must not
be limited to the COM or the European Parliament! The national parliaments of the member states must also decide on the agreement. Although
the EU has the mandate for foreign trade policy, the agreement with Singapore goes far beyond that: the rights of investors, for example in labor
law, are also regulated, and this falls within the remit of national legislators. To this day, the EU and the governments of the member states do not

follow the ruling. Motto: If we don't have a valid constitution, we can also break it.

Ongoing breach of the constitution II
The EU concludes agreements that it violates itself and allows others to violate. In 2014, for example, it concluded an association agreement with Israel on the Horizon 2020 research program. Via this agreement, about EUR 1.3 billion in subsidies have been paid to Israel up to 2020, for 1,500 projects. The beneficiaries include not only technological start-ups, but also, for example, the pharmaceutical group Teva - world market leader in generic drugs, in Germany Teva has bought Ratiopharm - and defense companies such as Israel Aerospace Industries IAI (produces, among other things, the Heron combat drone), Elbit Systems and Elta Systems. With the help of EU subsidies, they also boost their global exports.[214] The research program has a civilian character, but thus also promotes arms production. The agreement excludes recipients in Israeli-occupied territories - the West Bank, Golan Heights and also East Jerusalem - from the program. Israel stated in a supplementary declaration: We won't abide by this. The EU coughs up anyway.[215]

Disregard of supreme court rulings
The ECJ and the ECtHR occasionally issue rulings that are not to the taste of individual EU Member States. The judgments are then disregarded, not implemented. The EU model state Germany is particularly fond of doing this, for example in the case of the labor law status of German Red Cross employees, the recording of all working time (including overtime), the reduction of the subsistence minimum, the dismissed geriatric nurse Brigitte Heinisch and the occupational bans. The COM is silent on this.

Regulatory Capture
The EU, especially the COM, represents a systemic combination of state-bureaucratic functions with private capitalist actors. The COM outsources tasks to private entrepreneurs who perform state-sovereign functions, such as the rating agencies and the 'auditors'.

These operate according to the principle of regulatory capture: In their regulatory and supervisory tasks, private interests predominate because, first, the supervisors are themselves private companies and, second, they are at the same time perma-consultants for private companies, by whom they are handsomely remunerated.[216] This regularly enables criminal practices such as targeted fraud in favor of the private party.[217] This was evident, for example, in the complicity of the rating agencies and 'auditors' in the financial crisis of 2007, in the extreme over-indebtedness of Greece,[218] and most recently in 2020 in the case of the financial fraudster Wirecard.[219]

Systemic enforcement deficit
In addition, the EU maintains its own supervisory authorities. The anti-fraud agency OLAF, for example, has a great deal of knowledge about the misuse of subsidies and corruption among Eastern European governments and oligarchs. But abuse and corruption continue. The same is true of cross-border, carousel-like VAT fraud: Every year, EU Member States suffer losses in the order of EUR 30 to 60 billion.[220]

The sustained, mass violation of labor directives - for example, in the case of extremely exploited meat workers and truck drivers, in cabotage (rules on how much additional work may be taken on in between during an agreed cross-border transport) in international truck transport - is indeed known to the half-dozen EU supervisory authorities. But this is neither sanctioned nor abolished, in complicity with the similarly under-staffed national supervisory authorities.

National weakening of EU legal documents
The EU passes binding legal documents. These include the European Social Charter and the many directives. However, Member States can make significant changes. For instance, the Federal Republic ratified the Social Charter and adorns itself with it, but omits the regulations on notice periods, the minimum age for employment and the rights of pregnant women, mothers and the long-term unemployed.

Germany, the EU model state, leads the way in breaking EU law. For example, Germany violates the EU Fertilizer Directive. The poisoning of soils, groundwater, rivers, lakes and coastal waters is progressing most intensively here.[221] For years, demands of the Commission have not been implemented despite repeated threats of fines and remain without results or punishment.[222]

Statistical window dressing
You can call it window dressing, you can also call it fraud: In the EU budget from 2014 to 2020, EUR 102.8 billion of total agricultural subsidies are earmarked for climate protection. However, around 40 billion of this has nothing to do with climate protection, but is paid out to farms solely on the basis of their area. And even if only one percent of the funding amount is used for climate protection in a project, it appears as "40 percent for climate protection". This is because in the statistical three-stage model, Category I includes all funding shares from 0 to 40 percent, regardless of whether they amount to only 1 percent or 40 percent. Thus, the European Court of Auditors found: EU agricultural policy does not protect the climate, but destroys it; biodiversity of plants and animals continues to decline.[223]

Delivery of data to foreign powers
Protecting privacy: a noble EU value. But the EU is neither willing nor able to protect the private data of citizens, companies, governments and administrations from access by foreign powers. The US has secured access in the EU area through the Foreign Intelligence Surveillance Act (FISA, 1978) and the Clarifying Lawful Overseas Use of Data Act (CLOUD, 2018). Since corona, this also applies to the data of students, parents, and teachers in homeschooling, when carried out, for instance, using the Microsoft Teams application.[224]

Possible transition into criminality
The freedom of private owners and investors as the overriding principle, together with regulatory capture, has led to the weakening or complicity of legal and professional supervision in the EU and in the Member States. In individual cases, "scandals" erupt - financial crisis, Libor (London Interbank Offered Rate: fraud in the constantly redefined average interest rate in the financial center of London), money laundering for terrorists and drug cartels, falsified emission software, Cum-Ex, Wirecard, etc. – where judicial proceedings take an age and lead at best to the conviction of lower ranks.

Thus, the EU Directive on the posting of migrant workers could still be considered in line with the rule of law. But, first, the amendments of the directive in the Member States, second the dismantling of the supervisory authorities in the EU apparatus as well as in the Member States ultimately pave the way to permanent transition into area-wide criminality with multiple breaches of the law, as in the "scandal" of the extreme exploitation of East European meat workers in Germany, the leading EU slaughterhouse location.[225]

With its Charter of Fundamental Rights, the EU sees itself as a "civil" society. But: Not only refugees from third countries, but also citizens from EU Member States, and above all dependent employees, are practically denied the exercise of basic civil rights, such as equality before the law, the right to good administration and data protection, the right to free job placement and dignified working conditions - not to mention the denial of social and labor rights according to the ILO and the UN, the right to asylum and rescue from drowning.

Today's capitalist bureaucracy

The capitalist bureaucracy in today's EU emerged from the nuclei ECSC and EEC and, despite many changes, retains the same characteristics:

- The authoritarian High Authority became the authoritarian European Commission (COM).
- The Parliamentary Assembly, which was only consultative, became the European Parliament without the right to legislate and without the right to elect a government.
- The ECSC Court of Justice became the European Court of Justice (ECJ).
- The unelected ECSC Council of Ministers became the unelected Council of the EU (where representatives of governments act).

Overview: Today's EU institutions

The number and tasks of further EU institutions have been expanded enormously, as is usual in an uncontrolled bureaucracy. Here is a selection:

- European Commission COM
- European Council (Assembly of heads of state and government) EC
- Conferences of the ministers of the Member States
- European Parliament EP
- European Central Bank ECB
- European Banking Authority EBA
- European Investment Bank EIB

- European Bank for Reconstruction and Development EBRD
- European Investment Fund EIF
- European Globalization Fund
- Euro Group (currency supervision)
- European System of Financial Supervision ESFS
- European Insurance and Occupational Pensions Authority EIOPA
- European Securities and Markets Authority ESMA
- European External Action Service (Foreign Ministry)
- European Energy Charter (conference and secretariat)
- Agency for the Cooperation of Energy Regulators ACER
- European Environment Agency EEA
- European Agency for Railways ERA
- European Fund for regional Development
- European Agricultural Fund for Rural Development EAFRD
- European Cohesion Fund
- European Maritime and Fisheries Fund EMFF
- European Globalization Adjustment Fund EGF
- European Court of Auditors
- European Police EUROPOL
- Coast Guards FRONTEX und European Naval Forces/EUNAVFOR MED
- European Defense Agency, Military Planning and Conduct Capability MPCC
- European Defense Fund
- European Military Formation, Permanent Structured Cooperation PESCO
- European Court of Justice ECJ
- European Court of Human Rights ECHR
- European Innovation and Technology Institute EIT
- European Research Council
- European Anti-Fraud Office OLAF
- Trust Fund for Africa
- Statistical Office EUROSTAT, legal service, translation services, public relations and documentation

Authorities for labor rights and employment services

Several EU institutions are responsible for developing and monitoring labor rights and for shaping employment relationships. They promote increasingly differentiated forms of flexibilized work and labor migration, and breaches of the law are accepted.

- Senior Labor Inspectors Committee SLIC
- European Labor Authority ELA
- European Foundation for the Improvement of Living and Working Conditions EUROFOUND
- European Employment Policy Observatory EEPO
- European Job Mobility Portal EURES
- European Occupational Safety and Health Administration OSHA
- European Center for the Development of Vocational Training CEDEFOP
- European Training Foundation ETF
- European Social Fund ESF
- Free Movement and Social Security Coordination MoveS
- European Parliament Committee on Employment and Social Affairs EMPL

European Commission COM

The headquarters of the COM were moved from Luxembourg to the slightly larger monarchy of Belgium, to Brussels; many departments are still based in Luxembourg. The now 27 members (commissioners) are appointed by the governments of the Member States. The 32,000 civil servants, highly bureaucratically sorted into 16 salary grades, enjoy privileges in terms of comparatively high salaries, tax exemptions and legal immunity. In addition to the basic salaries, there is a complicated system of allowances for marital status, children, upbringing. Officials from outside Belgium receive an expatriation allowance of 15 percent, and higher ranks also receive a residence allowance and an expense allowance. Social insurance is more favorable than in the rest of the EU. The tax burden is one-third lower than the EU average, and all allowances are tax-free anyway.[226] With gradations, the privileges apply to all of the approximately 45,000 EU employees in total - they ensure that in the EU Member States, precisely such privileges are not available to the majority of the population.

In the EU, the initiative lies with the Commission. It subsequently involves the Parliament and the European Council. Although they can also introduce their own initiatives, nothing works without the Commission. The Commission has already stifled many an initiative, especially from the Parliament, such as the European Parliament's decision to establish an EU rating agency designed to break the dominance of the three large US agencies.

Revolving door between COM and corporations
The professional hypocrites of the business lobby, in Germany BDA, BDI, CSU, CDU, FDP, who otherwise polemize everywhere against "too much bureaucracy" and fight for "the reduction of red tape" - these loudest "bureaucracy critics" dearly love the biggest bureaucracy in Europe!

This also stems from the revolving door effect between companies and the COM: company representatives become agency heads - for example, the head of the rail agency comes from the leading rail manufacturer Bombardier. And former commissioners move on and up to banks and corporations: EU President Barroso landed at Goldman Sachs, Commissioner Reding at Bertelsmann and the mining group Nystar, Commissioner Kroes at Uber, Lockheed, Merrill Lynch and McDonald's.

European Parliament
The European Parliament emerged from the consultative Parliamentary Assembly of the Coal and Steel Community. In 1979 it was constituted: The supremacy of the "High Authority" passed to the COM. Gradually, the number of parliamentarians has climbed to 754 at present. This high number, as well as the high pay of the deputies - along with generous funds for staff and offices - are in inverse proportion to the political powerlessness.

The parliament cannot elect a government; it can only question the commissioners proposed by the Council, nod them through, or request new proposals if they are rejected.

European Council
Important decisions are removed from Parliament from the outset. Foreign and security policy, for example, is decided by the European Council, the

body of heads of state and government, also known as the EU Summit. In addition, the Council nominates the President of the Commission and the EU Representative for Foreign Affairs (EU Foreign Minister).

The decisions announced to the public result from intensive lobbying in advance. The Council's 150 working parties involve the lobbying associations and agencies of major banks, insurance companies, financial players and corporations, as well as industry associations. PR agencies such as Fleishman Hillard - most recently known for monitoring journalists, initiatives and politicians in the merger of Bayer and Monsanto[227] - arrange joint meetings of EU officials with representatives of governments and companies, such as the energy companies RWE, Total and Shell, prior to Council decisions. Trade unions and other organizations that are also represented in Brussels play virtually no role.[228]

Dominant capitalist players in the EU

The EU bureaucracy by no means acts sovereignly. It is subject to the influence of international institutions and players. They are also accepted by the EU as lobbyists, consulted as advisors and commissioned with expert opinions, but they also act without and, if necessary, against the EU and the COM. This must be borne in mind when criticizing the EU and the COM: Their "supremacy" is relative. Rather, in many respects, EU and COM are driven: e.g. against the tax, digital, labor law and spying practices of Google, Apple, Amazon, Microsoft, Facebook, BlackRock, PwC or NSA, the EU makes little headway, despite repeated attempts - not to mention the military demands of the US and NATO.

After Washington, Brussels has become the second largest location for professional influence agents since the 1980s. The early players American Chamber of Commerce in Europe, the law firm Cleary Gottlieb & Ball and European Round Table of Industrialists found hundreds of specialized successors until today. Via the Bilderberg Group, the Trilateral Commission, and more recently the World Economic Forum, close ties have been and continue to be cultivated with the elected and above all unelected leaders of the Western capitalist democracies and the COM.[229]

European Round Table of Industrialists

In 1983, 50 of Europe's most important, globally active corporations joined forces: Royal Dutch Shell (UK/Netherlands), Imperial Chemical

Industries (UK), Olivetti and Fiat (Italy), Nestlé and Ciba Geigy (Switzerland), St. Gobain and Renault (France), and Siemens and Thyssen (Federal Republic of Germany) formed the European Round Table of Industrialists. They accused the COM of "eurosclerosis" and "bureaucratic ossification" and called for innovation and "competitiveness". They enforced that the anti-trust provisions contained in the EEC Treaty no longer applied.[230]

Consultants, 'auditors'
Along with the US corporations promoted by the Marshall Plan, the McKinsey management consultants had come along in the 1950s. They and a good dozen others of their ilk advise most states and corporations in the EU - and also the COM itself.

In the same way, the EU has adopted the modus operandi of the Big Four, i.e., the world-market-dominating US auditing groups PwC, KPMG, EY and Deloitte, which together employ nearly one million people. The COM commissions them on privatization and tax issues and accepts them as members of advisory bodies. At the same time, the Big Four lobby in Brussels for systemic tax evasion by capitalists - after all, "tax structuring" is part of the Big Four's lucrative trade, along with 'auditing'. The Big Four have prevented the separation of auditing and tax consulting proposed by the EU. They themselves have their headquarters in various financial havens such as Luxembourg, Switzerland and the Cayman Islands. These COM consultants contribute to the permanent tax loss of the EU states amounting to billions.[231]

The professionals arguing with "the highest ethical standards" maintain a worldwide network of self-service and corruption for high society, as was recently revealed in the example of an African president's daughter (LuandaLeaks): For her hidden stakes also in companies in EU states, PwC & Co set up shell companies in financial havens such as Hong Kong, as well as in Luxembourg and the Netherlands - all unchallenged by the COM. In the EU as in the USA, the Big Four are exempt from money laundering regulations.[232]

Corporate law firms
The same is true of the most politically influential corporate law firm on the planet, Freshfields. Since the 1990s, Freshfields has advised states and municipalities in the EU in favor of fraudulent US financial products such as cross-border leasing[233], acts as a lobby for public-private partnerships,

and also negotiates the contracts on behalf of governments, as in Germany in the case of the Toll Collect contract to organize truck tolls on highways.[234] After the financial crisis, it drafted the laws for EU states such as Germany to bail out bankrupt banks and developed the concept for the EU's ESM stability mechanism. In Germany, Freshfields spent a decade issuing high-paying clean bills of health for the fraudulent Cum-Ex loan stock deals on behalf of two dozen banks.[235]

Investment banks
An important boost that spilled over into the EU was the activity of Wall Street investment banks such as JPMorgan and Goldman Sachs, initially in the Treuhandanstalt for the privatization of GDR enterprises. This continued with the EU-sponsored privatizations of railroads, postal services and media in other EU countries such as Germany and Italy. US investment banks such as Lazard, Rothschild and Australia's Macquarie now dominate mergers, acquisitions and infrastructure privatizations in the EU.[236]

Lobbyists
On behalf of individual large corporations and industry associations, some 25,000 lobbyists in Brussels work on the officials of the COM and MEPs with expert opinions and legislative proposals. For example, in 2019 the capital organizer BlackRock initiated the EU directive on private pensions.[237]

The representatives of trade unions, churches and consumer organizations in Brussels are also referred to as "lobbyists". But in terms of personnel and finances, they are a washout in comparison, and they are consulted by the COM to a much lesser extent. They do not exercise any counterforce because, despite all the occasional criticism, they want to be seen as "good Europeans" and have accepted the EU in principle.

US rating agencies
In 1999, the EU adopted the Big Three US rating agencies, Standard & Poor's, Moody's and Fitch, into its rulebook. Since then, the EU, its own budget, the budget of the European Investment Bank EIB and the EU Member States have been subject to the Big Three ratings. They have since been enshrined in the statutes of the ECB and the national financial supervisory authorities - in Germany, Bafin. Thus, credit conditions for

sovereigns as well as for the major banks and public companies in the EU are subject to the judgments of the US rating agencies.

The Big Three were partly to blame for the financial crisis of 2007 with their highly paid sweetener opinions on subprime securities, in Germany, France and England, but also in the particularly affected crisis states of Greece, Ireland, Spain, Italy and Cyprus. To make itself independent of these state-backed criminals, the European Parliament decided to establish a European rating agency. The US lobby prevented this, and the European Commission scuppered the decision. With their ongoing dependence on the Big Three, owned moreover by large capital organizers such as BlackRock, the EU, its states and companies remain crisis-prone.[238]

European Central Bank ECB

The ECB is a separate legal entity and is not subject to the COM or indeed the Parliament. The ECB is, after all, "independent". But it is all the more vehemently active for the interests of the banks and the capital organizers. The most important president so far, Mario Draghi, came from the investment bank Goldman Sachs. The current president, Christine Lagarde, comes from the US-dominated IMF; previously, she was head of the most important US business law firm for international corporate and tax law, Baker McKenzie.

To ensure that the ECB does everything right, it is advised by the largest capital organizer in the West, BlackRock. Thus, with its interest-free loans and bond purchases, it serves the large speculators BlackRock, Vanguard, State Street, Blackstone, Bridgewater & Co.[239]

Thus, the ECB surreptitiously became "Europe's most influential institution": "In the financial crisis, the ECB self-empoweringly expanded its competences, nolens volens assumed the role of the sweeper for reform-averse and spend-happy governments."[240] After the "corona crisis", this will continue on an intensified scale.

International Monetary Fund IMF

Without involving the EU, the IMF executed its shock program in Yugoslavia starting in 1989 (privatizations, cuts in wages and social benefits, layoffs). The EU enthusiastically adopted the disastrous result and has since continued to expand the small successor states, built on ethnic hatred, as a neocolonial periphery.[241]

In Russia, the IMF, accompanied by USAID and the Open Society Foundation of US speculator George Soros, supported the corrupt and drunken President Boris Yeltsin and his family clan, financed and organized his second election, and helped him succeed in the short term. Thus, the IMF-led West, with the help of local turncoats and oligarchs, ruined the country. Average life expectancy tumbled by eight years. Yeltsin's successor Putin, who insists on the sovereignty of the state, gets along without Western "help" and is economically successful, is, by contrast, hounded as an enemy by the IMF and the EU.

Troika

The IMF acts independently within the EU, but can also join forces with it. After the financial crisis emanating from the US and major Western European banks, the COM formed the Troika with the ECB and the IMF. This "triumvirate" was led by COM President Juncker, ECB President Draghi and IMF Director Lagarde. BlackRock, PwC and others were commissioned to carry out the work on the ground, for example in Athens.[242]

The Troika acts alongside and against the EU institutions: another form of the EU - as a legal gray area. The Troika is not subject to Parliament. Starting in 2010, it intervened in budgetary, labor, trade union and social legislation against the governments of the particularly over-indebted small crisis states of Ireland, Greece and Cyprus, had social benefits and minimum wages cut, suspended trade union rights and collective agreements, promoted "yellow" company unions, and ordered mass layoffs in the public sector, including in schools and hospitals.[243] In Greece, the unions were even deprived of their funding base.[244] Military spending was not cut: unsaid, NATO is ever-present.

Bank for International Settlements BIS

The BIS operates out of the financial haven of Switzerland. It has extraterritorial status there, i.e. it is not even subject to the lax Swiss financial supervision, and Switzerland is also not an EU member state: political uncontrollability is thus ensured in several ways. The BIS is the central bank of the central banks. It is widely unknown even among "globalization critics", although it is repeatedly described as the most powerful bank on earth.[245]

Most of the Marshall Plan funds were channeled through the BIS. In 1974, the "Group of Ten", which was not provided for in the statutes, was installed in the BIS. Since then, it has been dominated by the most powerful member bank, the Federal Reserve (Washington), and is the supreme decision-making body. This is where the international regulations for banks, the financial sector and insurance companies are agreed and also adopted by the EU. The Basel I regulations lowered the capital requirements for banks, and the Basel II regulations made the US rating agencies mandatory in the EU in 1999.[246] The BIS also housed the ECB's preparatory group. Likewise, on behalf of the G7 countries, the BIS "observes" the new "shadow banks" such as BlackRock, Blackstone, Elliott, so that they retain their special status to this day and are not regulated.

Intra- and extra-European financial havens
In addition to the financial havens Luxembourg, the Netherlands, Ireland, Cyprus and Malta, which belong directly to the EU, as well as Monaco, Andorra and San Marino, capital owners have other options. When they joined the EU, the United Kingdom and the Netherlands were granted special status for their former colonies as financial havens, now whimsically called "overseas territories". Unlike the "mother countries" they do not belong to the EU. For the UK, these are 12 island groups. However, the most important of these, such as the Cayman Islands, Bermuda, Anguilla, British Virgin Islands, Turcs and Caicos, are part of the established network of financial havens used by companies, banks, investors, and consultants. This also applies to the "crown colonies" directly assigned to the royal family: the Channel Islands of Guernsey and Jersey, the Isle of Man, and Akrotiri and Dekelia on Cyprus. Brexit has not changed their function as financial havens for companies and financial players.

Similarly, the Netherlands was granted that the outsourced financial havens, the Caribbean "overseas territories" of Aruba, Curacao and Sint Maarten, have special status and are not part of the EU. For France, these are Saint Barthélemy, Saint Pierre and Miquelon, Wallis and Futuna, and French Polynesia.

On the EU's "black lists" of financial havens, the most important ones are always missing: Luxembourg, the Netherlands, Switzerland and, above all, the small US state of Delaware. There, practically all banks, companies, auditing groups and large investors in the EU have branches or letterbox companies. This also applies to the largest owner of banks and companies in the EU, BlackRock.[247]

City of London: The Guantánamo of global finance

The traditional financial center of the British colonial empire - combined with the free trade area of Hong Kong (ex-Crown Colony) and the 14 financial havens in ex-colonies and current Crown Colonies - is the most deregulated financial center in the Western world. That is why all the important US financial players have maintained their European branches here at least since Margaret Thatcher's time, not least the new capital organizers such as BlackRock and Blackstone, but also all the important banks from EU countries and also from Switzerland, for example. The City as the "most competitive financial center" in the world (after Hong Kong) has accelerated the deregulation of the banking and financial world and the disempowerment of financial supervisors in the EU, thus opening up the financial sector to criminal practices. In London, financial players from the EU are allowed to do everything they are not (yet) allowed to do in their home countries: The City is "the Guantánamo Bay of global finance," according to the best British authority on the financial location.[248] Brexit won't change that much either.

European Council on Foreign Relations ECFR

With the onset of the financial crisis in 2007, ex-ministers of Christian, social democratic, conservative, liberal affiliations as well as former COM members founded the European Council on Foreign Relations (ECFR), modeled on the US Council on Foreign Relations (CFR). It too is a privately funded think tank. Its goal is to influence the EU, the COM, the European Parliament and governments, especially in foreign and military policy. The bogeymen Russia and China are the main focus.

Funders include Soros' Open Society Foundation, other foundations such as Mercator, corporations like Daimler and Microsoft, wealthy individuals - and NATO.

US foundations in Europe

In an extended continuation of ACUE and ACUSE, many dozens of US-led foundations operate. They award scholarships in Young Leaders Programs, issue invitations to conferences. In Germany alone, about a dozen are active: Atlantikbrücke, German Marshall Fund, Aspen Institute, etc.[249]

Together with the COM, the Bill and Melinda Gates Foundation organizes pandemic management and vaccine production. Soros's Open Society/Renaissance Foundation operates branches in Eastern and, more recently, Western European countries, and promoted radical right-wing upstarts such as the law student Viktor Orbán in Hungary from 1989. In France, then US Ambassador James Lowenstein and members of the CFR founded the French American Foundation. Its Young Leaders Program produced not only the Socialist and later President François Hollande and journalists from conservative to left-liberal newspapers, but also Emmanuel Macron, the current President of the Republic, and half his government team.[250]

Sponsors of EU institutions

EU institutions such as the European Council can be sponsored by private companies. For example, beverage company Coca-Cola sponsored the Council's 2019 Romanian presidency as its official partner, and in 2011 Coca-Cola sponsored Poland. Audi sponsored Austria, and BMW and the Beverage Industry Association sponsored Bulgaria. Beyond the mere fact of such sponsorship, this is also objectionable because several EU countries are discussing higher taxes on fattening sugary drinks like Coca-Cola.[251] Such proximity to large corporations is commonplace for the EU, but is only occasionally broached.[252]

5.
Economic policy principles:
Without labor rights

The EU organizes labor injustice throughout Europe and the world. It does this in many different ways. It also allows the independent organization of labor injustice by domestic and non-European companies and their consultants: they fight employee representatives and works councils even without permission, independently cut wages and social security contributions, violate applicable national laws and also EU directives. The EU legalizes, coordinates and globalizes labor injustice, which is pursued by capitalists anyway.

We first deal with indirect measures that do not explicitly interfere with labor rights and employment relations, but nevertheless (can, or are even designed to) change them.

Privatization

The EU, and its predecessor forms, has been gradually pushing ahead with the privatization of public enterprises since the 1980s ("completion of the internal market"). However, the term "privatization" is avoided; it is all about "market" and "competition".

It started with postal services (telephone, letters, parcels), media and railroads, i.e. the areas that are used practically on a permanent basis by the entire population. Thus, according to Directive 91/440, the governments of the EU Member States were to ensure that railroad companies could "behave in a self-sufficient manner in accordance with the requirements of the market". In the case of the media, political right-wing development and entertainment populism were also promoted: In Germany, it began in 1984 with RTL, via Luxembourg, which had already been privatized in terms of media policy, RTL = Radio et Télévision Luxembourgeoise.

State treason

At the same time - a characteristic of the privatization fake - the self-imposed principles such as "market" and "competition" are violated, through state subsidies no less. Example with EU approval: When privatizing the Bundespost in Germany, the "market" preachers of the CDU, CSU and FDP under Chancellor Kohl transferred the pension obligations of the several hundred thousand employees to the state budget for decades: a high three-digit billion sum that contributes to the covert, annual permanent over-indebtedness of the state until about the year 2060.[253] Not in a narrow legal sense, but politically, this is grave state treason, and the public, even most politically interested people and members of parliament, are blissfully unaware.

In such privatizations, the profits of the private owners are secured, in the case of Deutsche Post DHL also for the major shareholders, the state, Norges and BlackRock; the incomes of the board members and top managers, supplemented with bonuses and preferential shares, are topped up handsomely - while the rights, wages and pensions of the dependent employees, for example the postmen employed on a temporary and part-time basis and outsourced parcel delivery staff, are slashed.

Prevent re-nationalization
In 1994 the EU adopted the Energy Charter. The US law firm Clifford Chance was involved in drafting it. The reason for this was the privatization of energy companies in the ex-socialist states. The EU wanted to prevent emerging demands for re-nationalization.

For example, the Swedish company Vattenfall is suing the German state, citing the Energy Charter: Vattenfall calls the law to close nuclear power plants expropriation by the state. The government of an EU state that wants to take the energy industry back under state control - most recently the Labour Party in England in the event of its election victory - would be prevented from democratic nationalization by the EU.[254]

"Alternative investments"
In 1983, Directive 85/611 initiated the withdrawal of the state from the banking world. This really took off in 1990 with the help of deregulated capital organizers from the USA. They had already become active in Russia anyway. With directives 2003/41, 2009/65 and 2011/61, the EU promoted private aggressive investment practices. They are belittlingly called "alternative investments". In reality, private equity investors, hedge funds and capital organizers such as BlackRock were fostered. They buy and exploit not only companies and banks, but also apartments, hospitals,

nursing and retirement homes. These investors contribute to the Americanization of labor relations in the EU.[255]

Water is a human right - actually
The COM also wanted to privatize drinking water - Directive 2000/60. Based on 1.8 million signatures, the European Citizens' Initiative "Water is a Human Right" - it refers to the UN resolution - was only able to achieve that the "human right to water" is mentioned in the new directive, but in a non-binding way and not accompanied by concrete measures.

A resolution of the European Parliament had called for more far-reaching measures, but was brushed aside by the COM.[256] In addition, the much more cost-intensive area of wastewater was left out, even though more privatization is already underway there - the COM is speculating that the vast majority of citizens are not bothered about wastewater.

Aid to companies: Prohibited, but lavishly distributed

The EU wants the "free market", competition undisturbed by the state and trade unions. For this reason, Article 107 of the EU Treaty prohibits subsidies and state aid in principle. Support is to be given primarily to small and medium-sized enterprises in "structurally weak" regions, environmental protection projects, training, employment and culture.[257] But the biggest subsidies go to the biggest companies. In agriculture, for example, the amount of the subsidy depends on the size of the farmscape.

The "free competition" and the "self-regulating market" are a fake, a highly professional self-deception and deception of others. However, as is well known, private capitalist profits can only be secured and increased with state aid or state coercion. That is why the EU has built up a highly complicated system of subsidies and aid. It was brought up to date in Directive 1407/2013 and COM Communication 2014/C 188/02.

In other words, aid is actually prohibited, including direct subsidies, low-interest loans, tax exemptions, guarantees, state participation in private companies, rescue of insolvent companies, default payments in the event of corporate losses. But with the appropriate regulation, precisely all of these subsidies are allowed, and lavishly so. This was already made possible for US business investments with the Marshall Plan and the EEC Treaty, so it is not an innovation. Subsidies are the largest budget item of the EU. The COM organizes the second largest corporate subsidy program in contemporary capitalism,[258] after the USA.[259] This does not prevent the USA and also the EU from acting as major critics of "state capitalism" in China.

EU authorizes state command economy
Even direct state command economy is supported by the EU. Thus, in April 2020, the COM approved the State Treaty on the Modernization of the Media Order in Germany (Media State Treaty): It forces all citizens and companies to finance the state media ARD, ZDF, DLF and the state broadcasters such as WDR, NDR, BR, mdr through fees, moreover, regardless of whether these media are used at all. This also involves snooping: The state-owned subsidiary *"Beitragsservice"* (Fee Service) with 950 employees "tracks down unknown homes" in order to collect further contributions and initiates enforcements by writ.[260]

Pre-accession aid
The EU also grants aid to companies, authorities and groups in countries that are not members of the EU: "pre-accession aid". "Feeding up" is what they call it when the talk is of corruption. EU candidate states such as Montenegro, Serbia, Northern Macedonia and Albania are currently being fed, but also states that are only considered "potential" candidates such as Bosnia-Herzegovina and Kosovo. Companies can also receive subsidies in states with an even lower status, such as those in the "Eastern Partnership", Armenia, Azerbaijan, Georgia, Moldova, Ukraine and Belarus.

The goal of the subsidies is the establishment of a "market economy", adorned with demands for the rule of law, human rights and the fight against corruption. By market economy, however, this does not mean a national market and national economy with full employment, but rather the free movement of privileged private capital primarily of Western origin (including, for example, from Japan, South Korea and Taiwan) and the regulation of labor migration wanted by Western states and companies. Such an arrangement, which, as in the case of Bosnia-Herzegovina and Kosovo, even entails an EU protectorate (a High Commissioner appointed by the EU as head of state), can extend over many years.

Subsidies to ward off refugees
The EU now also awards aid to ward off refugees - all part of market and competition. The Trust Fund for Africa was launched in 2015 for this

purpose.[261] Eritrea, for example, has been receiving aid for road construction since 2017. Moreover, this is carried out with the help of forced labor. Human Rights Watch denounced this in its World Report 2020. As in other cases, the COM justifies itself by saying that it "hopes for reform". If this hope really existed, the condition that subsidies only be granted once forced labor has been eliminated would be more successful.[262]

Subsidies for oligarchs and populists
While EU officials criticize Hungarian Prime Minister Orbán as a "populist", the EU subsidizes precisely such politicians. For they support Western capitalists most fiercely. (see the reports on Poland and Hungary, page 223ff.)

For example, the Orbán government sold large areas of state-owned agricultural land, in subdivisions so large that ordinary farmers could not bid. The land went to the Orbán clan and to business partners - and they and also the Czech head of government Andrej Babiš are now the biggest recipients of EU subsidies in the states they govern. The situation is similar in Slovakia and Bulgaria. The subsidies result in small farmers having to give up.[263] The EU fraud investigation authority (OLAF) is helpless.[264]

Subsidies without conditions for labor rights
The subsidies go primarily to private companies in all sectors - and always without any requirements for labor rights.

Subsidies even in the event of plant closure and low-wage employment
In eastern Germany, for example in Saxony under the xenophobic CDU Prime Minister Kurt Biedenkopf, the US corporation American Micro Devices (AMD) received a subsidy to the tune of hundreds of millions for building a branch, along with subsidies from the Free State and the German government. The head of the Saxon government could boast that he had created new jobs - even though the branch was closed after the subsidy expired.[265]

In Saxony, BMW, Porsche and VW were also subsidized for the expansion as a new automotive location. As a result, the proportion of financially and legally disadvantaged contract and temporary workers was much higher than in West Germany. They complain about overtime and a lack of health protection. Their wages are partly "topped up" by the state - the EU does not prohibit this permanent subsidy either.[266]

Subsidies for Public Private Partnership
The EU has adopted the public-private partnership (PPP) privatization construct developed in the UK. Hidden in this are numerous state profit aids: tax advantages, additional claims by the entrepreneurs, default payments, and all this covered up by secrecy of the contracts. The EU also subsidizes the contracts through low-interest loans from the European Investment Bank (EIB).[267]

PPP practice includes the outsourcing of construction and operational work (facility management) to subcontractor chains organized by the prime contractor: they are an instrument of low-wage labor and the skimming off of cheap migrant labor.

Direct wage subsidies
The German state in particular, as the location with the largest low-wage sector in the EU, subsidizes low-wage earners with billions of euros annually, as it already did for the benefit of car companies in Saxony: the labor income of the average of between 1.3 and 1.1 million low-wage earners has been topped up by around EUR 10 billion annually since 2007; by 2018, this had amounted to EUR 117 billion.[268]

Subsidies for modern slave labor
Germany's leading slaughterhouse group, Tönnies, was also subsidized for investments in "rural areas". The main beneficiaries of subsidies are large industrial, environmentally harmful agricultural corporations that pay their few employees as poorly as possible.

Among the entrepreneurs promoted by the "Christian" Commissioner for Agriculture Phil Hogan (ex-minister in Ireland) were the mafia-infested plantation operators in southern Spain and southern Italy: they use refugees from Africa as slave laborers largely without rights or representation, house them in makeshift tent slums near the plantations, persecute trade unionists.[269] (See the chapter on Spain, p. 190ff)

Free trade agreements and global supply chains
The EU negotiates free trade agreements for its Member States: In recent years, these have included TTIP with the USA, CETA with Canada, JEFTA with Japan, the TiSA services agreement, with South Korea, Singapore, four South American states (EU-Mercosur) and, under the name Economic Partnership Agreements (EPA), with African states.

These do mention labor rights with reference to the eight ILO core standards - and only to these, not to the 180 other standards. And they are only non-binding declarations of intent. Violations, however, are not sanctionable. By contrast, investor rights are sanctionable and can be sued in private arbitration courts, resulting in damages.[270]

The EU thus also protects the unsanctioned violation of labor rights in global supply and service chains by corporations based on its territory. The EU, with German government support, has therefore blocked the Binding Treaty developed by the UN Human Rights Committee since 2014, according to which companies can be held liable and sanctioned for human rights violations.

A supply chain law that the EU and the German government have been striving for since 2020 already completely excludes supply chains within the EU in its planning and reduces human rights to the prohibition of child and slave labor and the like. But even that has not yet been decided.[271]

EU - that means worldwide legalized and also extra-legal labor injustice.

6.
Labor injustice:
Direct legal instruments

The EU works in all areas with directives and regulations. They are not laws, but represent extra- and supra-legal instructions, directives, regulations. The Member States must transpose the directives into national law or amend existing national laws.

PRIMARY LAW

There are some good-sounding passages in EU primary law, but they are mostly quite general and, above all, non-binding. Article 117 of the EEC Treaty, for example, stated that "efforts must be made to improve the living and working conditions of workers" and that "this should make possible their harmonization by means of progress". Well, the EU has been "making efforts toward" "harmonization" ever since - the result: harmonization downward.

The EU Treaty of Lisbon, in force since 2009, stipulates in Art. 153 that the EU "shall support and complement" the Member States in the following fields:

- Improvement in particular of the working environment to protect workers' health and safety,
- working conditions,
- social security and social protection of workers,
- protection of workers where their employment contract is terminated,
- the information and consultation of workers,
- representation and collective defense of the interests of workers and employers.

Then it goes on "including co-determination", but "subject to paragraph 5", and there it states: the provisions of this article shall not apply to pay, the right of association, the right to strike or the right to impose lock-outs.[272] There are no references to the ILO, the Universal Declaration of Human Rights, the UN Social Covenant and the UN Human Rights Committee or to control procedures in the UN. In order to classify the stipulations in Article 153 of the EU Treaty, we will take a look at further legal documents in the next section.

European Convention on Human Rights: Without labor rights
In 1950, the Council of Europe, convened on the initiative of the USA, adopted the Convention on Human Rights. It entered into force in 1953 and has been updated ever since.

The Council of Europe could have simply adopted the UN Declaration of Universal Human Rights, but it didn't. Thus, the Convention contains only the old "civil" liberties, reflecting primarily their status in the US Constitution and 19th century European nation states. For instance, the right to life, to liberty and security, to a fair trial in the judiciary, to respect for private and family life, and the right to freedom of thought, conscience and religion apply. The prohibitions of torture, slave labor and forced labor are mentioned. Freedom of movement in the choice of residence and profession, as well as movement within the state and EU Member States, are also important civil rights. Freedom of association, assembly, press and expression are highlighted. All these rights made and make good sense. However, they are subject to reservations: because of the protection of public safety and order, because of the prevention of crimes and because of the protection of the rights of third parties and generally under the reservation of a "state of emergency".[273]

Property is protected - but not state and municipal property
Civil rights include, not least, the "right to property", which was added later. Here, it is scrupulously avoided to describe more precisely the property that is protected by the state. The property of the dependent employees, the farmers and also the state and the municipalities is not meant at all.

What is meant, rather, is private capital ownership, but this is skillfully populistically not named in this way. As in the Basic Law of the Federal Republic of Germany, which was adopted at about the same time, where there is equally diffuse talk of "property", it can be expropriated for reasons of the "general good", with compensation. In practice, however, this applies only to land owned by farmers and other private individuals for the construction of roads.

From the privatizations promoted by the EU – the sale of public housing below market value, for example -state and municipal property was not protected by the 'human' right to property installed in the Convention.[274]

Therefore, without being explicitly mentioned, the rights to freedom of association, assembly, press and opinion are also subject to private property reservations: Free assembly within companies is impossible. Free expression of opinion on breaches of the law in private companies is not possible and can be punished by dismissal ("disturbance of industrial peace"). Public opinion in the EU is dominated by private media and digital corporations, and in Germany also by state-run compulsory media.

Most importantly, in the so-called human rights convention all labor and trade union rights are missing.

European Social Charter
In 1961, the Council of Europe adopted the European Social Charter. It was intended to supplement the Convention on Human Rights with "social" aspects: This includes labor rights. Even the "right to work" was taken from the UN Universal Human Rights. The following are listed: Just, safe and healthy working conditions, fair remuneration sufficient for

a decent standard of living for themselves and their families, free association and collective bargaining, special protection for working mothers, vocational guidance, vocational training, social security. Migrant workers - admittedly only those who are nationals of a contracting party - and their families have the right to protection.

In Article 6.4 it states: "The right of workers and employers to collective action in cases of conflicts of interest, including the right to strike." However, the Charter also makes no reference to the ILO and thus removes EU labor rights from the review procedures and also from the constitution of new labor rights in the ILO. There are also no provisions for sanctions in the event of violations.

Article 1 states that for "the effective exercise of the right to work", states must ensure "full employment". But the EU in particular does not ensure full employment, on the contrary: millions of employees work too much (including unpaid overtime), other millions work involuntarily too little (underemployment) and further millions have no work at all. This is another reason why the rudiments of the Charter have been suppressed and long since undermined by directives.

Germany in particular weakens the Charter
The Federal Republic of Germany in particular, which presents itself as a "model European state", was and is at the forefront when it comes to the non-recognition of occasionally democratic EU law, in this case the Social Charter. The mention of the right to strike goes beyond the German Basic Law. Accordingly, the German Federal Labor Court has repeatedly weakened this provision in the Convention.[275]

Although the Charter was ratified by the government of CDU, CSU and FDP under Ludwig Erhard and Labor Minister Theodor Blank (former Defense Minister, CDU), five rights were excluded and are not in the ratified version:

- The right of all workers to a reasonable period of notice for termination of employment (Art. 4.4)
- Minimum age of 15 years for employment (Art. 7.1)
- Protection from dismissal for women during pregnancy and until the end of maternity (Art. 8.2)

- Regulation of employment in night work of pregnant women, women who have recently given birth and women nursing their infants (Art. 8.4)
- The state must promote or provide special measures for the retraining and reintegration of the long-term unemployed. (Art. 10.4).

Moreover: The Additional Protocol on Collective Complaints was not signed or ratified by any German government.[276] And here began the development of the Federal Republic into the leading labor injustice state in the EU. (see p. 182ff.)

European Charter of Fundamental Rights and Treaty of Lisbon

So, the Social Charter had to disappear. The arch-reactionary lawyer and German President Roman Herzog, as head of a commission, drafted the replacement, the EU Charter of Fundamental Rights.

The Charter was adopted by the EU in 2000. It reverts to the bourgeois canon of values of the German Basic Law. "Fundamental rights" replace human rights. Thus, the six main fundamental rights are: the inviolable dignity of the human person, freedom, equality, solidarity, civil rights, fair justice, prohibition of torture and slavery. Modernized, the following were also included: Consumer and data protection, right to good administration, rights of children, disabled and elderly people, and still "dignified working conditions" - generic and legally diffuse. Nowhere are the UN Universal Human Rights, the UN Charter, the UN Social Covenant and the specifically codified ILO standards even mentioned.[277] The Charter is part of the Lisbon Treaty, which is not a constitution.

SECONDARY LAW I: DIRECTIVES

The concrete shaping of labor relations and labor law is done via directives. They have to be transposed into national laws. The states have several years to do this, can delay for a long time and also make changes and exceptions, and can also violate their own versions with impunity - a multifaceted gray area.

Directives can be violated and ignored

Especially the leading labor injustice state in the EU, the Federal Republic of Germany, also leads when it comes to not implementing directives. An example already mentioned is the slurry directive.

When Member States undermine the already low standards of directives, this is not criticized by the COM. This was the case, for example, with the frequent erosion of labor law seen in most EU states in the wake of the 2007 financial crisis. The Tory government in the UK overrode EU directives with impunity, made it even easier to dismiss people, imposed fees for going to an employment tribunal, and abolished existing rights of pregnant women.[278] The EU did not intervene.

Labor injustice from Member States is adopted by the EU
The EU also operates the other way around: capital-friendly practices developed in Member States are adopted in EU directives.

In labor law, the EU adopted the zero-hour contract, which was developed into a system in Great Britain and then in the Netherlands: work on call, without a guaranteed number of hours, whereby the person "employed" on call can also serve several labor pluckers. We will look at this in more detail in the European Pillar of Social Rights, the latest, comprehensive EU labor law directive of 2019. (see p. 147ff.)

Never a directive on compensation for forced laborers
The EU, starting with the Coal and Steel Community, never issued a directive on compensation for forced labor and concentration camp workers during World War II, even though since 1952 the six founding states had also subsidized companies that had benefited from Nazi forced labor.

Extremely exploitative labor, including forced labor in the African and Asian colonies of the EU founding states of Belgium and France as well as Portugal even after World War II, was never addressed, criticized or indeed abolished, not even in important cooperation states such as the dictatorships of South America and the apartheid state of South Africa.

Directives are sometimes revised several times and published as new directives. They are included in the trilogue, i.e. in the coordination between the COM, the Council of Ministers and the Parliament. As a rule, only the latest version is mentioned below. For better chronological classification, the complete year is given for the directive numbers, although the EC wrote e.g. 96 instead of 1996. This is a selection.

Migrant work
From the time of the Coal and Steel Community until 1968, essentially only guidelines for migrant labor were published. It was all about entry

and residence. There was no concern for labor rights; the "guest workers", so the fiction went, would gladly accept any job and would soon disappear again anyway.

With the collapse of the socialist states, the EU developed a new permanent reservoir of migrant workers. This is open to mafiotic and criminal practices when needed. This applies to various groups of migrant workers, which grew in size, such as construction, meat and agricultural seasonal workers, domestic care workers, hospital staff, truck drivers, prostitutes.

Posted workers directive and many loopholes

In 1996, the EU adopted the Posted Workers Directive (Posted Workers Directive 1996/71, since revised several times, most recently 2018/957). It is meant to ensure uniform "minimum standards" for workers temporarily working in another state, e.g. minimum wage in the state where the work is performed, compliance with the statutory working hours there, vacation entitlement, in each case at the lowest level. "Minimum standards": this indicates that deviations from the normal standard are involved. And minimum standards can also be undercut.

Loophople I: Multi-year transitional periods for Eastern Europe

For many years, social insurance - for unemployment, sickness, pensions - did not have to be paid as it was for native German, British, Dutch, Swedish, etc. workers, but could be arranged with reference to the low wages in Eastern Europe. The migrant workers were thus cheaper in any case, even if they had the same status under labor law as, say, contract workers. Companies in the rich states were thus granted multi-year transitional periods.

Loophole II: Normal implementation deadlines

When transposing this into national law, the EU states can specify a period of up to 18 months during which the standards of the recipient state do not have to apply. This encourages the constant exchange of posted workers and the flexibility defined by the entrepreneurs. If the deadline is exceeded, no sanctions follow.

Loophole III: Exceptions for certain professions

In Germany, the requirements of the EU directive initially applied only to construction workers under the subsequently implemented German Posted

Workers Act of 1996. It was not until years later that building cleaners, roofers, care workers, meat workers, etc. were gradually included in the scope - allowing entrepreneurs to conveniently develop workarounds with the help of labor brokers.

Loophole IV: No control
The EU does not exercise any control in the area of labor rights. It leaves the control to the national labor and trade inspectorates, fully aware and tolerant of the fact that they are understaffed, like customs, trade and health inspectorates in Germany. Customs officials pop up on construction sites from time to time for public effect. But there is no on-site supervision for the new million-strong groups of migrant workers, such as domestic and care workers, harvest helpers, restaurant and tourism workers, delivery workers, meat workers, and so on.[279] An unknown number of entrepreneurs do not report their posted employees to the authorities - never mind.[280] The many hundreds of thousands of prostitutes are not meant anyway, not recorded, officially non-existent.

Services Directive: Migrant pseudo self-employed as well
After low-wage workers for simple jobs, Western companies also call for cheaper skilled workers. That is why the EU issued the Directive on Services (Services Directive 2006/103, also called the Bolkestein Directive after the Dutch Internal Market Commissioner at the time). It regulates the temporary provision of services by craftsmen, freelancers and self-employed persons in an EU state other than the state of origin. Affected areas are e.g. skilled work in construction (type "Polish tiler"), hotels, tourism, care for the elderly, retail.

This directive also directly interferes with the labor rights of the nation states in an unconstitutional manner. For example, the country-of-origin principle applies in the sense of freedom of establishment for companies - in contrast to the Posted Workers Directive. Due to hefty protests, some areas were exempted, e.g. temporary employment agencies and health services. A common workaround: The Polish temporary tiler is registered with the Chamber of Commerce in Germany as a "self-employed entrepreneur" - the Chamber is happy to do this and gets new members.

Counseling centers for migrant workers
In 2014, the EU issued the Directive "Facilitating the exercise of rights conferred on workers by the free movement of persons" (Directive 2014/54). Member States must establish counseling centers for migrant workers and their family members: Advice on access to employment, social and tax benefits, vocational training and finding housing, along with labor rights. The European Social Fund subsidizes such counseling centers. Collective empowerment of migrant workers is not envisaged. (see p. 153ff.)

Three million truck drivers
A special group are the approximately 3.6 million truck drivers currently on the roads of the EU. They are not officially designated as migrant workers.

Initially, the EU promoted the deregulation of the logistics industry, for example through subsidies for road construction. Branches and suppliers of Western car and retail groups and supermarket chains needed more and more truck traffic. Working conditions were subordinate to this. The labor pool of Eastern European countries is exploited by Western logistics companies such as UPS, Deutsche Post DHL and Deutsche Bahn (subsidiary Schenker) as well as increasingly by Eastern European logistics companies such as Girteka (Lithuania): The transports are organized by an army of subcontractors registered there. They employ the precarious drivers from Poland, Romania, Bulgaria, Ukraine, Moldova. "Poles, Czechs, Romanians, Russians drive trucks with German and Austrian license plates, German forwarders establish branches in Romania."[281]
To regulate this, the EU has issued numerous directives, e.g.:

* 2002/15: Working time of persons performing road transport activities
* 2003/59: Requirements for the initial qualification and further training of professional drivers
* 2006/561: Driving and rest times for long-distance drivers
* 2009/4: Prevention and detection of tampering with tachograph records.

That was of little use. Alarmed by accidents involving overtired drivers and by union protests against criminal practices, the COM and Parliament have wanted to adopt a new directive since 2016. Actually, the Posted Workers Directive also applies, but it is being circumvented across the board.[282] A study on accidents and traffic fatalities caused by tired truck drivers, announced by the EU back in 2010, has still not materialized - in 2020, ver.di and the European Transport Workers' Federation ETF organized an online survey on the subject.[283]

EU mobility package: Unclear future
The compromise reached in 2019 (EU mobility package) provides for the recognition of minimum wages applicable in the state of the work performed; in addition, the legal right to monthly trips home to families in the countries of origin; restriction of cabotage (additional jobs accepted abroad in between); and the ban on spending the newly regulated breaks in drivers' cabs.

However, this is where the EU mechanism kicks in again: There are exceptions in the compromise, for example if the driver declares that he by no means wants to spend the night in a hotel instead of the driver's cab. Moreover, there are not nearly as many and, moreover, affordable hotel rooms along the highways, nor are there any truck parking spaces in the neighboring cities. And finally, the Eastern European governments, with Western corporations breathing down their necks, have not given their approval to the mobility package - it is not supposed to apply until 2021 anyway. And above all: Neither the EU nor the EU states would actually have the staff to be able to monitor compliance with the new rules.[284]

Labor migration in favor of rich countries
Since the economic crisis of 2007, the number of officially posted migrant workers has almost tripled. The highest proportion in relation to the number of employees is posted by the small ex-Yugoslav state of Slovenia: 5 percent of its dependent employees work in another EU state.

Most are posted to the rich EU founding states, in this ranking: Germany, France, the Netherlands, Belgium. The highest proportion of posted workers in relation to its own population ends up in the low-wage sector of the richest EU state: Luxembourg. The state in which its own citizens have by far the highest per capita income in the EU allows itself to be served most intensively by posted workers from other states.[285]

60 years delay, and with exceptions
As early as 1949, in the face of global labor migration after World War II, the ILO decided on equal treatment for migrant workers. This includes

social insurance, paid leave and paid overtime. It also includes the obligation to prevent misleading recruitment (ILO Standard 97 "Migrant Workers").[286] The Federal Republic of Germany, for example, ratified the Convention in 1959.

But what does the EU make of it? Only 50 years later did it adopt selected rights, allows exceptions and delays, does not impose controls.

No collective labor law

The EU has no collective labor law that is even remotely in line with UN human rights and the ILO, or even that in Western European countries such as France, Belgium, Luxembourg, Italy, Germany, Austria, the Netherlands and the Scandinavian countries. The directives are never about collective labor law, never about support for unions, as was the case, for example, in Roosevelt's New Deal in the 1930s in the United States and in the Western and socialist states in Europe after World War II, each in a different way.

Collective labor law - i.e. the rights to the establishment and permanent operation of independent trade unions, works councils and other employee representation bodies, including forms of co-determination: This does not appear in EU directives, with one - apparent - exception: European Works Council. However, it has no rights whatsoever to co-determination, only to information and consultation.

European Works Council (EWC)

Directive 2009/38 is called Establishment of a European Works Council or a procedure in Community-scale undertakings and groups of undertakings for the purposes of informing and consulting employees. Sounds complicated, bureaucratic, and it is. And regulates only subordinate rights: information and consultation of employees.

The directive regulates a procedure for establishing a "European Works Council" (EWC). The very term is a deception. First, a "special negotiating body" of the employees must come into being: Either on the initiative of the management (!) or it is requested by the employee representatives to the management (!). The body may then enter into negotiations with the management: How should the works council be composed, how often should it meet, how much money will be allocated?

The EWC only has the right to be consulted and informed.[287] And this is only the case if management decisions have a cross-border impact on employees, e.g. if further training becomes necessary. If entrepreneurs prevent the election of a works council or obstruct an elected works council, this is a criminal offense under the German Works Council Constitution Act (BetrVG) § 119 - nothing of the sort with the European Works Council.

"Can anybody hear us?"
A similar arrangement has existed since 2004 with Directive 2001/86 for the new legal form created by the EU for stock corporations, the Societas Europaea (S.E.). It is available to companies with several locations within the EU. Here, too, employees only have information and consultation rights.

Article 1 of the German Works Constitution Act (Betriebsverfassungsgesetz, BetrVG) states: "Works councils are elected in establishments with at least five permanent employees entitled to vote, three of whom are eligible for election." By contrast, a European Works Council must have at least 1,000 employees, with at least 150 employees in each of two Member States. Tens of thousands of smaller companies are therefore excluded. In 2015, there were 1,300 EWCs and an additional 161 in a S.E. Trade unions such as IG Metall support the networking of EWCs.[288] Particularly active EWCs can also agree on "site protection" in Europe, as at General Motors (Opel, Vauxhall, Saab, plants in 7 EU countries). However, this means little in the event of a conflict.[289]

Co-determination, as in Germany, is undermined with the S.E.: Workers and unions have no representatives on the supervisory board. A survey of 365 such bodies revealed: we are not involved in important decisions. The mood among the powerless works councils: "Can anybody hear us?"[290]

Only individual defensive rights against entrepreneurs
The EU promotes the collective rights of private entrepreneurs; it encourages their institutional self-organization, for example in the growing number of lobby groups used for COM consultation. Start-ups are subsidized, but the formation of trade unions is not. Nor does the EU promote collective representation as under the co-determination laws in Germany.

The EU establishes rules for recurring labor disputes. Here is a selection of guidelines:

- 1977/187: Approximation of the laws of the Member States relating to the safeguarding of employees' rights in the event of transfers of undertakings, businesses or parts of businesses
- 1998/59: Protection in the event of collective redundancies
- 1991/533: Employer's obligation to inform employees of the conditions applicable to the contract or employment relationship
- 2001/23: Safeguarding of employees' rights in the event of transfers of undertakings, businesses or parts of undertakings or businesses
- 2002/14: Informing and consulting of employees in the EU. (This directive was triggered by job cuts at firms in France such as Renault, Panasonic, Sabena, Marks & Spencer)
- 2008/94: Protection of employees in the event of insolvency of their employer

So here too: merely defensive rights, compliance with which is not monitored by the EU.

Flexicurity: Flexibilization without security

The EU has progressively driven fragmentation, limitation, precarization of work and its legalization:

- *1990/70: Fixed-term work.* This directive considers fixed-term contracts to be permissible, but does not lay down any rules of its own. The Member States are merely called upon to prevent *abuse* that is not defined in more detail.
- Directive 1997/81 urged *part-time work*. In the FRG, the two directives were implemented in 2000 - long before Hartz Act No. 1 - with the Part-Time and Fixed-term Employment Act. This also made unfounded fixed-term employment permissible, although it was limited to two years. This was a breach of the dam.
- *1991/383: Temporary work,* recast by Directive *2008/104.* It was implemented in the FRG in 2011 by the Temporary Employment Act (AÜG). Temporary employment had been regulated in Germany since 1972 and only applied under precisely defined conditions. The EU directive stipulated that the working conditions for temporary workers should be equal to those of directly employed workers. That sounded

good. But the loophole was built in: According to Article 5, Member States are allowed to derogate from equality, for example by collective agreement between the "social partners". The German government exploited this: According to the AÜG, the same status does not need to apply until after 9 months, and by collective agreement it can take even longer. The German government had already done the groundwork with the Hartz I law. Thus, temporary work became a large-scale labor market policy instrument: temporary work as a permanent status for years, also with the help of "Christian" trade unions.[291] In Germany, the number of temporary workers, which has risen to one million, serves as the first available resource for quick layoffs - and new hires - whenever there is a crisis in the automotive industry.

- *2003/88 Aspects of the organization of working time.* The average working time per 7-day week was set at 48 hours, including overtime. The emphasis is on "average", so the number of hours may be higher if, for example, a one-year working time account is kept. However, unpaid overtime is not covered, nor is on-call time. The 48-hour rule is all the more unfair because the EU promotes more and more part-time work with other directives. This means that employees in the same company can work 60 hours a week alongside those who work only 4 hours.

Directive 2007/359: Flexicurity
In 2006, the COM blended the various forms of precarization into an overall concept: Green Paper - Modernizing Labor Law to Meet the Challenges of the 21st Century (2006/708). After consultations with the business lobby, parliament and trade unions, the Commission turned this into Directive 2007/359.

Establish common principles for the flexicurity approach: More and better jobs through flexibility and security
"Flexicurity" - the combination of the terms flexibility and security - was supposed to mean that we can make work more flexible and at the same time more secure. However, this only resulted in greater flexibility for employees, while the security is very much tilted towards employers.

Role models in EU countries

The EU cited examples from Member States for this purpose:

- In the Netherlands, private employment agencies had been established since 1982, also for voluntary part-time work by women. The Flexibility and Security Act of 1999 promoted the reduction of full-time jobs and leads to a high level of employment.
- Denmark organized rapid job rotation: The low level of protection against dismissal promotes rapid changes from one job to the next and forces the unemployed to look for a new job. While employees continue their training, the unemployed can take over their jobs for a short time.
- In Ireland, the Towards 2016 program, agreed by the social partners, promoted rapid qualification with basic skills such as literacy and numeracy and workplace learning. This created new jobs for unemployed young people, disabled people and migrants.[292]

No social security

Flexicurity was geared toward the interests of companies, which were impelled to "organize themselves on a more flexible basis" due to "globalization".[293] To this end, the Commission constructed a fake scenario: according to OECD criteria unemployment in the Netherlands, Denmark and Ireland was about three times higher than according to the manipulated EU statistics.[294]

That is why the flexicurity approach was not translated into a directive. The verifiable social security especially for the mentioned flexibilized target groups of women in part-time etc. could not be achieved. In addition, at that time the SPD/Green federal government had fulfilled (almost) all the wishes of the COM with the four Hartz laws. Voluntariness in accepting precarious jobs was replaced by coercion, exercised by the job centers or by the growing lack of full-time jobs.

The Hartz laws with legalized forms of flexibilized and precarious work were later adopted in other "reform" programs of social democratic governments in important EU countries such as France and Italy.[295] Youth unemployment, working poverty and the pension poverty that follows it in the 'reform' states such as Spain, Germany, Italy, the Netherlands, Ireland, France, Greece are particularly high.[296]

Safety and health at work?

With the cheapening and disenfranchisement of dependent labor, workplace hazards were already on the rise in the 1980s: For one thing, entrepreneurs were on the scrimp here too; for another, EU Member States took the axe to their inspection agencies. Therefore, the EU rightly saw an increased need for countermeasures. It founded the Senior Labor Inspectors Committee (SLIC) in 1989 that still exists to this day. At the same time, the COM attempted a compact approach with the framework directive 1989/391 Safety and Health at Work.

Problem identified...

This includes, among others, the following implementing directives:

- 1989/654: Minimum safety and health requirements for the workplace
- 1989/655: Minimum safety and health requirements for the use of work equipment at work
- 1989/686: Approximation of the laws of Member States relating to personal protective equipment
- 1990/269: Manual handling of loads where there is a risk particularly of back injury
- 1990/270: Minimum safety and health requirements for work with display screen equipment
- 1992/85: Improvement of health and safety of pregnanz workers, workers who have recently given birth or are breastfeeding.
- 1994/33: Protection of young people at work
- 2004/37: Protection of workers from the risks related to carcinogens or mutagens at work– exposure limits.

... but no solution

The EU had somehow recognized the problem. The directives pinpointed actual danger areas in a very differentiated way. The EU established further agencies, such as the Occupational Safety and Health Agency (OSHA). However, it is not the EU agencies, but the Member States that "ensure adequate control and supervision". "Adequate" – one of the EU's favorite words. But the EU tolerates further cuts in labor inspection in the Member States, even for the most vulnerable workers.[297]

Equal rights for men and women at work?

Here, too, the EU relies on delay. Neither the 1950 Convention on Human Rights nor the 1961 Social Charter include the right to equal treatment of women in working life. It is only in the Charter of Fundamental Rights of 2000 that equality between men and women "including employment, work and remuneration" also appears in Article 23.

Directives 2002/73 and 2004/113 were implemented in the Member States with further delays and exceptions. The German Bundestag passed the General Equal Treatment Act (AGG) in 2006. And there, again, many exceptions and complicated conditions apply.

Practical development: Disenfranchisement for the majority of women
However, the development promoted by the EU is simultaneously going in the opposite direction. The traditionally discriminated "weaker sex" is further discriminated against by the flexibilized breakdown of work volume and jobs into ever smaller parts:

- First, even in "normal" full-time jobs, women are permanently and consistently paid less throughout the EU: In Germany, women earn 21.5 percent less than men on average - not including part-time work - while the EU average is 16.2 percent.[298]
- Second, the share of women in forced part-time work, temporary work, 450-euro jobs, catering and cleaning, domestic help, full-time home care work, and the like is maintained at traditionally high levels.
- Third: Equal rights for women are promoted with practical measures only for a tiny minority, namely for advancement to management positions in companies, law firms, banks, political parties and the public sector. There, a women's quota of mostly 30 percent - 50 percent would be too bold! - which, for example, is to be *aimed for* in supervisory boards of stock corporations, without obligation, at some time in the future.

Perverted women's movement
Where the advancement of women really takes hold: Never before have so many women risen to minister of "defense" and labor in the EU. In Germany, for example, women are now being admitted to male-dominated bodies such as the Advisory Council of Economic Experts: Prof. Veronika Grimm, for instance, who then uses feminist posturing to advocate the

same neoliberal economics and the advancement of women (only) into leadership positions.[299]

Every single female who rises to the leadership of a company, a party, a government, a central bank, a board of advisors, and even the COM is celebrated: she contributes, smiling all around, to keeping the majority of dependent women mired in labor injustice.

Whistleblowers or corruption in EU bureaucracy

With Directive 2019/1937 *Protection of Persons Reporting Breaches of Union Law*, the EU aims to protect whistleblowers. It covers crimes such as corrupt contracting, money laundering, food and product safety violations; in keeping with the times, terrorist financing was also included. The confidentiality of whistleblowers' identities is to be preserved, and they are to be protected from retaliation. To this end, "internal reporting channels" are to be set up in companies and public authorities.

The top ten EU countries, like Germany, have no legal protection for whistleblowers so far. In the leading financial haven of Luxembourg, they are treated as criminals.

The directive was triggered by the tax fraud via the financial havens of Panama and Luxembourg published by whistleblowers: it had been organized by professional, state-commissioned 'auditors' such as PwC.

In fact, because of the supervisory failings that contributed to the 2007 financial crisis, the EU had already adopted Whistleblower Directive 2013/36. This was then forgotten: the new scandal provided an opportunity to innocently start over!

Inbuilt hurdles

The intention sounds good (maybe). But the inbuilt hurdles become apparent at first glance:

- Violation of labor rights is not meant.
- Much-used financial havens that are not on the EU blacklist, such as Luxembourg, the Netherlands and Delaware, are excluded.
- The tip-offs are to go through "internal reporting channels". There are to be no public discussions and no court hearings. The information should remain under the wraps of the companies and authorities concerned - including the COM - for as long as possible.

- The directive must be transposed into national law by 2021. The two governing parties in Germany, especially the CDU/CSU, have stated: We do not want such "far-reaching" protection for whistleblowers.[300]

Deep-seated corruption in the COM

The directive would have made sense two decades ago. After all: In 1999, the entire leadership of the COM - i.e. all elected Commissioners - resigned under President Jacques Santer. Commissioners had funneled high offices and contracts to relatives and friends. Contracts had been awarded without mandatory auditing. Subsidies for projects in Bosnia and Africa had seeped into "dark channels". Over many years, Santer & Co. had disregarded tip-offs from COM employees. Nepotism at its best!

To prevent public scrutiny, the COM quickly resigned in unison. OLAF, the anti-fraud agency, was established to investigate corrupt practices. COM staff were now encouraged and reported violations. But they were harassed, neutralized: Paul von Buitenen, Bernard Conolly, Marta Andreasen are some of the names that became known by chance.

Numerous whistleblowers were demoralized

One whistleblower who lasted longer was Guido Strack. The model lawyer had been promoted to COM by the Federal Ministry of Economics in 1995. From 2001, he was responsible for the linguistic coordination of EU legal texts. These had to be translated on an ongoing basis into the eleven languages of the prospective new Member States of Eastern Europe: a tall order. Strack reported that a private translation agency failed to meet specifications for quality and punctuality, but the COM paid anyway and did not impose the contractual penalties.

In 2002, Strack informed the new anti-fraud authority OLAF. OLAF investigated and repeatedly called off the investigation. The EU Ombudsman confirmed: OLAF had also violated the rules. Strack dutifully continued to inform the OLAF Supervisory Committee, as well as the European Court of Auditors: No reaction. Strack wanted to use the last option and filed a complaint with the ECJ. The Court refused to accept the complaint. Strack was mobbed and demoralized. He became depressed. In 2005, he was sent into early retirement at the age of 40.[301]

Whistleblower Network established: Against COM and Federal Government

Strack recovered and founded the Whistleblower Network in 2006, remaining chairman until 2015. At a hearing of the Grand Coalition in the Bundestag, he proposed a law to protect whistleblowers: Rejected.[302]

German state broadcaster celebrates corrupt EU president

The corrupt COM President Santer was a member of the Christian Social People's Party in Luxembourg and co-founder of the European Coal and Steel Community with Monnet, later Member and Vice-President of the European Parliament, co-founder of the European People's Party (here Christian parties and also the Hungarian Fidesz/Orbán as well as the nationalist Forza Italia/Berlusconi are members): he was therefore an "EU old hand". No one in the EU objected to Santer running for mayor of Luxembourg City a few weeks after resigning. He lost the election because locally his corruption was all too well known, but he remained a much sought-after talking head in the Luxembourg and EU mainstream media and the Brussels business lobby. He rose to become president of the European Business Confederation, which represents 18 million SMEs across the EU.[303]

In 2017, the pro-government Deutschlandfunk (DLF) celebrated Santer as an EU pioneer and "European visionary". The DLF editor-in-chief praised the Christian-painted crony leader as a "politician close to the people and a forward-looking European".[304]

SECONDARY LAW II: JUDGMENTS OF THE EUROPEAN JUDICIARY

The European Court of Justice (ECJ) and the European Court of Human Rights (ECHR) are repeatedly involved in labor law disputes. If in a few cases the ruling is in favor of dependent employees, this is usually not implemented.

European Court of Justice (ECJ)

ECJ: Wage dumping is legal

The ECJ does not protect the rights of dependent employees in important matters, such as in the case of the whistleblower Strack.

Reflagging to a state with lower wages? Yes!

The shipping company Viking Line from Finland planned to have one of its ships sail under the Estonian flag in order to hire employees from Estonia at the lower wages there.

The Finnish Seamen's Union FSU threatened a strike and boycott. It was supported in this by the International Transport Workers' Federation (ITF), which fights wage dumping via the flag of convenience (FOC) practice worldwide. The FSU wanted to reach a collective agreement to ensure that the shipping company observed Finnish labor law when reflagging for Estonian employees and refrained from dismissing Finnish employees. Viking Line sued the FSU and the ITF to stop the strike and the collective bargaining demands because they violated the freedom of establishment in the Union.

On December 11, 2007, the ECJ ruled (C-438/1905) that trade unions have the right to strike. But the freedom of establishment of companies must not be hindered. Strikes and similar measures had to be "proportionate"; strikes and boycotts went too far in this case. The ITF's support had also shown that the union's main gripe was with freedom of establishment.

Pay construction workers according to the labor laws of the country of assignment? No!

A similar ruling was issued a few days later on December 18, 2007. Under the Posted Workers Directive, states must ensure that employees posted from another EU state are subject to national labor law, i.e. are paid roughly the same as locals.

The construction company Laval from Latvia had sent several dozen workers to a construction site in Sweden - renovation of a school, i.e. a public contract. Laval wanted to pay the workers, on the basis of a collective agreement with a Latvian trade union, according to the lower Latvian low wage. The Swedish construction workers' and electricians' unions blocked all Laval construction sites in Sweden.

The Swedish trade unions thus followed the labor law in Sweden. Here, the regulation of employment relationships is largely left to the "social partners", including the setting of minimum wages. Laval sued the Swedish unions for damages. The ECJ ruled (C-341/2005): Laval is right, the unions' actions are illegal, violate companies' freedom of establishment and the Posted Workers Directive.

Collective bargaining agreements for public contracts? No!
The German state of Lower Saxony had stipulated in its public procurement law: Contracts for construction services may only be awarded to companies that pay their employees at least the collectively agreed wage applicable at the location and also oblige subcontractors to do the same; in the event of non-compliance, a contractual penalty is due.

In the case of the contract for the Göttingen correctional facility, it emerged that a Polish subcontractor had not paid its 53 employees even half the applicable standard wage. The German general contractor received a penalty order of EUR 84,934 (1 percent of the contract amount). The state of Lower Saxony terminated the contract. The general contractor refused to pay the penalty and declared insolvency.

On April 3, 2008, the ECJ ruled (C-346/2006): The Lower Saxony Public Procurement Act conflicts with the Posted Workers Directive. Moreover, it makes a difference whether the employees work directly for the state contractor or for a subcontractor.

Can an EU state decide independently on labor rights? No!
The COM itself sued the state of Luxembourg, claiming that in its 2002 labor and social law it had adopted too many labor laws that violated Union law, in particular the Posted Workers Directive and the freedom of establishment of companies.

The ECJ followed the COM and ruled on 19.6.2008 (C-319/2006): Luxembourg may not inspect or even check a written contract concluded by a foreign entrepreneur with his employees - the contract in the country of origin is sufficient. Information on names, addresses, employee insurance, etc. is inadmissible. Collective bargaining agreements for Luxembourg employees may not be applied to foreign companies. It also said that Luxembourg's minimum wage could not be imposed on foreign companies. It would also be illegal to demand an adjustment of wages to the high cost of living in Luxembourg. Otherwise, entrepreneurs from other states would be "discouraged" from exercising their right to freedom of establishment.

Luxembourg's 2002 labor and social law is largely due to the traditionally strong trade unions in the Grand Duchy. At the same time, however, they were integrated into a "social dialogue" by the mostly "Christian"-led governments, such as Santer and Juncker. They pulled this off with reference to the central role that Luxembourg had had for "Europe" from the beginning, also with reference to the many jobs created by the EU bureaucracy and the branches of foreign banks and consultants.

13 successive fixed-term contracts permissible? Yes!
In its ruling of January 26, 2012 (C-586/10), the ECJ dismissed the action of a judicial clerk. She sued for permanent employment after 13 successive fixed-term contracts in the office of the Local Court of Cologne. The ECJ rejected the complaint: recurring fixed-term contracts without factual justification are also permissible if they serve to cover a temporary need for replacements - due to illness, vacation, other time off of regular employees. This is not permissible in the case of a permanent need - but what the difference is between these two needs remained open.

In 2016, the ECJ issued somewhat milder rulings in two cases (C-184/15 and C-197/15). In one case, a Spanish nurse had demanded a permanent position after seven successive fixed-term contracts. The ECJ ruled: Member States must ensure that the *abuse* of fixed-term contracts is prevented. In addition, fixed-term employees would have the same right to compensation as permanent employees if the contract is terminated.

Fixed-term contracts, including successive fixed-term contracts, are therefore still legal even without factual justification. Only abuse is to be prevented - but this is not defined by the court.

Hungarian low wages in Austria and Germany? But yes!
The Austrian Federal Railways ÖBB had awarded the catering on the trains between Budapest, Salzburg and Munich to an Austrian company from 2012 to 2016. They handed on the contract to the Hungarian company "Henry am Zug". During an inspection at the Vienna train station in 2016, it turned out that the employees were working according to Hungarian low wages and conditions regarding working hours and vacations. The Austrian labor inspectorate imposed an administrative fine because Austrian labor laws apply under the EU Posted Workers Directive.

The entrepreneur challenged this all the way to the ECJ. The Court ruled on December 19, 2019 (C-16/2018): The penalty is illegal! Because a significant part of the catering does not take place in Austria, the work begins and ends in Hungary and the administration is done in Hungary.

Thus, the ECJ violated the EU Posted Workers Directive. In the 2018 revision of the directive, the protective provisions were strengthened, but are not implemented.[305]

ECJ: Friendly judgments in individual cases
In addition to and after initially harsh fundamental rulings, the ECJ is increasingly making rulings in favor of dependent employees. These rulings concern individual rights, never the strengthening of collective rights, such as those of trade unions or works councils, and never co-determination. This is always gratifying for the plaintiffs. However, the rulings, even if legally binding, do not mean that the employers and the respective national judiciary will abide by them - except in the individual case that ended up in court.

Notice periods in Germany unlawful (C-555/2007)
The complaint was filed by a 28-year-old woman who had been dismissed. The German Civil Code (BGB) § 622, 2 provides for a staggered right of termination: In a business-friendly manner, when calculating length of service, the years before the employee's 25th birthday are not taken into account. There are no rational reasons for this. The ECJ, with reference to Directive 2000/78 against age discrimination, ruled: Inadmissible! Discrimination!

No forfeiture of leave entitlement (C-350/2009 and C-520/2009)
The court ruled on the German Federal Vacation Act: the provision that vacation not taken by the end of March of the following year is forfeited violates the Working Time Directive 2003/88. Likewise, the vacation entitlement is not forfeited if the employee has not applied for vacation. The employer must inform the employee of the vacation entitlement. The Federal Labor Court concurred with this ruling.

Companies may not deduct anything from the minimum wage (C-522/2012)
In Germany, the minimum wage law was delayed for a particularly long time due to resistance from the BDI, BDA, CDU, CSU and FDP, and was only passed in 2015 on the initiative of the SPD. As a result, numerous companies undermined the meager minimum wage of initially EUR 8.50 gross per hour by deducting costs for uniforms and the like. An employee brought an action against the state-owned DB Services GmbH. The ECJ

ruled: Company-related expenses such as the provision of uniforms, company cars, company telephones, company housing or discounted personnel purchases as well as capital-forming benefits and, above all, vacation and Christmas bonuses may not be deducted from the minimum wage.

On-call duty is working time subject to remuneration (C-518/2015)
Interpreting the Working Time Directive 2003/89, the ECJ dealt with an action brought by an employee of a municipal volunteer fire department in Germany. He sued for recognition of guard and on-call duties as paid working time. The ECJ ruled: The company determines the place of residence for on-call duty, sets the conditions, such as that the employee must be at the place of work 8 minutes after being called. The employee must be available for operational purposes. Therefore, guard and on-call duties are considered working time.

Freedom of expression at Christian employers (C-414/2016)
The separation of state and church/religion is theoretically part of the self-conception of Western capitalist democracies, but it is often undermined, for example in military chaplaincy, military services and the consecration of tanks and other weapons. The two main Christian churches in Germany are often exempt from current labor law, such as the Works Council Constitution Act (BetrVG). Church enterprises have over one million dependent employees, the Catholic Caritas 450,000, the Protestant Diaconia 600,000. However, the churches provide less than 2 percent of the necessary funds, the state subsidizes. Nevertheless, church employers often require employees to belong to the church and to behave in an ecclesiastical manner, for example in marriage.

A woman therefore sued the Evangelisches Werk für Diakonie und Entwicklung e. V. The ECJ ruled in her favor on April 17, 2018: The obligation to behave in an ecclesiastical manner is only justified if the professional activity is closely related to the Christian mission of proclamation - teaching and spreading the faith. This compulsion therefore does not apply to medical and nursing employees, to jobs in the office, in the kitchen, in cleaning, in the kindergarten and in the janitor's office. Despite the ruling, the two churches are not dissolving their special labor jurisdiction.[306] The Diaconia took the ruling to the German Federal Constitutional Court in 2019.

Uber: not an intermediary, but a transport company (C-434/2015)
The US digital company Uber, like other digital companies and digital employment agencies, is trying to portray itself as a mere placement platform that has no responsibility for employees. Uber also claimed in Spain: We are not a transportation company. We merely broker a connection between non-professional drivers and customers via smartphone app. No driver was employed by Uber. They do not have a license and are therefore not subject to Barcelona's cab regulations.

A professional association of cab drivers brought an action against Uber Systems Spain. The ECJ ruled in favor of the cab association: Uber is a transport company and also determines the working conditions of drivers. Therefore, the EU states must determine the rules under which the drivers work.

Rulings that are undermined nationally
In the EU, rulings of the ECJ can be considerably watered down or undermined, even reversed, in the respective national implementation. The model Europeans in Germany are particularly willing to give their beloved EU the finger.

German Red Cross nurses: normal contract workers? Not with the SPD
It was only on the basis of an ECJ ruling (C-2016/2015) that the Federal Labor Court found: Nurses of the German Red Cross (DRK) who work as nurses at clinics are employees within the meaning of the Temporary Employment Act (AÜG).

The DRK, which presents itself as a Christian aid organization led by former CDU Chancellery Minister Rudolf Seiters, now by CSU politician Gerda Hasselfeldt, took a different view: the 18,000 nurses were loaned out to hospitals on a secondment basis, but not with the status of temporary workers, but with the even lower status of honorary members of the DRK association, which is considered a non-profit organization. They were therefore not paid according to the collective wage agreement, were not allowed to take legal action before the labor court, and were not allowed to participate in works council elections.

Following the ECJ ruling, DRK nurses are now subject to the Temporary Employment Act. They may therefore be hired out for a maximum of 9 months. They are therefore allowed to take legal action against unlawful treatment before the state labor court, to participate in the election of works councils and to be elected as representatives themselves.

But German Labor Minister Andrea Nahles negotiated a loophole with the DRK president. And the majority in the German Bundestag followed her lead: the DRK law was amended. According to this, the 9-month limitation according to the Temporary Employment Act does not apply to DRK nurses.

However, works councils, labor lawyers and the ver.di trade union have succeeded in ensuring that DRK nurses are at least treated as (semi-)normal employees at several hospitals, such as in Essen, Coburg and Hamburg.[307]

Note: Men and women are equal at work and before the law? No! Get an SPD woman as Minister of Labor, so that the women of the DRK still remain below the status of temporary workers. Criticism from the COM for disregarding a supreme court ruling? No.

Record all working time - but not in Germany!
The Spanish trade union Federación de Servicios de Comisiones Obreras CCOO filed a lawsuit on behalf of some of its members against Deutsche Bank's subsidiary. The union wanted to oblige the bank to record the daily hours worked by employees and thus ensure compliance with the agreed and applicable working hours. By the union's count, 53.7 percent of overtime hours had not been recorded to date.

The ECJ ruled in favor of the trade union on May 14, 2019 (C-55/2018). According to the Working Time Directive 2003/88 and with reference to the Charter of Fundamental Rights, "the fundamental right of every worker to a limitation of the maximum weekly and daily working time and to daily and weekly rest periods" must be safeguarded. This, it said, is only possible with a "system" for recording the total daily working time. Member States must establish such a system.

The capitalist lobby, in Germany as well, was furious. The BDA complained about "too much bureaucracy". The (un)Christian Minister of Economics Altmaier obediently declared: We will not simply accept the ruling! The Social Democratic Minister of Labor, Hubertus Heil, declared: We will "not turn everything upside down" because of the ruling.[308]

The Federal Labor Court had in fact already ruled in 2003 in exactly the same way as the ECJ. But companies and governments alike are violating this supreme court ruling. For a long time now, employees in Germany have been asked to work at least one billion hours of unrecorded and unpaid overtime each year - an extorted gift to employers of around EUR 40 billion annually.[309]

But the government is eagerly looking for ways to undermine the ruling. It commissioned two leading union busting professors, Volker Rieble of the corporate-funded Center for Labor Law and Industrial Relations ZAAR and Professor Gregor Thüsing, who works for the special church labor courts, to provide expert opinions.[310]

Thüsing interprets the ruling as follows: There must be a system for recording working time. But each employee is free to decide whether he or she wants to be recorded. For their part, the parties to the collective bargaining agreement and the company could find "intelligent solutions". For example, certain employees, especially those in the upper echelons, could be exempted from recording altogether.[311]

Judgments that are not observed at all
In the unjust grey area that is the EU, it is also possible for ECJ rulings to remain without significance - as if they did not even exist.

The subsistence level must not be reduced
The Federal Constitutional Court in Germany had ruled in November 2019: The subsistence minimum for the unemployed can be reduced as a penalty, in individual cases even completely, by 100 percent. A week later, the ECJ ruled, not in the case of an unemployed person, but of a refugee: the subsistence minimum for a dignified standard of living may not be reduced (C-233/18). Member States must guarantee this on a permanent basis. The ECJ referred to the Refugee Protection Directive (2013/33).

In principle, this decision is a good one, but it would then also have to lead to the end of the sanctioning of unemployment benefit II recipients, which is legally possible in Germany.

The ECJ ruling is above all in contradiction to the EU's handling of refugees at the EU borders, which breaches human rights. This happens (mostly) outside the borders of the EU and affects (only) people who are not EU citizens. In this respect, the judgment does not apply in the narrow legal sense. With EUROPOL and FRONTEX as well as the refugee agreement with Turkey, the EU ensures that the injustice takes place outside the EU - the US-American method: We only torture abroad.

Free trade agreement: Inadmissible because labor rights are also affected
On May 16, 2017, the ECJ ruled on the EU-Singapore Free Trade Agreement (C-376/2017): ratification must not be confined to the COM or the European Parliament! The national parliaments of the 27 EU Member States must also decide on the agreement.

This is because, according to the EU Treaty, the Commission has the mandate for foreign trade policy. But the agreement with Singapore also regulates investors' rights and private arbitration, and this falls within the remit of national legislators. And the conditions for investment - for example, labor, tax and environmental laws - are decided in the EU by national parliaments.

However, the ruling is ignored by the COM and the Council.

European Court of Human Rights (ECtHR)
Some labor law conflicts reach the ECtHR via the detour of "freedom of expression", but only a minute fraction. Article 10 of the European Convention on Human Rights (ECHR) mentions the general right to freedom of expression.

Freedom of expression in the company?
The geriatric nurse Brigitte Heinisch had reported inhumane conditions in a nursing home of the Berlin hospital group Vivantes, caused among other things by staff shortages. Legal violations were frequent, and the Medical Service of the Health Insurance Funds (MDK) had also pointed these out. Vivantes demanded documentation of care services that were not provided at all. Another eight employees filed complaints. After they went unheard by management, Heinisch went public with a flyer and filed criminal charges against Vivantes. She was dismissed without notice.

In early 2005, the Group dismissed Ms. Heinisch, and the dismissal without notice became an "ordinary" termination. Heinisch took legal action against this before the Berlin Labor Court, the Regional Labor Court, the Federal Labor Court - she was rejected by all of them.[312]

With the help of her lawyer Benedikt Hopmann, she went before the ECtHR - and was proven right in 2011. Her freedom of expression at work was protected with reference to ECHR Article 10. In this case the

ECtHR interpreted this article, which makes no mention of freedom of expression in the company, broadly. Heinisch was awarded compensation of EUR 15,000.[313]

However, Vivantes did not rehire the successful plaintiff - the industrial peace had been permanently disturbed. In 2013, the German labor court pressed for a settlement: Vivantes bought itself off with a severance payment of EUR 90,000 without admitting to a violation of the law.[314] So after eight years, the result: the wrongful termination remained in place in Germany. The injustice remained injustice. Job loss, nervous breakdown, hospital, early retirement.

Note: If you tell the truth in the company, if you are fired for it and are even proven right before the highest EU court - you will not get your job back in Germany. The entrepreneur retains the upper hand, and is not penalized for his violation of the law. The EU will give you justice, but it will not enforce it.

The occupational ban in Germany: Violation of human rights
In 1972, the government led by Willy Brandt (SPD) in the Federal Republic of Germany, together with the minister presidents of the federal states - the SPD-led state of Hamburg had taken the lead - decided to ban public employees who violated the "free democratic basic order" from their jobs ("*Radikalenerlass*" Radical Decree).[315] It was directed primarily against actual or suspected "communists". Three and a half million people were checked by the domestic secret service for "loyalty to the constitution" (i.e. about 1,000 times more than there were communists). 1,250 teachers, university lecturers, postal workers, train drivers and the like who were judged to be "left-wing extremists" were not hired, and 250 were fired. The teacher Dorothea Vogt, who was affected and filed a complaint against this, was proven right by the ECtHR after many years.[316]

An apology, compensation and rehabilitation - for the successful plaintiff only to a small extent, she was only taken on as an employee, not as a civil servant - for the other victims, however, never took place in Germany.[317]

7.
In the crisis: Even more labor injustice!

On November 17, 2017, "the EU" proclaimed the *European Pillar of Social Rights (EPSR)*. It was proclaimed in Gothenburg, Sweden, "unanimously and solemnly" by the then 28 EU states, it was reported. However: no head of government was present. The declaration was signed by only three people present: COM President Juncker, Estonian Council President Jüri Ratas and EU Parliament President Antonio Tajani.[318] These three figures: That is "the EU"!

Juncker explained: Unfortunately, despite all the successes in the EU, there is also "social dumping and social fragmentation". In southern Europe in particular, "with high unemployment, rampant poverty and a weak economy, we are facing the biggest crisis in generations". It was time to take countermeasures, not least, according to Juncker, to "take the wind out of the sails of populists and EU opponents". So, while Juncker had indeed identified a problem, his "solution" further exacerbated the crisis - as well as the populism he denounced.

European Pillar of Social Rights (EPSR, 2017)
The 20 new rights in the EPSR are divided into three sections: 1. Equal opportunities and labor market access, 2. Fair working conditions, 3. Social protection and social inclusion.

Under Right No. 3, "Equal Opportunities", the usual anti-discrimination criteria are reeled off: "Irrespective of gender, racial or ethnic origin, religion or belief, disability, age or sexual orientation, everyone has the right ..." Sounds good, right? But one criterion is missing: social origin!

Young people: Right to an apprenticeship
Right No. 4 is entitled "Active support to employment". This proclaims, for instance: "Young people have the right ... to an apprenticeship". Blow me down! It doesn't have to be a real apprenticeship or job. Whether the graciously provided apprenticeship is paid is unimportant. Further: "Unemployed people have the right to personalized, continuous and consistent support": Hartz IV fulfills these criteria well: The support is personal and

somehow also consistent, isn't it? How much the support is, doesn't seem to be that important.

Atypical contracts yes! But they mustn't be "abused"
Right No. 5 is called "Secure and adaptable employment". It states: "The transition towards open-ended forms of employment shall be fostered": So the initial assumption is temporary employment, and then somehow permanent employment is fostered - but it doesn't have to come about. It continues: "Employment relationships that lead to precarious working conditions shall be prevented, including by prohibiting abuse of atypical contracts." Atypical contracts are therefore permissible and normal, they just must not be "abused". "Probationary periods should be of reasonable duration." Reasonable. Should.

Private dispute resolution instead of state labor courts
Right No. 7 states: "Workers have the right to be informed at the start of employment about their rights and obligations." Wow! That is almost on a par with China! And it continues: "Prior to any dismissal, workers have the right to be informed of the reasons." That is, before you are kicked out of the door! There are further gems: "Workers have the right to access to effective and impartial dispute resolution." This fulfills the long-cherished wish of the entrepreneurs and as it is already enshrined in the labor law chapters of the free trade agreements CETA etc.: Away from the state labor courts, rather the internal, private, non-public dispute resolution!

"Fair" working conditions
Working conditions should be "fair". But: Fair - that is legally vague. Fair - that comes about through consensus. It is possible, for example, when two sports teams from the same league meet and a referee moderates the match. But what is fair when dependent employees and entrepreneurs meet as essentially unequal parties? And when the referee, openly or covertly, is on the side of the employer anyway?

"Long participation in the labor market" – how long is "long"?
Right No. 10 declares: "Workers have the right to a working environment adapted to their professional needs and which enables them to enjoy long participation in the labor market." In plain language, this means that migrant workers from Romania and refugees (who have not drowned or starved to death) are deployed in Germany and France by entrepreneurs

and intermediaries and job agencies wherever their demands and perhaps recognized qualifications fit best.

And what does "long" participation in the labor market mean? How long is "long"? For life? Until the statutory pension? Or just until the worker is worn out - as in the meat factories?

Social rights must be "adequate"
Rights No. 11 to 20 come under the heading "Social protection and inclusion". They concern children, the unemployed, pensions, health care, minimum income, disability, care, housing, etc. Again, the rights are not only non-binding, but particularly vague.

In the case of labor rights, the term "adequate" is already often used vaguely: "adequate time off and flexible working time arrangements", "adequate notice period". But when it comes to social rights, this vague criterion gets out of hand: "adequate minimum wages", "adequate standard of living", "adequate social protection", "adequate benefits of adequate duration" (for the unemployed), "adequate pension", "adequate housing and services" (for the homeless).

Collective labor, collective bargaining and trade union rights, co-determination and employee representation are missing from the "European Pillar", as are decent pensions, free education and affordable housing. However, in the spirit of the times, the term "social inclusion" must not be missing.

Directive implementing the "European Pillar" (2019)
The EPSR was transposed into Directive 2019/1152 and has the skillfully misleading title "Transparent and Predictable Working Conditions".

"Atypical" forms of work: All permissible and legalized
Thus, zero-hour contracts are permitted, they are just not to be "abused". And there is now the right to multiple jobs: Casual, mini- and part-time workers, zero-hour contract workers, gig workers and, in Germany, for example, 450-euro workers are to be given the "right" to take on a second, third, etc. job on the side.

"The directive has a broad personal scope. It aims to ensure that all workers in all employment relationships – even in the most flexible atypical and new forms such as zero-hour contracts, casual work, domestic work, work based on vouchers or work through platforms – benefit from these rights."[319]

BlackRock & Co: Private pension provision

BlackRock leads the financial lobby that has already made some headway in the US with the goal of private pensions. George Osborne already advocated private pensions when he was the British Tory finance minister: The ETF financial product marketed by BlackRock is particularly suitable for this purpose. This "people's share" can be bought for as little as a few hundred euros. Because ETF is managed automatically, the fees are low. The previous providers of private pensions - in Germany for the "Riester pension" - have thus been pushed aside.

The EU has also opted for BlackRock, or rather, BlackRock has opted for the EU. After his term as finance minister, Osborne became BlackRock's pension lobbyist in Brussels with an annual salary of EUR 750,000. In 2017, BlackRock CEO Fink had criticized the inadequate performance of the state-organized pension in the hall of the German Stock Exchange and promoted retirement provision with the help of ETFs in the EU.[320]

The lobby team of BlackRock and Osborne in Brussels also includes the PR agency Fleishman Hillard, which had already monitored critical politicians and journalists during the merger of Bayer and Monsanto led by BlackRock. On June 14,2019, on the proposal of the COM, namely the Finance Commissioner Valdis Dombrovskis, who was worked on intensively by BlackRock - six publicly registered meetings in 2016 alone - the European Parliament and the European Council adopted the regulation on the Paneuropean Private Pension Product PEPP.[321]

Thus, the dwindling pensions of dependent employees in the EU are to be improved by the purchase of BlackRock's People's Share. Its attractiveness is to be further boosted via tax subsidies from the Member States. The amount of the pension payment does not have to be guaranteed by the sellers; it depends on the performance of the shares. And it is precisely those who need it most who do not have the money to finance additional share purchases from their poverty incomes anyway.

Eight EU institutions to enforce labor injustice

Several EU institutions are responsible for the operational implementation of labor injustice. In many cases, they overlap in a non-transparent manner.

European Job Mobility Portal EURES

Since 1993, the "European job network" EURES has been arranging migrant work, internships and any form of employment between EU states. EURES has a good 1,000 employees. The COM, employers and trade unions are involved. Migrant labor is dressed up as "occupational mobility".

Special target groups are "young people throughout Europe" who are placed in "internships, apprenticeships and training courses". EURES organizes public forums in EU countries. For example, the portal brought together "emigrants, expats, students, job seekers and entrepreneurs" at the Emigration Expo in the Netherlands in February 2020, which lasted several weeks.[322]

In January 2020, the portal offered 3.2 million vacancies at 15,225 employers. Motto: Any job - even an unpaid internship counts as such - is better than no job. This includes, for example, the supply of Christmas seasonal workers from southern crisis states to Amazon in Germany and Poland.

European Agency for Safety and Health at Work (OSHA)

The agency is named after the US Occupational Safety and Health Agency. Since 1994, it has been tasked with making workplaces in the EU "safer, healthier and more productive". However, it limits itself to collecting information on new risks in line with the times: stress, bullying, sexual harassment in the workplace, psychological risks associated with digitalization. However, only companies are surveyed and then advised. Companies, governments, but also "workers" are represented on the committees.[323]

Senior Labor Inspectors Committee (SLIC)

The committee was installed as an EU body by Directive 1995/319. It regularly brings together representatives of the COM and the labor inspectorates from the EU states. An improvement of labor inspection in the EU is not known.

European Competence Center for Labor Law, Employment and Labor Market Policies
The center was established in 2016 and oversees the "Program for Employment and Social Innovation". Like EEPO, the Center is integrated into the "European Semester" and continuously prepares reports on the implementation of the directives in all EU states, candidate and aspirant states, as well as in the European states with special status: Norway, Iceland, Liechtenstein, Switzerland.

European Labor Authority ELA
The European Labor Authority started its work in 2019. Its headquarters are in Bratislava, Slovakia. It is concerned with the "market" of migrant workers, estimated at 17.5 million, who move back and forth between EU states. This does not include migrants from non-EU countries.

The migrants are to be qualified and guided, crime and moonlighting are to be prevented. For example, caregivers for the elderly and nursing assistants are to be qualified in a crash course of a few weeks with work-specific handgrips, practices, regulations and bywords. But technical school and university graduates, such as engineers, doctors, and information technicians, are also placed as low-paid specialists, especially in Western EU countries.

Free Movement and Social Security Coordination MoveS
The agency organizes labor migration primarily on the basis of the Posted Workers Directive. Its network of experts from 32 European countries extends far beyond the EU Member States. The agency is advised by the US 'audit' group Deloitte.

European Employment Policy Observatory (EEPO)
The European Employment Policy Observatory is a "network of experts". It is primarily responsible for the Youth Employment Initiative: to help young people, who are most affected by unemployment in many EU countries, find employment, across the spectrum of precarious and atypical forms of employment identified in Directive 2019/1152 "Transparent and Predictable Working Conditions". This overlaps with EURES. The frame of reference is, on the other hand, the "European Semester", i.e. the monitoring of the national budgets of the EU Member States by the COM.[324]

European Parliament: Committee on Employment and Social Affairs (EMPL)

As in all EU institutions, labor law and labor relations are not a separate area. As in the EPSR, they are sorted into the secondary area of "social affairs". This is also followed by the responsible committee of the EU Parliament.

It collaborated on the EPSR and committed itself to advancing its implementation. At the time of this declaration, the committee was headed by Thomas Händel,[325] formerly a functionary of IG Metall, who had switched from the SPD to Die Linke: in terms of trade unionism, no trace remains.

European Social Fund ESF as soft power

The EEC Treaty of 1957 established the ESF. It continued the management of labor migration that the Coal and Steel Community had used to bring mostly unskilled men from poor regions like southern Italy into the hard and dangerous jobs of the steel, iron and coal companies.

Promotion of external and internal labor migration

Since then, the Social Fund has been gradually expanded into a comprehensive labor market policy instrument. Tens of thousands of individual projects are currently funded here throughout the EU. The funds are distributed via the governments and regional administrations - in Germany, the federal states.

The Social Fund claims that "every EU citizen should be given a job perspective". There is no shortage of other euphemistic phrases either: "Intelligent, sustainable, inclusive growth" and "Shape.Future.Together". The reality looks different. One major ESF project was the promotion of the German employment agency in the wake of the Hartz laws: Trying out *workfare*, i.e., under the title of "citizen work", the unemployed were made to do public work for EUR 1 per hour.

Now to the general characteristics of the ESF:

- First, the ESF operates outside of any human rights-based labor rights;
- second, the sociality of work is not promoted, e.g. not the ability to self-confidently stand up for collective representation in the company or beyond; rather, only the isolated individual is promoted, with his or her respective "disadvantages" - unemployed, disabled, migrant back-

ground, young, single parent, poor, female. Thus, *within* the class of dependent employees, the particularly disadvantaged are tracked down and made the object of treatment;

- third, the principle of "any job is better than none" is applied. The goal is to "increase the employment *rate*", even if this leads to a division into smaller and smaller jobs with fewer and fewer hours and to precarization. Every part-time job, no matter how small, counts as a job in the EU statistics and contributes to meeting the quota.

Populist modernization of eligibility criteria

The criteria for support were modernized in line with the times. Because the EEC was expanding its reach beyond the coal and steel industry to include more and more industrial sectors, the Social Fund promoted the retraining of migrants in other occupations in the first period from 1958 to 1971. Retraining had not yet been necessary for the low-skilled toilers in the lower ranks of the coal and steel industry. But now at least a makeshift rapid retraining of 850,000 Italians was promoted. They found jobs, for example, in the automotive industry, especially in the FRG, France and Belgium, especially at Ford and VW - 80 percent of the funds were spent on this, while migrants from Portugal and Turkey, which were not EEC members, were not qualified.[326]

ESF accompanies unemployment, precarity, migration

After de-industrialization in Great Britain, Northern Ireland and Ireland, for example, and then also in the sold-out ex-socialist states such as the GDR, the vocational retraining of the unemployed was promoted. It was not aimed at creating new jobs there, but it did enable emigration to West Germany, for example. In this way, domestic unemployment was kept at a high level, creating new promotional opportunities for the Social Fund.

In the 2000s, long-term unemployment was added as an eligibility criterion - also due to EU directives - as was non-discrimination in the labor 'market' on the grounds of gender, age, ethnic origin, religion, sexual orientation. Unemployed youth, single parents, start-ups and refugees became new target groups. "Social inclusion" and "combating poverty" were added. In the meantime, projects involving initiatives from several EU countries are also being promoted.

The now very lavish funds and tens of thousands of projects are failing to prevent working poverty and precarity - see the EPSR specifications - from spreading further.

How critics are subsidized and ensnared

NGOs, trade unions, works councils, professional and social associations are now also receiving more and more funding. Out of a fairness impulse, the projects often pursue goals that tend to contradict those of the EU. In order to receive subsidies for this, it is certainly permissible to kick against the goads. But in the long run - for example, with the second or third follow-up funding application - the criteria of the ESF prevail, have to be adopted, internalized.

In this way, the projects become part of a reassurance strategy. This also creates a thoroughly creative milieu of tens of thousands of jobs: The happy job owners in the projects must continue to be creative in order to make their own goals compatible with those of the almighty funder. After all, the follow-up application is supposed to extend the temporary job at least for the next year.

DGB project "Fair Mobility"

For example, the DGB in Germany receives funding for the "Fair Mobility" project for several dozen mostly young creative workers. For many years, this project provided advice to migrant workers from Eastern Europe, for example the repeatedly exploited contract workers in the German meat industry.

It is important to know: The slaughter company Tönnies was subsidized by the EU because it bought up slaughterhouses even in structurally weak areas and continued to operate them (in part), for example in Weißenfels/Saxony-Anhalt in eastern Germany: after all, Tönnies creates jobs. The fact that the jobs had the lowest status in Germany until 2020 – work contract - and at the same time the work contract was fraudulent (in reality a temporary employment contract), did not bother the EU. But the DGB did not criticize it either.

The DGB project "Fair Mobility" in nine regional advice centers was intended to "support" mobile workers from Central and Eastern European EU countries in enforcing fair wages and working conditions on the German labor market. In addition, studies were conducted on the situation of those affected.[327]

Counseling of the few frightened victims who were reached was limited to the individual. Collective strengthening, for example through the election of works councils, was not promoted. The fear that was stoked by extortion was not overcome - only a handful of the migrants dared to go to court with DGB support.

Soft power: Only aroused by "surprise" corona infections
Thus, the ESF became an instrument of soft power in the EU's labor injustice. Not the project "Fair Mobility", but only the "surprisingly" high, suddenly and belatedly revealed Corona infection of Eastern European meat workers at Tönnies, Westfleisch, Vion & Co woke up the federal government in June 2020. Because of this "scandal", it frantically decided to now abolish not only work contracts, but also temporary employment in the meat industry as of Jan. 1, 2021.

Even if that were to happen, why not do the same in the construction, security and cleaning industries? Why not abolish the at least equally exploitative labor prostitution for construction workers?[328]

No member of the COM and no member of the eight EU agencies concerned with labor law, health and safety at work, and migrant workers has commented on the "scandal" in Germany, even after the "Tönnies scandal" in 2020.

Labor migration between poor and even poorer states
The rich EU states like Luxembourg, Belgium, the Netherlands, Germany and France have been on the lookout for even cheaper and even more willing labor migrants from outside the EU for some time now, between Mexico, the Philippines and Kosovo. But now the Member States of Eastern Europe, particularly impoverished by the EU, are doing the same.

Initially, the EU encouraged mass emigration from these countries. And after decades of Western "employers" simultaneously outsourcing low-wage work to branches and suppliers there, the work there is now becoming too expensive for them in some cases. Moreover, with the switch to e-cars, labor skills previously required there will become obsolete, because assembling e-cars is much easier. In addition, local employees in Poland, Hungary, the Czech Republic and Slovakia have now enforced higher wages and better working conditions in some cases. (see p. 230)

The impoverished EU states are therefore looking for new low-wage workers in even poorer regions of the world, with even lower low wages, and occasionally skilled workers - but also those with the lowest possible incomes.[329]

Poland: Migrant workers from Ukraine, Nepal, Bangladesh, Vietnam
Poland, which is heavily subsidized by the EU, has admitted about a million migrants from Ukraine in recent years - Ukraine had been heavily subsidized by the EU, together with the US and the IMF, while being nationally impoverished for the benefit of friendly oligarchs. Ukrainians are mainly employed in low-wage agricultural sectors of agriculture and simple services.

Moreover, in 2018 alone, Polish authorities issued 635,335 residence permits to people from other, even poorer third countries. These include about 40,000 labor migrants from the Philippines, Nepal, Bangladesh, Vietnam, and India. The Christian fundamentalist government pays attention to religious selection in violation of human rights: No Muslims! The EU does not protest.

Czech Republic: Migrant workers from the Philippines, Ukraine, Vietnam, Mongolia
The Czech Republic, led by entrepreneur and EU subsidy recipient Andrej Babiš, is negotiating a bilateral labor migration agreement with the Philippines. Workers have already been recruited from the Philippines and Mongolia, and for some time also from Ukraine. The branches of VW subsidiary Škoda, Toyota, Hyundai, PSA, Daimler and many suppliers at the Mnichovo and Ostrava car plants in particular are scrambling to recruit workers. Lufthansa was looking for 400 Filipino support staff for its outsourced catering subsidiary LSG Sky Chefs.

Hungary: Labor migrants from Ukraine - and from the "Far East"
About 600,000 able-bodied Hungarians have migrated abroad. The nationalist Orbán government initially encouraged ethnically determined immigration of Hungarian minorities from Romania, Serbia and Ukraine, including Christian immigrants from the Middle East. Some better qualified people also came from Ukraine. But this is not enough. Above all, the Western car industry in Györ and Kecskemet is urgently looking for new

low-wage workers: the government is also, as it announced, sounding out "the Far East"!

North Macedonia: "Bangladesh" in Europe
The states associated with or aspiring to the EU offer even lower standards than those already admitted. Western textile traders in particular take advantage of this, and not only for the cheap goods, but also for the upper quality levels, which are brought to market by the luxury companies Seidensticker and Strellson, for example. A shirt produced in North Macedonia, the Bangladesh of Eastern Europe, and sold for EUR 3 to the retailer in Germany costs EUR 60 in Paris and Berlin and EUR 10 in Serbia - and most people in Eastern Europe still cannot afford the shirt.[330]

The labor regime tolerated by the EU is harsh. The local entrepreneurs are played off against each other, they are allowed to enrich themselves moderately, the labor inspectorate does not work, there are no works councils - workers have to work through without a break with diapers in their underpants.[331]

European minimum wage?
The COM proposed a European minimum wage in 2019. "An EU legal framework for minimum wages can help fight inequalities and avoid a destructive race to the bottom in labor costs," said Nicolas Schmit, the Social Affairs Commissioner responsible, a Social Democrat from Luxembourg.[332]

At the beginning of 2020, 22 of the 28 EU states had minimum wages - ranging from EUR 1.72 in Bulgaria to EUR 11.97 in Luxembourg. In principle, the EU does not want to change such differences. However, the minimum wage is to be 60 percent of the respective national median income.

But if the labor incomes of the majority are too low anyway, which is already evident in the millions of poverty pensions, then this is not a meaningful benchmark. Apart from that, minimum wage earners are also the ones who most often get temporary and part-time jobs.

But even the public discussion about it is too much for the business lobby like Business Europe and the German BDA. They invoke the EU Treaty Art. 153, which prohibits EU intervention in pay matters. This is hypocrisy, of course, because other illegal interventions by the EU in labor rights are welcomed by the lobby.

The European minimum wage is designed at least to improve the EU's image. COM President von der Leyen is also counting on this. As German labor minister, she had rejected a minimum wage. Partly because of this delay, the German minimum wage is one of the furthest away from the 60 percent mark in an EU comparison.[333] (On the criticism of the minimum wage by the Scandinavian trade unions see p. 219)

Current wages are also no basis for a minimum wage for another reason: In the EU and especially in the ex-socialist states, labor incomes are increasingly decoupled from labor productivity:[334] This power-based, unproductive appropriation of even more added value from exploited dependent labor must end!

Part Two

Stirrings against exploitation and disenfranchisement

In all EU states, including candidate and associated states, which have been "fed" or mangled with subsidies for years, resistance is stirring. In Brussels, it is treated as non-existent.

What stirrings? Slumbering injustice
By stirrings, we do not mean here the resistance directed against "the EU" proffered by right-wing, racist, nationalist governments of EU Member States such as Viktor Orbán/Hungary and Jarosław Kaczyński/Poland. Nor does it mean the criticism from similar political actors like Brexiteer Boris Johnson. Nor does it mean the opposition of secondary populists like the AfD in Germany, which wants to keep EU capitalism in place. What is meant here is the democratic resistance to the labor injustice that is mostly ignored in the criticism.

Of course, there is also and above all dormant injustice that does not (yet) make itself publicly felt - and there is a lot of it.

Necessary selection: A start
In the following, some selected examples of stirrings in ten EU states, one candidate state (North Macedonia), one associated state (Switzerland) and from the United Kingdom, which has now left the EU, are presented. For reasons of space, a selection had to be made not only among the states, but also among the stirrings described.

Among the states not included here are Greece, the Czech Republic, Romania, Bulgaria, Serbia, Bosnia-Herzegovina, Slovenia. The rich founding and leading states France, Germany are only briefly touched upon. Italy and the Benelux countries are not dealt with - there would be a lot to say about them. Thus, the following presentation should nevertheless be seen as exemplary and a start.

On the situation of the working class in the EU

Since the embryonic forms of the EU in the 1950s, indeed directly after the Second World War, the European Nazi collaborators in the companies, banks and above all "Christian" parties then very quickly battled, infiltrated, divided, de-ideologized the anti-fascist and democratic forces - trade unions, left-wing parties, intellectuals and others - together with the USA. The welfare state, which was then also militarily and anti-communistically secured, with enforced, depoliticized social partnership, was only a temporary concession also in the Western core and founding states of the EU and its early forms - as long as the enemy of real socialism on the doorstep posed a challenge.

The stewards of the welfare state: Emaciated early on ...

The main stewards of the welfare state, mainly social democratic parties and their associated trade unions - some of these parties, see England, France, Spain and Portugal, called and still call themselves socialist - had had the critique of capitalism trained out of them. They were already obsolete when the indirect props of class compromise, the Soviet Union, the GDR and the other socialist states collapsed in 1990.

That is why the trade unions and political parties meant here have proved and still prove to be incapable of responding to the new demands since the 1990s. They sit with their representatives in the EU capital and are happy when they get project funds from the ESF. But they do not resolutely fight the labor injustice that they sometimes document and criticize in copious brochures.

... then perverted

Perversely, moreover, social democratic and socialist parties in the EU after 1990 - following the example of the "Democratic Party" in the US, beginning with the youthful William Clinton - became the political pioneers and executors of neoliberally unleashed Western capitalism.

In the EU, this is particularly true of "New Labour" with Anthony Blair in England, the German SPD with Gerhard Schröder, the Socialist Workers' Party with Felipe González in Spain, the Portuguese Socialists with Mário Soares, then the French Socialists with François Hollande, the Italian Social Democrats with Matteo Renzi and the like - and by no means to be forgotten, albeit less conspicuous, the clichéd long-praised Social Democrats in the Scandinavian welfare model.[335]

Important parts of the trade unions and union-oriented institutions were and are interwoven and paralyzed with these parties.

The new era of social and political organization
This perversion is all the more true with and since the eastward enlargement of the EU and NATO. The exploitation and impoverishment of the Eastern European and ex-Yugoslav states, above all the necessary reorganization of the dependent employees there and in the EU as a whole, are confronted helplessly, but also spinelessly, by the discredited stewards of the sinking welfare state, who have withered to the point of disappearing. The beginnings of a nationalist-patriarchal-Christian welfare state are offered by governments like those in Poland and Hungary, which are heavily subsidized by the EU.

A reprise of the failed welfare state and the old US-led and only temporary class compromise does not promise success. The actors for this are lacking anyway. Therefore, an era of social, political, cultural reorganization for democratic, human rights, international law, rule of law values and rights has begun. It began long ago, suppressed and distorted by the established public, from a deep defensive position that has so far worn some down and driven them to give up.

"Food is the first thing, morals follow on" – that is over
Western-style capitalist democracy has run its course. Corrupt government parties and the EU, anti-democratic from the outset, have largely destroyed the previous wobbly democracy.

The capitalists, in organized self-blindness, have rested on their unproductive perma-profits, subsidized also by the EU, and driven ahead with the visible destruction of labor, environment and sociality. These capitalists are desperately lashing out and waging more declared and undeclared wars in their defense and preparing more, internally and externally.[336]

"Food is the first thing, morals follow on" – went the saying in better times, in reference to capitalists. Today the saying goes: "Food is the first thing, then comes more food."

"The first victim of war is the truth" - so went the saying in better times. But for a long time now, wars are no longer needed: The truth is the first victim of the perfectly "normal" EU capitalism, led by US capitalism – with the pace stepped up even further since 2020 with "corona".

On the situation of the working class
The working class, what's more as a class conscious of its situation, exists in the classical form of the unionized and party-organized worker with a fulltime job secured by collective bargaining or fought for, only in very diverse remnants. But even there, class awareness and class knowledge were barely present. And the bulk of the binding force of these formations has dwindled; membership is individualized. And the knowledge and awareness of one's own situation is largely confused, exhausted. Many union members in Germany, France, etc. vote right-wing, in Eastern Europe and the US even more - if they vote at all.

"You can't change anything anyway" - this is the prevailing doctrine of dependent employees in the Western capitalist democracies, also in the EU.

Multiple, deep fragmentations

The status of dependent labor in the EU has been fragmented into many dozens of variants and combinations of variants, legal, financial, local, social, ethnic, national, gender.

The working class today is the social class of the dependent employed, excluded from seminal ownership, but also of the involuntarily non-employed, the unemployed, the overworked and the underemployed, the temporary and permanent employees, those changing between these states, with or without a formal employment relationship:

- Between permanent full-time to regular employment of one hour or more per week, which is statistically counted as employment in the EU
- Between full-time work with paid and unpaid overtime and forced underemployment down to zero-hour contract
- On-call work with varying guaranteed hours starting at zero, flex contracts starting at 10 hours per week, part-time work with guaranteed hours but varying hours of assignment
- Temporary work and the even lower status as work contract labor

- Fixed-term and part-time work in a variety of combinations according to hours, pay, taxation, social insurance, and additional benefits or non-benefits such as paid vacation, paid sick days
- Pseudo self-employment, for example, of cultural workers, truck drivers, cab drivers, food couriers, outpatient care workers
- Diverse semi-legal/illegal work of domestic helpers, refugees, prostitutes with different degrees of (un)freedom up to mafiotic dependencies
- Streetwalking not only for prostitutes, but also for construction workers
- Paid and unpaid internships and probationary periods, in small companies as well as in prestigious engineering and architecture firms
- One-euro jobs, either "voluntary" or as state forced labor
- Gig and crowd workers, whose contractless, project-based casual labor can be broken down into tiny portions of a few euros each
- Millions of long-term and short-term unemployed or as more or less frequent switching back and forth between working and not working
- Unsecured low-wage employment in the science and education sector: permanent student assistants, teaching assistants, temporary and partly untrained substitute teachers in "general education" schools ("lateral entrants")
- Unsecured and temporary low-wage employment in public administration, also in the labor (unemployment) administration, in ministries, also in the German Bundestag and the EU Parliament.

Injustice laws are also violated by entrepreneurs
A further hallmark of the often juridified injustice status is the fact that even this is constantly violated by capitalists with impunity: For example, in the case of mass non-payment or undercutting of the statutory minimum wage, in the case of non-payment of mandated overtime, in the case of illegal state sanctions against the unemployed, in the case of fraudulent additional exploitation of contract workers, temporary workers and migrant workers (deductions for placement and transport, exorbitant rents).

In the upper engine room of capital
At the same time, on the upper floors of the engine room of capital, where annual salaries start at EUR 60,000 or even 80,000: Highly paid work of varying degrees, which, as in the case of Romanian meat cutters, also

amounts to 60-80 hours per week and can also exceed this, as in the case of the approximately half a million academically highly educated employees in business law firms, consulting and auditing companies, PR agencies, corporate foundations, investment consultants, brokerage firms, outsourced subsidiary groups of large media and software forges in Germany: Squeezing out the young workforce combined with sumptuous privileges, which, like the exclusive and exotic vacations befitting one's status, can often only be enjoyed in a hassled and cheerless manner.[337]

"Bullshit jobbers"

Many privileged people in these groups do not understand their situation, despite or because of their academic (mis)education. They take refuge in the pseudo-proletarian, diffusely critical attitude that they have to do a bullshit job, as the academic anarchist David Graeber, who is popular in the managerial milieu, documented in a misunderstood but comprehensive way.[338]

State civil servants

Hierarchically ordered, privileged civil servant status in ministries, the judiciary, intelligence services, public administration, state media, academic and state-subsidized cultural life, public and private schools, private and state universities. The employees who subjectively feel free do not necessarily have to notice anything of their legally secured but unconsciously practiced dependence - on the contrary: the majority of them simulate the system-relevant "spiritual freedom", believe in it (even if often only half-heartedly) and spread this (half)belief, similar to the remaining members of the complicit, eroding major Christian churches.

"Young creatives"

A particularly ambivalent milieu are the "young creatives" who, as self-employed or pseudo-self-employed, today form a diverse army of millions and often work in no formal relationship of dependence. Their status ranges from permanent poverty to sudden super-wealth as a successful start-up entrepreneur who founds the next zeitgeisty charitable foundation at the age of 30.

Everything precarious?

The claimed commonality of the many, diverse, lower groups and the pseudo self-employed as the "precariat", which, moreover, is the main source of the new right-wing radicalism, contributes not to clarification but to confusion.[339]

Such diverse forms of dependent work are also mixed in a variety of ways with

- more or less frequent changes between status and locations
- the partially simultaneous exercise of multiple, main and side 'jobs'
- partial or total state or private subsidy, including from the ESF or, in the short term, from "corona" aid programs
- longer or shorter lasting or also permanent labor migration
- legal uncertainty due to constant changes in EU directives and national laws
- varying degrees of legal knowledge/ignorance
- varying intensity of voluntariness and coercion
- varying intensity of illnesses, treated and untreated
- with time-consuming life activities such as caring for relatives, childcare - with institutional help or not
- Finding housing, struggling to maintain housing, paying for housing.

We are not running out of work - we need to change it
"We" are by no means running out of work - this fake prognosis is also part of the prevailing taboo.

On the contrary: concrete, conscious, formative work for the production of the necessary "food" of society - food in the broadest sense - and just as much for the organization of cohabitation and the state is more necessary than ever, instead of the flexibilized, disenfranchised "jobs" that destroy communality as well as the environment, and pervert products and services.

From the defensive against the capitalists
The real situation of dependent labor, the injustice of labor and the resistance against it are the big taboo - before corona, during corona, after corona. Breaking the taboo, through associated, collective, national and, at the same time, internationalist organization, with the associated, inevitable experiments, successes and defeats, with old and new actors - this is the project we need.

The depths of the long slumbering injustice

The depths of the long slumbering injustice have hardly been explored. As if out of the "blue", in reality out of evil, denied, distorted reality, mass protests then suddenly break out like the Yellow Vests in France and Black Lives Matter in the USA - to the (alleged?) surprise of the self-blinded elitist system defenders, also worldwide in protests of millions from Chile to India.

The tactics of the capitalists, in cahoots with governments and the dying and the new mainstream media ("social media"), to date managed to distract, divide, mollify, make such upheavals disappear - or instrumentalize them – example "Arabellion". Such tactics are more visible in the "corona crisis", have become more vulnerable. Statues of ostentatiously exhibited slave traders in the UK and southern state generals in the USA are suddenly and finally overthrown after centuries of public sleep - other, as yet unseen statues can also be in line!

Upward mobility, for women as well, at the expense of new underclasses

The extreme diversity of the working class in the EU harbors easily ignitable and calculated, instrumentalized conflicts and animosities.

Complicated alliances are necessary and possible. But in many cases, they are rendered difficult or even impossible. In addition, as already seen in the Coal and Steel Community, a part of the traditional working class is promoted a bit upward - the bit is subjectively very important, however - by the new underclasses moving in from poor regions. In the rich EU countries, for example, many millions of private households of the middle and upper classes currently employ domestic help from Poland, Hungary, Romania, Albania, in many cases, moreover, unregistered. And in these impoverished states, the tiny upper class does the same. Sick parents can thus be cared for at home around the clock, while the adult children indulge in their cosmopolitan-ecological "self-realization". Middle-class women emancipate themselves at the expense of the non-emancipation of an army of servants - not to mention the global supply chains of cheap and luxury textiles.[340]

Labor rights are human rights

The exploitation and disenfranchisement of dependent employees, which have taken on a diverse and extreme form in today's capitalism marked by the furies of hyperglobalization, are only one dimension of the entire state of the world associated with it: thus, this class society also damages bodies in their individuality, sociality and health, also damages individual property, however small, and nature with plants, animals, water, earth and atmosphere.

Working poor = living poor = working sick

Thus, working poor is connected with living poor and working sick. But: Dependent employees must have an apartment, must be able to go to work and come home again, must take children to kindergarten and school and pick them up again, must eat healthy food, need insurance against unemployment, illness and for retirement, need free time for rest and sleep, for conversation, devotion, care, love, music, literature, knowledge of the world.

In earlier phases, the working classes have always developed networked forms of organization: For work, culture, sports, knowledge, recreation, consumption, housing. The trade union as an organizer only of wage demands is unsuitable for this, if it does not at the same time operate forms of organization for the other areas and also the state or other social associations do not support them - in the appropriate way. By the way, social and labor rights evolved from this, including, for example, the right to housing, education, and so on.

Opponent research: Recognize and name your owner

Today, the owners of the capitalist enterprises are as unknown as never before in the history of capitalism - the class opponent does not seem to exist. The EU helps in hiding them in the occult parallel society of four dozen financial havens. The established trade unions like the DGB in Germany including its individual unions, also their research institutions and those of the European trade unions in Brussels, have, with slight differences, no idea about the present capitalism in the EU.

And, behind the much-vaunted "globalization", movers and shakers also hide. Globalization is a successor term to earlier terms that also suggested that capitalism, classes and capitalists had disappeared: Industrial society, consumer society, service society, risk society.[338]

Hence, what is needed is research on opponents. Trade unionists, democrats, leftists, the woke and awakening often know neither the owners nor their agents of influence in their state, in the EU, in the company where they work, in their own home. Therefore: Who owns not only my data, but also "my" company, "my" apartment, "my" state? How do they "work", against me and us?

Unconditional Basic Income (UBI)?

Especially the ideologists of the dangerous precariat often advocate UBI as a solution. The acclaimed, confused diagnosticians of bullshit jobs like David Graeber also look for this comfortable way out: We should cease this senseless work, let the state support us!

But: First, the recipients of such state welfare remain supplicants. However, it is a matter of following the essence of humanly necessary work, that the human being changes from being a supplicant and a recipient of mercy to a self-confident creator, who associatively regulates his circumstances himself. Second, UBI recipients would be dependent on payments from others who continue to do bullshit jobs and pay taxes for the UBI. Third, this is quite uncertain, especially in today's capitalism: How much work paid by the capitalists will there be at all, and how much tax will the state take from low labor incomes and from rich tax evaders? Fourth, the ultimate key is that those who are meant by precarious and bullshit jobs do not remain in their lack of understanding of the causes of their perverted work, but understand it and change it together.

20-hour week for all!

Those who exploit, disenfranchise, wear down and make people ill at work also exploit, wear down and make nature and the environment ill. Therefore: The movements for human rights at work belong together with the movements for the reproductive preservation of the natural preconditions of human life.

In every company, products and services must begin to be examined for their relevance to the lives and survival of communities large and small, and ultimately to global society.

In the same way, the distribution of work and the volume of work must be changed. The current spread in the EU between about 48 hours per week with further paid and unpaid overtime on the one hand and the digitally fragmented work portions in minutes on the other hand is as unfair as it is performance-inhibiting. It perverts and destroys human labor power, health, creativity, and the ability to innovate. In the capitalist West, the 30-hour week is no problem from the point of view of meaningful work volume, and with fairly distributed digitization, the 20-hour week is no problem either.

Company takeovers by the workforce

Precisely in the current crisis, the activities needed include the takeover of insolvent companies by the workforce and the establishment of new democratic forms of enterprise such as cooperatives and collective start-ups.[341]

Labor, peace, security

Those who exploit dependent labor also exploit dependent states and, as is well known, overrun them with war if necessary. The self-organization of dependent workers must also act as part of the overarching global peace movement, in cooperation with the Non-Aligned Movement and all resisters who are geared toward the original international law of the UN.

The metamorphosis of the EU, together with the USA, towards an aggressive stance, calls for a reconstitution of the EU's security architecture, with the inclusion of Russia. No parliament of a European NATO member state voted on changing NATO from a defense to an offensive alliance after 1990. Nor has the European Parliament ever approved it. NATO must be dissolved.

Associate entrepreneurship

On its way down, Western capitalism has also perverted entrepreneurship, with mass pseudo self-employment, that is, pseudo entrepreneurship. Personal data and personal ownership have been disbanded. From "normal" employees from the very bottom up to top consulting and managerial positions, "entrepreneurs of themselves" are created or simulated, called Me plc or the like - in order to then be unequivocally determined and exploited by someone more powerful. This also signals an end of the badly perverted capitalism.

Hence: The dependent employees from the bottom to the top must become associate entrepreneurs themselves, with the right to ownership. The task is big, very big, it is necessary, it corresponds to the current situation, human dignity and human capabilities.

1.
United Kingdom:
Where the new labor injustice began and will not end with Brexit

"We want to take back control": This abstractly correct slogan of the Brexiteers was directed against "the EU" as a bureaucracy, but not against the capitalists backing it, especially not against the capitalists ruling in the UK in a particularly anti-social way and their monarchical-aristocratic-corrupt accomplices. Brexit - this is the most effectual form of populism and political right-wing development in Europe so far. And integration into the EU is being replaced by more direct dependence on the USA.

Rise of the working class and its humiliations

The working class in Great Britain had gained political weight through its struggles after the First World War. Churchill, the war hero orchestrated by the mainstream media, proved to be not so popular as soon as the war ended. He suffered a crushing defeat to the Labour Party in the first post-war election.

The capitalists, blinded in their war profits, had to make concessions on a scale not achieved anywhere else in Western Europe: The war profiteers in the mining, steel, coal and automobile industries were expropriated. The trade unions gained in prestige, the public infrastructure with a largely free health care system and cooperative housing was expanded, as was water, rail transport, the postal service and the BBC broadcasting service.

There was majority support for the reforms. The unions became more self-confident. Up until the 1970s, subsequent Tory governments still had to grudgingly live with fierce strikes, wage increases and improved working conditions for miners.

Humiliation of the working class I: The Tories/Thatcher

The counter-revolution slowly got underway. The ruling class had to recover from the shock. This usually takes a while. Private TV led the way. Starting in 1979, the new Tory prime minister, Margaret Thatcher, demonstratively waved the neoliberal bible - Friedrich von Hayek's "The

Constitution of Liberty", first published in London in 1960 - at her party conference appearances. When Thatcher's bosom buddy Ronald Reagan became president in the US in 1981, this gave a new boost. Reagan immediately showed how to break up a united, striking union acting in a central position: With strategic preparation, with the help of police beatings, the army as strikebreakers, secret service employees infiltrated into the union, dismissals, imprisonment, non-payment of wages, all staged as a "national emergency".[342]

Coal supplies from abroad, police, secret service
The Thatcher government prepared its counterattack as soon as it came to power in 1979, in secret. First, the political, symbolic core of the working class was to be destroyed: The National Union of Mine Workers, NUM. The orchestration: "20 nationalized mines are unprofitable, they must be closed!" There was no negotiation with the unions. It was not about the mines, it was about the miners, about their union. The 20 mines were chosen from among the 70 mines because that was where the fight against the NUM promised the best success. They were to be the beginning.

The government built up huge coal reserves by buying coal abroad ("strikebreaker coal") and expanded ports to this end. The state-owned electricity industry was obliged to replace coal with oil - for which the fraudulent US corporation Enron received the orders.[4] Special mounted police squadrons were established, the secret service eavesdropped, non-union truck drivers were recruited. Social legislation was changed: Families of strikers were not to receive allowances. The confiscation of NUM assets was also prepared. The dockers' and railroad workers' unions, which showed solidarity with the miners, were granted wage increases without fuss. By contrast: 11,000 strikers were arrested, and 8,300 were investigated for breach of the peace.[343]

---

[4] Enron, the energy company that had grown with Governor George W. Bush in Texas, caused the biggest corporate scandal in the USA to date in 2001 through systematic accounting fraud. Bush, who had also promoted the company as US president, only escaped criticism because the terrorist attack on the World Trade Center submerged the scandal. The bosses were sentenced to prison, and the group became insolvent. The complicit auditing company Arthur Andersen, the largest at the time, was also dissolved.

Class struggle from above - surprising for those at the bottom
The union was not prepared for this differentiated, underhanded and brutal class struggle from above. With its successes, it had settled into the welfare state, in which there were supposedly no longer any classes.

The sacrificial strike, which lasted several months and was supported by many groups in England and internationally, including many women's groups, collapsed, partly because the struggle quickly became a system struggle. As a result, the leaderships of the Labour Party and most other unions withdrew. The fact that the US, with the help of the CIA, had turned Labour and the TUC anti-communist after the war had an impact.[344]

For the class struggle, the government piled up enormous debt, no neoliberal austerity dictates applied: coal reserves, port expansion, more police, then the expensive mine closures, more social welfare, regional aid for the doomed coalfields. Since then, coal has been imported on a grand scale from Australia, Colombia and the US, where labor standards are low: "globalization".

The defeat - permanent, with ripples throughout Europe
The strike and the defeat also had an impact on the continent because the UK had been a member of the EEC since 1973. At the same time, the government initiated a more radical de-industrialization than in any other European state - and gradually expanded the City of London into an EU financial center instead.

"The strike was the largest and arguably the most important labor dispute in post-war European history.... Industries have disappeared, communities have been destroyed. Many things would have been different in Europe, too, if the miners had won."[345]

Humiliation of the working class II: "New Labour"/Blair
Nowhere else in Europe was a self-confident and organized working class defeated and humiliated at its core as hard as in the UK. And the neoliberal fanatic Mrs. Thatcher was only the beginning.

After her inevitable moral demise, it was the socialist 'labor' party Labour that won the elections, following the alternating pattern of Western capital democracies and the US Democrat/William Clinton model. But under demagogue Anthony Blair and his successor Gordon Brown with

"New Labour", the humiliation of already humiliated workers was taken a step further. "My greatest success was Tony Blair," Thatcher mused.[346]

Humiliation of the working class III:
The Tories/Cameron

That was not the end either: After the ritual demise of "New Labour", too, there followed an escalation. The new Conservative "government of the rich"-23 of the 29 ministers were millionaires - under Tory David Cameron insulted the unemployed as "chavs", as "fat, lazy and stupid", and on other occasions as welfare cheats, drug addicts and alcoholics. The government demolished social housing because "squalid families" were living there.[347]

The anti-social and corrupt millionaire pack, alimented by the City of London, expanded the zero-hour contract introduced by New Labour: Work on demand without fixed working hours, if necessary without a single working hour a week. Back in 2013, the UNITE union estimated the number at 5.5 million workers under this fearful waiting regime.[348] More people than in any other EU country have to work at weekends; 30 percent of all employees are now affected.[349] Precariousness extends far into the academic staff: fixed-term contracts for teachers and lecturers at institutions of higher education that are not elite universities.

While the Western "quality" media reported on the Royal Family's spiritual and pregnancy woes, the UN special envoy Philipp Alston reported widely unheard: In the last decade, the number of billionaires doubled; 14 million people live in poverty, including millions of low-wage earners also in the public sector; 1.5 million vegetate as destitute. Public libraries and youth centers are closed. And Brexit will hit low-wage earners and the unemployed the hardest.[350]

Bought Brexit Campaign: The EU as a surrogate enemy

Both capitalist parties, Labour and Tories, were now more unpopular than ever before. Against gradually spreading criticism, against mounting trade union protests and against the resurgence of an only tentatively renewed Labour Party under Jeremy Corbyn, young upstart entrepreneurs, gutter press and conservative radicalized politicians set up the EU as a surrogate enemy.

It was clear to the Brexiteers that if reforms, indeed expropriations and re-nationalizations, were to take place in England, if low wages were to be combated as promised by Corbyn's Labour Party, then US capital in particular would be affected, in addition to the domestic elite.

Transatlantic financiers
The Brexit party UKIP and the Leave.EU campaign were funded by aggressive young British entrepreneurs and bankers, including Richard Smith, Christopher Harborne, Jeremy Hosking and George Farmer - all former Tory donors.[351] The best-known sponsor of the Brexit campaign was Arron Banks. In just a few years, the young multimillionaire had pulled together a financial and insurance holding company that included diamond mines in Africa and numerous shell companies in the Caribbean. He donated over GBP 7 million to the Brexiteers and opened his Bristol offices to the campaign.[352]

Most donations came from US foundations, including the Chase Foundation, Templeton Foundation, and Rosenkranz Foundation. The clandestine money flowed through British think tanks such as the Institute of Economic Affairs, Policy Exchange, TaxPayers Alliance, and Adam Smith Institute.[353]

Capitalist lobby as simulated proles
The Brexiteers succeeded in directing the anger of the humiliated against "the EU". Spearhead Johnson posed as a class warrior after his model Trump. They hypocritically wooed the working class, surrounded themselves with workers, visited factories, in hard hats and work gear they grinned at workers, and promised new jobs and new prosperity[354] - if the shackles of the EU were finally broken.

In colonial tradition, the British upper class had brought a particularly large number of migrant workers from poor regions to the country of high unemployment, from Pakistan, India, Bangladesh, and then from Eastern Europe, especially Poland, Romania and Lithuania. Especially in the capital London, populated by oligarchs from all countries between Russia and Israel, people like to be served cheaply. But the rich, their politicians and the media quickly turned this around and agitated against foreigners who stole the jobs of "our workers".

Hypocritical re-industrialization à la Trump

The demagogues knew: support for our regime is more fragile than ever. If the criticism turns into the right channels, we are gone. That is why Johnson & Co. act as the makeshift representatives of the capitalist class and as the radicalized new edition of Thatcher. The gutter and capitalist press of the multi-billionaire Murdoch (The Sun, Times, Wall Street Journal), which incites against gays and leftists, is an important bastion. Johnson&Co therefore want to do what Cameron failed to do last time: Shut down or privatize the state broadcaster BBC, which is languishing with remnants of liberalism. Johnson banned all ministers from giving interviews to the long-since lame BBC: How scared one must be!

US investors had already registered their condition for the free trade agreement hoped for with the United States: sell the still not completely privatized health service as well! But only the lucrative parts! Thus, Johnson could lie to the public that he did not want to privatize "the NHS".[355]

EU labor law: Still too worker-friendly

The old relationships with Commonwealth countries such as Canada, Australia and New Zealand are to be expanded, especially with the former crown colony of Hong Kong: From there, access to China is to be intensified, as well as to Turkey, for example, in order to exploit the consequences of Trump's trade war. Like Trump, Johnson wants to build up new industries - with the help of the otherwise denounced deadly sins, namely large government subsidies.

At the same time, Johnson wants to further curb the right to strike with a new trade union law: workplace ballots are to be banned. Even the low standards of the EU directives on labor have always gone too far for the Tories, for example on break times, annual leave, parental leave, temporary work, maternity leave.[356] The radicalized "conservatives" want something similar to the Polish government populists: first destroy the leftists, then grant a few benefits to the particularly well-behaved - especially the native-born - among the impoverished. After Brexit, Johnson promised: We'll raise the minimum wage by 53 pence!

Corbyn's lax social democracy

The short-lived and at the same time lukewarm social democratic renewal under Corbyn was no match for the deep humiliation of dependent employees. The "Labour Party Manifesto 2019" dutifully lists all the social inequalities in wages, pensions, rents, health care, and Internet access, and declares that the Labour-led government would change all that.[357]

The manifesto trumpeted the largest infrastructure investment program of modern times and a "green industrial revolution". The English state should become "fairer", one that "cares for all" and "shares wealth and power with all". "We will all win." This was the new communality in "post-capitalism" advocated by the ultra-radical and equally opportunistic globalization critic and Corbyn advisor Paul Mason.[358]

Criticism of capitalism? None of it

There is not the slightest hint of the class struggle that needs to be waged here, not with but against the "rich". The term capitalism and capitalists does not appear anywhere. No corporation, no bank, no investor, no matter how aggressive, is named; not even the City of London is mentioned: it disappears behind the abstract term "the financial industry". Corbyn/Mason wanted merely to curb the subjectless, psychologized "short-term greed" of the otherwise unnamed.

The manifesto did not call for a stronger, new organization of dependent employees. No: "Only if we find our way back to our old strength" would we be able to make progress again in the "proud tradition of the historic trade union movement": nostalgia was cultivated. The decades of adaptation and the humiliation of the dependent employees by "New Labour": ignored.

The proposals for labor and trade union rights were correspondingly lax. The minimum wage was to be raised to GBP 10 (EUR 11.20). Unions and employers' associations were to negotiate "minimum standards", for example, on the zero-hour contract, working hours and "decent wages". This soft language with "fair" and "decent", favorite terms in the EU and among the business lobby, focuses on compromise rather than legal entitlement backed by sanctions.

Employees were to acquire "up to 10 percent" of the company's shares, make up one-third of the members of the supervisory board and have a say in the pay of directors. How pathetic! The EU was highly praised: Unlike the Tories, Labour wanted a return to the EU labor directives after all! Could it be any more hopeless?

Criticism of the EU? Of the military buildup? No way!
The manifesto had nothing to say about the EU, as was the case with Labour throughout the Brexit conflict. Labour vacillated between getting out of the EU and staying in the EU, without even hinting at the pro-capitalist nature of the EU and the systemic labor injustice.

From Labour and in the manifesto, not a word about military buildup and the threat of war. There is no mention of the fact that, after the United States, the UK already has the highest arms budget in the EU, measured in terms of gross national product, that it repeatedly joins the United States in wars that violate international law, and that it actively participates in the deployment against Russia.

That was not the language for the long exploited and disenfranchised. Hundreds of thousands of young people in their first new awakening enthusiastically participated in the Labour youth organization Momentum, but they could not comprehend the real class struggle and then the defeat.

Strikes, new unions, self-organization
What went unmentioned in the prevailing Brexit coverage, and while the transatlantic Israel lobby played up Corbyn's supposed "anti-Semitism", is that for a decade many unions have been regenerating themselves, new forms of self-organization are emerging.

In areas of precarious and digitally organized work, where traditional unions are hardly present, new small, militant unions and initiatives are being formed. In part, membership is being remixed, with more women and migrants.

Students: Action against tuition fees
The working class was also humiliated by the exclusion from higher education. In 2010, the Tory government introduced tuition fees for all universities, following the example of its elite Cambridge and Oxford universities -where Cameron, May, and Johnson also studied.

A nationwide protest movement of students developed against this over many months. Tens of thousands demonstrated repeatedly across London. Universities were occupied in all university towns. The offices of the Tory Party in London were also occupied. The government repeatedly unleashed police on the students. The protests dragged on for two years. Without results: defiance requires more than a spontaneous, albeit mass, uprising.

Since then, studying the cheaper social sciences and humanities costs EUR 11,500 a year, studying medicine costs EUR 38,000. In addition, the cost of housing and other necessities of life starts at EUR 12,000 a year, and even more in London.[359] Not only the working class is excluded. Even the middle class, generously supported so far to maintain capitalist society, often cannot send their children to study, or they have to take on debt.

Several unions successful against outsourcing
Things look different with professional defiance. Success is possible, even if it is on a smaller scale. But for those directly affected, the stakes are high.

Both Labour and Tory governments had pushed ahead with the outsourcing of services - cleaning, security, transport, offices - from public administration, ministries, universities, hospitals. In 2012, the new Independent Workers Union of Great Britain (IWGB) was formed. It primarily represents migrant workers, including those in the care, bicycle delivery and gig economy sectors. It also organizes language courses and training.

For the first time in 2018, several unions joined forces to strike against outsourcing, including the IWGB, the United Workers of the World UVW and the older Public and Commercial Services Union PCS. After selective strikes, blockades, occupations and months of negotiations, a thousand janitors, canteen workers and cleaners at London's Imperial Healthcare NHS Trust, with its five hospitals, achieved direct and permanent employment - the first time industrial action has reversed outsourcing on this scale. Wages and working conditions were brought into line with permanent employees. UVW co-founder Petros Elia pointed out: The fight was also for the benefit of the patients! When services were outsourced, it was shown: Infections spread much faster![360] The IWGB achieved a similar outcome at the University of London, supported by university staff[361] and the PCS at the Ministry of Justice and the HMRC Royal Tax Office.[362]

As early as 2006, outsourced cleaners from the London School of Oriental and African Studies SOAS had joined forces under the motto *justice for cleaners*. Gradually, outsourced workers in catering, janitorial, reception, hospitality, repairs, security, and postal services joined. In 2018, through strikes and other actions, they achieved their goal: the contracts with the subcontractors were terminated. The workers were put on an equal footing with permanent employees, in terms of wages, vacation and sick pay, pensions. The initiative renamed itself: *justice for workers*. It is now active in other institutions and companies.[363]

How do we analyze our surroundings together? Forget about Twitter!
Others are starting at the bottom and from scratch, for instance the *Angry Workers of the World*. They write: "There's a lot of people out there despairing – hoping for struggles for a better world, but feeling isolated and unsure of where to focus their political action...

- We can't just 'start where we are', we have to move our ass. It's only a few of us, we have to be where it's at. For us that's where working class people come together, day-to-day. Big workplaces are central, neighborhoods are not irrelevant. Dig in, get a job and learn. Or go to new places and ask. Discover how people organize and why they don't. Slowly help build structures. Our initiative SolNet is getting off the ground. We meet weekly, at McDonalds, in an Indian tea house, in the 24h Asda cafe. Form small gangs at work.
- Keep all this together in a regular publication for the area – this is central! Become a mirror for the class, help to look ahead. Forget about Twitter, create working class papers. Pick up the small stories of resistance from the packaging department.
- Circulate workplace reports. Analyze your local working class surroundings. Look for concentrations, conflicts, current divisions.
- We will need this rooting process. Headless chickens will get eaten."[364]

Gig workers are organizing themselves - but with Soros' help

Platform companies in the gig economy - food delivery companies such as Lieferando, Deliveroo, Foodora, UberEats, cab services such as Lyft, Grab, Uber - use apps to tie up orders between customers and executors. The companies see themselves purely as intermediary services. The workers are not employed and, if possible, bring their own bikes, cars and other paraphernalia: In many cases, work on call, paid per delivery, unpaid waiting time, no insurance. But since 2015, there has been diverse resistance to this fake pseudo self-employment.

Bicycle couriers went to court and sued as regular employees. In the end, this was of no use, because they were not employed afterwards. In 2016, 200 riders in London began a wildcat strike, supported by the

IWGB, triggered by the switch from hourly pay to piece rate. The strike was successful: a return to hourly pay and an additional pound bonus per delivery.

Based on the English example, similar court actions, strikes and demonstrations by riders followed in Italy, Spain, Belgium, the Netherlands and Germany. Some ex-riders have now founded their own cooperatives with permanent jobs, such as Mensakas in Barcelona, Spain. Admittedly, the fixed income is low.[365] Deliveroo & Co dominate the market with their large investors.

Soros/Open Society Foundation are organizing the new working class
Many millions of gig workers are involved, in the EU and around the globe. An awakening like that of the bicycle couriers also bubbled up among the cab companies Uber, Lyft, Grab and Bolt.

So, the IWGB convened an international conference in London on January 29-30, 2020. Organizer Nicole Moore of the US-based Rideshare Drivers United RDU explained, "We are all at the mercy of exploitation by multinational corporations like Uber. Global exploitation demands a global strategy of resistance."

The ruling class has also understood that a politically important movement is underway. For years, it has been looking for initiatives that would renew contemporary capitalism in an affable way. To this end, Soros' Open Society Foundation founded the *Fair Work Initiative*. Its director welcomed the conference, where "strategies for new forms of global collective action" were to be discussed.[366] *Fair* - the EU's favorite fudge word.

For this, multi-billionaire Soros provided a few million: Initiatives from 23 countries were invited, from all continents, from the UK, France as well as from Australia, Bangladesh, India, Cambodia, Indonesia, Malaysia, Pakistan, from the USA and Canada, from Panama, Argentina, Brazil, Chile, Costa Rica, Uruguay, from South Africa, Kenya and Nigeria.

Soros and his foundations, the organizers of extreme capitalist individualism who have already opened up many a state, such as Hungary and most recently Ukraine, to Western capital and military, are now organizing the new collectivity of the new working class. They are attempting it.

Toppled statues – better late than never
The ruling class of Great Britain has rendered its practices invisible many
a time - this is the other side of the populistically staged monarchical
spectacle. Slavery was abolished in 1830, and the slave owners were
compensated: As late as 2015, the state paid the final installments to their
descendants.[367]

In anti-racism protests in 2020 some slave trader statues were finally
toppled. It can take that long. There is more toppling to come!

2.
EU founding and core states

The six founding states have remained the richest and most powerful.
Only brief information on them is possible here: very briefly on the Benelux states, in more detail on Germany and France, Italy is left out.[368]

Benelux: Rich, at the expense of the other EU states
The two smallest states, Luxembourg and Belgium, which are at the same
time monarchies and strongholds of a secretive financial and power elite
and particularly close US vassals, are home to the most and the most important EU institutions: European Commission, CJEU and numerous
agencies, as well as the most capital lobbyists.

Luxembourg and the Netherlands are at the same time the largest financial havens in the EU and enable corporations from the USA, but also
from Germany, Italy, the UK, etc. to evade taxes. The Netherlands alone
inflicts a tax loss of at least EU 10 billion on EU Member States every
year.[369] The tax loss promoted by the state of Luxembourg at the expense
of other EU countries is higher still.[370] Their governments are right-wing
populist, regardless of whether they call themselves Christian or liberal.
The European Commission is an accomplice: Luxembourg and the Netherlands never appear on the "black lists" of tax havens.

The majority of indigenous workers, especially the older generations,
are doing very nicely, especially in Luxembourg, which has by far the
highest per capita income in the EU. But everywhere a tabooed, silenced

working class serves and, as part of it, a legal and illegalized army of migrants: in no EU state is it so numerous in relation to the native population and at the same time so invisible as in Luxembourg.

Germany: Leading labor injustice state

Starting in 1990, the Federal Republic of Germany developed into the leading labor injustice state in the EU with its takeover the former GDR.

The German employee: heteronomous, personally dependent

"Through the employment contract, the employee is obliged to perform work in the service of another in personal dependence, bound by instructions and determined by others." This is the wording of the German Civil Code (BGB) § 611a Employment Contract.

Is that clear enough? Social partnership? Freedom? No. When the going gets tough legally and on a daily basis in the capitalist enterprise, the core emerges: the "employee" is "heteronomous", "bound by instructions", and "personally dependent", working "in the service of another". This new version in the BGB was adopted in the CDU/CSU/SPD coalition in 2016, Labor Minister Andrea Nahles and Justice Minister Heiko Maas belonged to the SPD, under Chancellor Angela Merkel (CDU).[371]

Basic Law: Animal protection yes, labor protection no

The 1949 Basic Law of the Federal Republic of Germany fell behind labor standards that had been achieved in Germany after World War 1. The Basic Law lacks all provisions from the Weimar Constitution on trade union rights, works councils, freedom of expression in the company, equal pay for women and men. With regard to labor law, therefore, the claim that the Basic Law was based on the Weimar Constitution is a lie.[372] Later, in a zeitgeisty populist move, environmental and animal protection were included, but not the protection of workers at the workplace.[373]

Economic constitution: cowardly omitted and in breach of the law
The chambers of commerce demanded by trade unions and the British military government after 1945, in which entrepreneurs and employees were to be equally represented, were rejected by the USA. Out of cowardice, the issue was left out of the Basic Law. In 1956, the Adenauer government passed the Act for the Provisional Regulation of the Law of Chambers of Industry and Commerce. All companies, even the very smallest, are compulsory members: compulsory bureaucracy is thus com-

patible with "free market economy". At the same time, the vast majority of those working in industry and commerce, the dependent employees, remain locked out. The law was meant to be provisional. The final regulation was to come later - but cowardly and in violation of the law, all federal governments prevented this. Thus, 65 years later, the provisional nature of the law is still valid: an eternal provisionality. Unjust state.[374]

No compensation for forced laborers
The Federal Republic was the successor state of the Nazi state. But not a word was said about compensation for the 7.5 million forced laborers or the return of aryanized company property. Aryanized property was returned or partially compensated only in a few and only in individual isolated cases, such as works of art. Moreover, only pressure from abroad brought this about, along with the late compensation of the last surviving forced laborers. Aryanized art is still in German museums, mostly hidden in depots. But expropriations of large companies were not reversed.

Constitutional breach with the ex-GDR
According to the Unification Treaty of 1990, the Federal Republic must adopt a uniform labor code. Such a code existed in the GDR, while the FRG's labor rights were scattered over three dozen different labor laws adopted at different times and under different conditions (Works Constitution Act, co-determination, dismissal, working hours, disability, Hartz I to IV...) and still has. 30 years later, the labor code still does not exist. And the dependent employees in the conquered territory of East Germany are still paid less than in West Germany: This has nothing to do with qualification, with performance and with equality before the law: East Germany is a modernized colony within Germany. In addition, the more than one million employees of church enterprises as well as civil servants are exempt from general labor rights.

The four Hartz laws: Legalized labor injustice
Germany leads the EU in the legalization of labor injustice. This began systematically again in 2004 with the four Hartz laws:
* low-wage, part-time and temporary jobs
* extended temporary work, which was then further developed to the even lower status of the contract for work and services

- reduction of unemployment benefits by amount and duration of entitlement, combined with drastic sanctions, up to and including withdrawal of unemployment benefits; also combined with the compulsion to accept poorly paid and distant work, even if it is only short-term.

Under Labor Minister von der Leyen - today's President of the European Commission - the unemployed were even deprived of their pension contributions; likewise, under von der Leyen, state supervision of the employers' liability insurance associations - responsible for health protection at the workplace - was scaled back.

Germany thus created the largest labor-injustice, low-wage and low-pension sector in the EU.

Eponym Peter Hartz was a member of the SPD and a functionary of IG Metall. On behalf of the SPD-led federal government, he headed the commission that drafted the Hartz laws with McKinsey. On the board of the VW Group, Hartz had introduced low-wage work in the car company with the help of systemic corruption of the works council leadership.[375]

The regulations were later adopted in other EU countries such as France, Belgium, Spain, Italy, Greece and Eastern Europe.[376]

The Americanization of labor relations

The Hartz laws were based on the US model of the '*job*':[377] Free disposal of the entrepreneur over the dependent worker, "heteronomous, personally dependent, in the service of another" (Civil Code § 611a).

Since the 1970s, extremely anti-union US companies such as UPS and McDonald's have used the Federal Republic as a gateway for their expansion in the EU. No other EU state has adopted the professional service of union busting - preventing and obstructing works councils - from the US to such an extent as the Federal Republic. US law firms such as Allen & Overy, Hogan Lovells, Freshfields and DLA Piper maintain their own departments for this purpose in Germany, while German law firms such as CMS Hasche Sigle and Kliemt&Vollstädt have adopted the methods.[378]

Minimum wage, overtime: Millions not paid

In 2015, Germany was the last major EU country to introduce the statutory minimum wage. In relation to purchasing power, it is the lowest among the rich western EU states. In addition, newspaper publishers succeeded in exempting newspaper delivery staff from the minimum wage.

And what is more, the judiciary and governments allow millions of other entrepreneurs not to pay the minimum wage or to undermine it, with impunity. The approximately one billion unpaid overtime hours per year can also be usurped by the entrepreneurs without punishment as an annual extorted gift worth billions.[379]

At the same time, the Confederation of German Employers' Associations (BDA), with close ties to the governing CDU party, is agitating against the ruling of the European Court of Justice, which requires the complete, legally secure recording of working hours, including overtime. The BDA is also fighting the tentative project of a "European minimum wage", according to which the minimum wage in the EU states is to be just above the respective national poverty line.[380]

Leading the way in discrimination against women
Despite or because of the fashionable hype for "women's rights" and the figurehead of the female head of government, women are particularly disadvantaged in German working life. They make up the vast majority of precariously employed and forced under-employed (involuntary part-time work and work on call). This also percolates down into the particularly dire poverty among women pensioners.

In terms of labor income inequality, German women rank 26th among the 28 EU countries, with 20.5 percent lower incomes; only in the Czech Republic and Estonia are women's incomes slightly lower.381

Likewise, German women are only in the bottom third of the EU in terms of the proportion in management positions.382

Germany: Europe's "pigsty"
The legalized labor injustice is open to various forms of criminality, as can be seen in the unsanctioned non-payment of the low minimum wage. With EU subsidies, Germany became the leading country in the multiple exploitation of meat workers: Fraudulent contracts for work (faked temporary work); working conditions harmful to health; unpaid overtime; deductions for placement costs, for alleged misconduct, for transportation and excessive rents (rent usury): modernized slavery. Those affected remain fearfully silent and dare not go to court.

Up to 80 percent of employees are on work contracts. Market leader Tönnies sourced them from at least 12 different intermediaries in 2020. The workers come from states impoverished by the EU: High unemployment, lowest low and minimum wages, in Moldova EUR 200 a month. They often come for two, three years, then they are replaced, exhausted.[383]

Thus, Germany rose to become the "pigsty of Europe".[384] That's why slaughter companies Vion of the Netherlands and Danish Crown of Denmark set up large slaughterhouses in the leading labor injustice paradise - German practices are banned at home. Germany's leading slaughter company, Tönnies, promoted by the EU, attracted further labor injustice. Germany became the largest exporter of cheap meat after the USA.

Minimal enforcement of the law: Only 1.3 percent works councils
Another form of legalized injustice is the mass non-implementation of laws, as already seen with the minimum wage. "With, as a rule, at least 5 permanent employees entitled to vote, works councils are elected" is stated in §1 of the Works Constitution Act (*BetrVG*). In Germany, there are 2.16 million companies with more than 10 employees: if we take these as a basis (and not already the companies with 5 or more employees), then the 26,000 works councils that came into being in the last works council election in 2018[385] represent only 1.3 percent.

Especially in the auto and pharmaceutical industries, works council chairpersons are corrupted by high managerial salaries (see the Hartz system at VW). And a highly paid union-busting service industry is deployed to obstruct and prevent the other, militant works councils. In this way, little remains of the good law.

According to §119 of the Works Council Constitution Act, the obstruction and prevention of works councils by employers and their agents is a criminal offense: It stands lonely at the top of the list of crimes not prosecuted by the judiciary.[386] The Works Constitution Act is subject to a similar enforcement deficit as sexual abuse in the (systemically relevant) Catholic Church.

No freedom of expression for dependent employees
There is no freedom of expression in the companies, but extorted silence. Whistleblowers also have no protection; despite decades of demands, there is still no law on the subject.

Even someone who reports fraud committed by management to the public prosecutor's office, which can be proven in court, can be dismissed in accordance with the law for disturbing industrial peace. Before the labor courts, "the protection of trade secrets" and the employee's cap-doffing "duty of loyalty" apply here.[387]

The Federal Republic is the only EU state that, in 1972, with a formal "radical decree", had 3.5 million public sector employees - or those seeking entry - investigated by the domestic intelligence service because of suspected "left-wing extremism", did not accept 1,250 people into the civil service and dismissed 250. The European Court of Human Rights' ruling to the contrary is not heeded in Germany.

Stirrings against exploitation and disenfranchisement

For this reason, uprisings on a larger scale and with a longer-term effect have hardly been possible so far. Important approaches are, for example, the concentrated, also internationalized struggles organized by verdi against the union hater Amazon[388] and the strikes of hospital employees for more jobs under the motto "More of us is better for all".[389]

The *Aktion gegen ArbeitsUnrecht* (Action against labor Injustice) supported and documented the elections to works councils, which have now become dangerous adventures in some cases, especially in areas where trade unions are not present, such as food delivery services and supermarket chains. *Aktion gegen ArbeitsUnrecht* contributed to the exposure of the meat company Tönnies as a particularly criminal exploiter through its nationwide campaign day "Black Friday the 13th", which was directed against the company in 2019.[390]

France: The leading movements against capitalist Europe

After World War II, left-wing and anti-fascist forces in France resisted the influence of the US manipulators most successfully in a European comparison (along with Belgium and Italy). A high minimum wage, the 35-hour week and the highest short-time working benefit within the EU, early retirement for women and particularly stressful professions were among the achievements. That is why today, in the phase of even further radicalized neoliberalism ("hyper-globalization", figurehead Macron), the most important battles in the EU are also being fought in France.

The renewed resistance began with the mass protests against the "reform" of labor law initiated under the "socialist" President Francois Hollande.[391] Starting in 2016, Hollande wanted to catch up with what his role models Blair and Schröder had done.

Hollande's successor Emmanuel Macron, ex-co-owner of the Rothschild investment bank, had already served the racist President Nicolas Sarkozy and had been an advisor and economics minister under Hollande. With the help of the oligarchs Arnauld, Lagardère, Hermand and Niel and various private foundations, the extreme political opportunist Macron built a new political movement - La République en Marche (LRM) - on the remains of the socialist and conservative parties, which had been deeply discredited by their complicity with capitalist forces.[392]

Banker Macron gathered together all available ideological remnants of "bourgeois" society. He teamed up with the oldest reactionary forces: He renewed the feudal alliance with the Catholic Church. In LRM he mopped up defectors from the "conservative", "bourgeois" as well as "socialist" parties and, with the decline of his prestige since 2020, helped by the revived Sarkozy, he is also courting the supporters of the far-right Rassemblement National. Of course, there is also a green-faced new female environment minister.[393]

Above all, Macron is developing the network with the most powerful capitalists of the new generation. In the Elysée Palace as well as in the monarchical splendor of Versailles, he holds exclusive meetings with the representatives of the largest international corporations, with preferential position for BlackRock. His goals: Multiple favoritism for the super-rich, downgrading of dependent employees in the areas of taxes, income, health, pensions, transport, infrastructure.[394]

La convergence des luttes – The convergence of struggles
Against this, a system of resistance has developed that is as broad, widespread as it is deep: yellow vests[395], trade unions, the left-wing party La France Insoumise, farmers, mayors, lawyers, students, artists.[396] The convergence of struggles, even without a directorate, is the goal.[397]

At the same time, and continued during the "corona crisis", there were strikes in countless companies, occupations: In hotels, at Amazon and Coca Cola, in refineries, hospitals, post offices, metro and railroads, judicial buildings, in the Paris branch of BlackRock.[398]

By contrast, the president, who presents himself as softly liberal – "autonomy of labor", "freedom of the individual" - is relying on French nationalism along the lines of the kindred US president Trump: "France first". Like Trump, he brutally deploys the heavily armed police, and the police, of course, are exempt from pension "reform". Macron's downfall is also significant for the further development of the EU.

3.
Later EU Member States

The UK, Ireland, Denmark, then Greece, Spain and Portugal were the next EU members up until 1986. The UK has already been discussed. Denmark is presented along with the other Scandinavian states. Greece's plundering by Goldman Sachs, the US rating agencies, then the Troika, Blackrock&Co has been widely documented elsewhere.[399] This section is about Spain, Ireland and Austria.

Spain:
Migrant organization in EU vegetable garden
The USA, along with the UK, the Vatican and Nazi Germany, were among the first to diplomatically recognize the fascist coup regime of General Francisco Franco, married to a wealthy noblewoman, in 1939. Even during the war, the US and Britain intensified trade and investment, developed tourism, did nothing to stop exports of tungsten, a precious metal vital to the war effort, to Nazi Germany.[400] From 1953, the US continued this, expanding economic aid to develop military bases here.

After the dictator's death in 1982, Spain joined NATO, and in 1986 the EU. King Juan Carlos, appointed by Franco as his successor, led the country into democracy, it was said. Fascist criminals, including those who remained active after Franco's death, were exempted from prosecution and expropriation, victims of the dictatorship were not even dug up from mass graves, there was no talk of compensation for injustice. All judgments and hundreds of laws from the dictatorship are still in effect today.[401] The EU celebrated this as a return to democracy and, as in the case of other Member States, suppressed the reappraisal of the fascist past and its current aftermath.[402]

Recreated social democrats as new hope

The Spanish Socialist Workers' Party (PSOE) was reinstalled after Franco's death, purged of communism. It now had nothing to do with socialism or workers, but kept its name and target group. The first secretary general, the young Felipe Gonzalez, became a beacon of hope, supported by the CIA.[403] He successfully pushed through the referendum on remaining in NATO against a general strike: The unity of the EU and NATO was preserved.

The EU continued US economic aid, celebrated the corrupt monarchical clan as guarantors of democracy, and promoted the country's "modernization", especially in transport infrastructure, tourism, and agriculture. The EU subsidized the construction of high-speed rail lines, local and regional airports, and toll highways operated by private companies. The EU subsidized the development of agribusiness with monocultures and day labor.

Conservative populists particularly corrupt

The corruption of the populist People's Party, Partido Popular, PP, did not bother the EU any more than in the case of the oligarchs in Eastern Europe. Regional airports and rail lines, underutilized, are now permanently subsidized by the state. For more and more Spaniards, rail tickets and tolls are far too expensive anyway.[404] Financial speculation by Western banks robbed 2.5 million Spaniards of their homes. Unemployment continued to rise. Any form of labor supervision is virtually nonexistent.[405]

"Labor reforms" stabilize high unemployment

In line with EU doctrine, the state now had to "save". Starting in 2010, the alternating governments of the Socialists and the "conservative" populists therefore pushed through far-reaching "reforms" under pressure from the Troika. The PP crooks were happy to bail out the construction groups and banks they had been bribed by, according to the Troika's instructions.[406] At the same time, BlackRock&Co were able to snap up major stakes in the most important banks and construction groups in Spain.

Old and new media: Against trade unions

The TV business is majority-owned by the Berlusconi Group/mediaset and Bertelsmann/RTL. The newly founded, originally left-liberal daily El Pais was bought by the Liberty Fund of US investor Nicolas Berggruen.

All these media, with numerous specialized subsidiaries, are anti-union and pro-EU in different ways.[407]

With the help of the media, the Socialist government under José Zapatero initially pushed through the "labor reform" against the will of the majority. The reform included the relaxation of protection against dismissal, temporary and project-based employment contracts, and the transfer of collective bargaining to company level. Through a "social dialogue", parts of the unions were integrated and dissuaded from strike action.[408]

Old privileges and even more injustice for the younger generations
The old privileges are also evident in the highest proportion of private schools in an EU comparison, around 30 percent. At the same time, the state is allowing state schools to fall into disrepair. Trained teachers are among the 13,000 Spaniards who applied for 34 jobs as quickly trained assistant train drivers for Deutsche Bahn in Germany.[409]

The property and class relations inherited from the Franco era also have an effect on employment relations. Under the old labor law, long-serving employees were particularly well protected against dismissal. This privilege was left untouched. But everybody else with a short employment record was abandoned for dismissal.

This is why work and unemployment are more unequally distributed between the generations in Spain than in any other EU country ("dual labor market"): the average unemployment rate in 2016 was 26 percent, but 56 percent for those under 25. Both figures would be even higher if emigrants were included.

And among the 44 percent of young people who have jobs, various forms of precarity prevail. The UGT union noted that in universities and other state institutions, some 900,000 young people, many of them students, are employed without employment contracts, without social security and with low wages. They replace nearly 300,000 regular jobs.[410]

Fragmentation of employment - dissolution of the workplace
This created an extremely fragmented labor landscape with the groups of dependent employees and the many temporarily unemployed separated from one another. As a result, counteraction took on countless forms and shapes.

At the same time, digitization is blurring the previously clear boundaries of the workplace. Another contributing factor is that the owners of the companies and subcontractors are becoming increasingly invisible. This calls for new forms of collectivization.

36,000 strikes in one year - ever heard of that?
In 2012, for example, an estimated 36,000 individual actions such as strikes, occupations, rallies, collective bargaining and the like took place. In the face of the patriarchy, which is still widespread as a legacy of the dictatorship, women organize a host of feminist-flavored actions.

Las Kellys became the most famous: The cleaning women employed by subcontractors in hotels organize strikes, also in tourist centers like Mallorca, joining forces with British and French trade unionists. They have hired a lawyer who has developed an equal treatment directive to submit to the EU. In some cases, they have won pay increases.[411]

And how many "convinced" Europeans have heard about the 2017 strike of care workers in the Biscay region? 5,500 workers in privatized nursing homes went on strike for 360 days against the low wages imposed on them. 360 days! After the year-long strike, they actually achieved their goal: minimum wage EUR 1,200 per month, 35-hour week, breaks as paid working time, full sick pay. And how was this success possible? Only through the support of the ELA union: it created public awareness, organized food and money, linked the strike with feminist groups and social movements.[412]

Almeria: Unprecedented strikes in Europe's vegetable garden
With EU subsidies, the largest agribusiness complex on earth was built in southern Spain, near the coast at Almeria in the region of Andalusia. Peppers, tomatoes, cucumbers, lettuce, grapes, strawberries, avocado, garlic, onions, eggplants are exported all year round to the EU and worldwide.

Largest and most modern intensive agriculture on earth
This intensive agriculture in thousands of large-scale greenhouses includes groundwater pumping, automated irrigation systems, heavy use of pesticides, seed breeding, plant, pesticide and fertilizer research, standardization of the size and texture of vegetable products (for automated packaging and pricing), and sophisticated global transportation logistics using vans, trucks and airplanes.

Under the greenhouse plastic tents, called "the plastic sea", the heat accumulates and, in combination with the other factors, allows multiple harvests a year.[413]

The representatives of the supermarket chains - in Germany REWE, Lidl, Kaufland, Aldi and others - play off the farmers, subcontractors and companies against each other in relentless price dumping. The small ones are constantly on the verge of insolvency, sometimes working below production costs.

Cost factor labor
Part of the intensive economy is the pre-modern exploitation and disenfranchisement of labor. Discriminating against illegal workers, ostracizing them and at the same time blackmailing them into slave-like labor - the US model. There is no criticism in Brussels of the electoral gains of the far-right and anti-migrant VOX in Almeria, for example.[414]

Among the 130,000 employees, 90 percent are migrants, mainly from North Africa, and about 30 percent are illegal.

- Even Spain's meager labor laws, such as the minimum wage of EUR 5.45 and the payment of social contributions, are violated across the board and with impunity. Overtime: Often not documented at all and not paid. Even in organic-labeled farms, piecework of up to 14 hours is required.
- Scant medical care although needed for the frequent injuries, on contact with pesticides.
- The workers cobble together their own makeshift dwellings from plastic sheeting and discarded wooden pallets. Electricity and water connections are usually lacking.[415]
- The streetwalking patch for the workers is concentrated in the small town of El Ejido: Days of anxious waiting to see if a minibus will take those waiting to a plantation - without a work contract, with vague promises.

International solidarity
The Andalusian trade union Sindicato Andaluz de Trabajadores/as, SOC-SAT, founded in 1976 after Franco's death, is part of the worldwide organization of small farmers and landless *La Via Campesina*. Migrants hardly ever become members of the union, for lack of language skills and

money, because of short duration of stay, also because of fear of their mafia-like intermediaries, but they increasingly participate in SAT actions.[416]

SAT can only keep this up because the union is supported by several NGOs from Spain and other countries, from Germany for example by the Berlin-based Interbrigadas.[417] Activities range from labor law advice in small local offices, help with criminal charges, organizing protest marches and limited strikes. SAT activists occupied a deserted finca for a year and farmed the several thousand olive trees until they were evicted.

The Interbrigadas also organize from scratch what a representation of dependent workers needs: research. When the activists are on the ground, they research the ownership structures of agribusiness, the middlemen, the supply chains, summarize workers' complaints, draft leaflets, prepare meetings, establish links with political parties and initiatives such as Podemos, Izquierda Unida and Anticapitalistas.

Ireland:
Against Ryanair - First Europe-wide organization of pilots

The colony of Ireland was exploited by the British Empire, impoverished, condemned to underdevelopment. To save themselves, the majority of the inhabitants had to emigrate: From 6.5 million inhabitants in 1841, the country shrank to 2.5 million by the 1980s. Even the courageously and bloodily-won independence as a free state in 1923 did nothing to change this. People emigrated permanently to the US and Canada, and in the colonial master England they often worked as seasonal laborers in the industrial centers and in private households, separated from their families for six or nine months a year.

Independent Ireland remains British colony
After World War II, industrialization was belatedly nurtured, following the pattern of the poorest "developing" countries: Governments lured Canadian, US, Finnish and Swedish investors with tax exemptions and loans from London to extract and export mineral resources such as ore, mercury, silver, lead, oil and gas: these were processed abroad. Gulf Oil and Total were the dominant oil companies from the USA and France. The collecting tankers did not have to pay port fees. The local workers were poorly paid. Environmental and marine pollution went unpunished.[418]

With the EU: Ireland becomes a modern US colony
In 1973, the UK and Ireland joined the EU. Irish migrants returned home
to do simple work for low wages in the branches set up mainly by US
corporations such as Dell, IBM, Microsoft, Pfizer, and so on. In the still
agrarian country, the corporations, who were also lured with low taxes,
were able to buy land cheaply. Ireland was transformed from a British
colony into a modern US colony, and for US corporations it became the
customs-free trade gateway to the EU.

The EU reinforced the development from 1987 onward with lavish
subsidies to develop Dublin as a global financial center: tax exemptions
for companies and asset managers from other countries, extremely low
corporate tax of initially 10 percent (which is rarely paid), deregulated
financial supervision, no investigations into financial crime, lowest data
protection in Europe. This attracted, for example, the big digital corporations like Apple, Microsoft, Google, Amazon, Facebook, Paypal, Twitter.
They operate their European headquarters here. The state expanded the
huge Dublin Airport with EU aid, as well as the road network and business infrastructure, according to the needs of the corporations.[419]

More and more automotive, pharmaceutical, technology, industrial and
consulting groups, also from EU countries, opened branches and subsidiaries. They mostly leave their operational headquarters in their home
country, but move their tax domicile to Ireland and process loans and
licenses primarily via Luxembourg and the Netherlands.[420]

After the financial crisis of 2007, to which the small Irish banks and,
above all, the large US, French and German banks that showered them
with loans had contributed, the COM, the ECB and the IMF in the Troika
called on the Irish state to rescue the banks, with stringent measures:
Among others, the US Rothschild banker Wilbur Ross profited from this
with 500 million, which also qualified him to be President Trump's Treas-
ury Secretary.[421]

This impoverishment program included cuts in pensions, welfare benefits and labor income. For example, the Troika demanded that the minimum wage be cut by one euro and that sanctions be imposed on the unemployed who do not accept jobs offered.[422]

In the same way, Irish governments and the EU cannot or do not want
to prevent the unprotected forwarding of European data from Face-
book&Co to their central US storage sites – where intelligence agencies

have access. The Irish data protection authority DPC allows any transfer of data from the EU to the US. After 2015, the ECJ overturned the lax EU data protection for the second time in 2020,[423] but in Ireland the data is still being passed on.

Zero tax and low labor costs

Apple is Ireland's largest company by revenue: all sales worldwide, except in the US, are handled through Ireland, with only 6,000 employees. Around this European Apple headquarters are about 300 suppliers and a few thousand disenfranchised clickworkers. Ireland has an extreme spread between the highly paid top managers, the well-paid middle managers and those at the bottom who vegetate with a few temporary crumbs of work. Opulent luxury apartments in the trendy parts of town, slums and desolate villages are all part of this antisocial model. The majority of precarious workers do not come from Ireland itself, but from other poor regions, from the Baltic States, Romania, Poland, India, Bangladesh.[424]

At the same time, these largest companies are the ones with the highest profits and the lowest tax payments. At 12.5 percent, the tax on profits is now one of the lowest in the EU. But it can be lowered by much more. For years, for example, Apple paid only 0.005 percent. The Irish government doggedly defends this loss of revenue, and the EU has so far been unable to do anything about it despite various attempts - after all, it created the conditions for this practice.[425]

Around 1,000 corporations benefit from the low labor rights and labor costs with outsourced subcontracting. The top 100 are dominated by US corporations: Medtronic (medical technology), Accenture (the world's largest consulting firm with 450,000 employees), Adient, Eaton and Johnson Controls (automotive suppliers), Seagate Technology (storage media, hard drives), Allegra, Pfizer, Johnson&Johnson and Merck (pharmaceuticals), Smurfit Kappa (packaging), Kerry Group (food).

"While the profits of foreign corporations increased and gross domestic product GDP grew by 11 percent, at the same time the national income shrank by almost 2 percent. It is a good third lower than GDP", this is also known in EU circles, without doing anything about it.[426]

Against Ryanair - First Europe-wide organization of pilots

A typical product of these practices is Ryanair. Founded in 1985 by KPMG's Michael O'Leary on the model of US low-cost carrier Southwest

Airlines, Ryanair says it is now the largest airline with 200 destinations and 140 million annual passengers. It is expanding with the help of the EU and leads the world in this industry in the exploitation of dependent employees, states and the environment.[427]

EU subsidies for labor injustice
Ryanair takes advantage of Ireland's location, but also of the EU's deregulation of air traffic. It buys up abandoned small military and provincial airports in poor areas. They are up to 100 kilometers away from the nearest larger airport, but passengers are fooled about this by labeling, for example, Weeze on the Lower Rhine as Düsseldorf and Girona as Barcelona. For the few jobs there, the EU pays subsidies from its regional fund. Nowhere does the EU impose labor law requirements, even though Ryanair practices violate EU directives.

Low-cost airline Ryan Air
Airfares are low, seats on the plane are tight - but the additional fees for baggage are high. The poorly paid cabin crew is under pressure to sell as many snacks and other goods as possible to passengers at the highest possible price: Anyone who sells too little gets a black mark.

Until 2019 the company refused to negotiate with trade unions. 70 percent of the workforce is made up of temporary workers, mainly recruited through the Irish temporary employment agencies Workforce and Crewlink. Wages are on average EUR 1,000 lower than those of the competition.

The pilots, also increasingly temporary workers and pseudo self-employed, are hustled to complete as many flights per day as possible with the shortest possible layovers of 25 minutes. In 2009, the salaried pilots were outsourced to a separate company so that Ryanair does not pay social security contributions for them either. Ryanair is a pioneer in the precarization not only of cabin staff, but also of pilots.

Extreme gender inequality
The management under founding CEO O'Leary has even topped the usual EU measure of inequality between men and women. In 2017, men accounted for 97 percent of the top earners. Women - including many from poor regions such as North Africa - earned 72 percent less than men on average in the workforce.[428]

The annual growth of this type during the last decade is 10 percent. Annual profits now exceed one billion. Although only the loudmouth O'Leary, who is popular with the media, appears in public, the dumbed-down public have to grapple with his provocations. But here, too, the profits flow to the now invisible, ubiquitous major owners such as Baillie Gifford, Harris, Capital World, Capital Research, Fidelity, BlackRock and the private bank Lazard, or ultimately, for the most part, to their anonymous investors.

First pan-European organization of pilots and cabin staff

On August 10, 2018, pilots went on strike for the first time in the 34-year "success" story of the anti-social upstart, across borders in Ireland, Germany, Belgium, the Netherlands and Sweden. A year earlier, overworked air traffic controllers in France and Spain had already gone on strike, forcing Ryanair to cancel thousands of flights.

Until then, O'Leary had kept employees under his thumb through organized national fragmentation. But in 2018, European pilots' associations formed the transnational Ryanair Transnational Pilot Group RTPG in Luxembourg. Its collective bargaining committee set uniform Europe-wide demands:

- Recognition of collective interest groups.
- Fixed contracts instead of temporary work and pseudo self-employment
- Contracts according to the respective national law instead of Irish law
- Payment of waiting periods and transfers.[429]

In July 2018 the International Transport Workers' Federation (ITF) had prevented 600 flights by two days of strikes by cabin crew in Portugal, Spain, Italy and Belgium. ITF organized a conference of Ryanair cabin crew from Europe and North Africa under the banner Cabin Crew United 2018 in Dublin. They earn between EUR 700 and 1,300 per month, with constant fluctuations due to changing working hours. Wages are paid by Ryanair according to the cash situation, sometimes months late. Among the 34 demands:

- Regulated and predictable working hours
- No obligation to set up a salary account in Ireland
- Free food and water while on duty
- Free work materials and uniforms

- Sick pay.

First collective agreements
O'Leary had become known for his pithy saying, "Hell will freeze over and I'll chop off both my arms before Ryanair negotiates with unions." That's why he tried to prevent the emerging strikes. He threatened the striking pilots and flight attendants in Ireland that he would outsource them to Poland. The Bremen site was to be closed down altogether. In the Netherlands, he wanted to have a strike banned by the courts. Then he initially switched to negotiating with yellow unions.

But Ryanair also had to conclude its first collective agreements with proper unions. Hell froze over. However, the loudmouth did not chop off his arms after all, a pity - but a sign of flexibility. Verdi in Germany pushed through significant improvements for 1,100 flight attendants in March 2019:

- EUR 600 increase in basic pay
- Sick pay
- Protection against dismissal under German labor law
- The regulations also apply to the 700 temporary workers.430

"Lex Ryanair": Bundestag improves Works Constitution Act
Members of the Bundestag - except from the CSU and FDP - took on sponsorships for strikers. Suddenly, due to an intervention by the trade union Verdi, it was recognized in the Bundestag: Section 117 of the Works Constitution Act (BetrVG) previously stated that airline employees were excluded from the right to elect works councils. This was changed. Since May 1, 2019, these employees also have the right to elect works councils. "Employers were able to exploit the previous regulation to prevent co-determination. That's over now," said Ingolf Schumacher of the pilots' association Cockpit. And this applies not only to Ryanair, but also to Eurowings, Air Cargo Global, Sundair, DC Aviation...[431]

However, Ryanair has still been able to prevent the establishment of works councils. Nor is the COM intervening, and certainly not under the new President von der Leyen. Companies are allowed to continue breaking current labor law.

Hell has not really frozen over yet. The international, internationalist self-organization of the workers continues.

Austria: 30-hour week for carers!

The State Treaty of 1955 with the four victorious powers of World War 2 stipulated: Austria is sovereign again and remains neutral. After the collapse of the Soviet Union in 1990, the Social Democratic Party and the business-friendly ÖVP took up the EU's lengthy courtship: Austria joined the EU in 1995. Criticism came from the Greens and the Left, saying the EU was a capitalist affair, linked to NATO and not environmentally friendly. The Freedom Party/Haider also criticized the EU, but only because of its "bureaucratism" - the FPÖ had nothing against capitalism, environmental pollution and the military.

Although Austria is not a NATO member, unlike the other EU states, just two years after joining the EU, Austria joined the more flexible organizations established by NATO, the Euro-Atlantic Partnership Council (EAPC) and the Partnership for Peace (PfP), and has since taken part in military missions in Bosnia and Kosovo, for example, as well as in Afghanistan, Mali, Lebanon and others - 13 in all so far.

Springboard for modern Balkanization

The EU subsidies triggered a twofold development: First, foreign direct investment increased, especially from Germany, e.g. Porsche, MAN (trucks), BMW, Benteler (automotive supplier), Siemens. Other investors came from Italy, the Netherlands and Switzerland; from outside the EU, the USA, Canada and Abu Dhabi dominated. The subsidiaries of corporations from these countries now account for one-third of the country's sales and half of all research and innovation.[432]

Second, the new EU member became the hub towards Eastern Europe. Thus, companies and banks from their base in Austria are now in first place in Bosnia-Herzegovina, Northern Macedonia and Slovenia, and in second place in the other new states of former Yugoslavia.

Thus, the dependence of the "backyard" Balkans from the old Austrian monarchy, the subsequent Kingdom of Yugoslavia and the Nazi occupation was revived, modernized and integrated into the larger EU area.

This destroyed the catch-up industrialization by socialist Yugoslavia - as well as the infrastructure of schools and hospitals accessible to all citizens. This spawned new unemployment, mass emigration and also the new class of local rich oligarchs.

US devotion: Cross-border leasing

With EU accession, from 1998 state and municipal enterprises quickly opened their doors to the latest, also fraudulent US financial products, such as cross-border leasing: bogus sale and hundred-year leaseback of power plants, streetcars, trains and train stations, sewer networks. Austria became a leader in the EU after the model pupil Germany, ahead of the Netherlands and Belgium. US commercial law firms such as White & Case offered their advice for good money. The cities of Vienna, Innsbruck and Linz took part in these undisclosed contracts, as did the Austrian Federal Railways (ÖBB), the Tyrolean hydroelectric power plants and the state air traffic control.[433]

BlackRock

With its Vienna branch, BlackRock also used Austria as a location "for expansion into Eastern Europe", for example in the sale of funds and for private pension provision.[434] BlackRock holds equity stakes in Austria's flagship companies Voestalpine (steel, industrial equipment) and engineering company Andritz, which are spread across 35 and 37 shell companies respectively between Delaware, the Cayman Islands, Jersey, Amsterdam, etc. for the benefit of anonymous investors.[435] In 2018, Vonovia, the German housing group dominated by BlackRock, bought Austria's largest private housing group, BUWOG, with 51,000 apartments, beginning its expansion beyond Germany into the EU.[436]

Dismantling of labor rights and the welfare state

For longer than in Germany, for example, the trade unions, together with the Social Democrats, formed a bastion for good, permanent jobs, at least for the locals. But it was only a gradual difference. Pensioners benefit from this: Their pensions are 40 percent higher on average, with gross wages similar to those in Germany. In addition, pensions are paid out 14 times a year. Employer contributions are two percent higher. All employees, including civil servants, are in the same system. Even the leading pension privatizer in Germany, Bert Rürup, has to concede: Such a system, which he successfully fought against in Germany, is possible in the middle of the EU - and "not to the detriment of the economy".[437]

However, the precarious labor conditions advocated in the EU and by corporations have altered the picture for younger generations and migrants.

The new labor injustice of ÖVP and FPÖ
With the EU, governments and corporations gradually intensified the management of cheap immigrants from the impoverished and newly "balkanized" states of former Yugoslavia. Meanwhile, the catchment area is being extended beyond the EU.[438]

The latest highlight was the new labor law pushed through by the two business parties ÖVP and FPÖ in 2017, in partial compliance with EU directives:

- Increase in the maximum daily working time from 10 to 12 hours
- Increase in the maximum weekly working time from 50 to 60 hours
- Increase in additional annual overtime by 100 to 416
- Shortening of rest periods in individual industries such as catering
- Abolition of co-determination of works councils
- Abolition of the Youth Councils of Confidence.[439]

In part, this is even more anti-social than the Hartz and follow-up laws in Germany and Macron's "reforms" in France. The EU, which criticizes Austria for not taking in refugees, remains a silent accomplice in the escalation of labor injustice.

The Austrian Trade Union Federation ÖGB was unable to agree on countermeasures at its federal congress. As with their counterparts in other countries, this was not the first step by the SPÖ and the ÖGB towards digging their own grave. A one-off large-scale demonstration in Vienna with 130,000 participants - the largest in 15 years - organized at the last moment because of pressure from the grassroots failed to prevent the law's passage.

Labor rights and housing: Human rights!
However, there is still democratic potential in what remains of the social partnership.

Human rights review of the EU!
Thus, the ÖGB, together with the Vienna Chamber of Labour, commissioned the report that would have suited the democratic and left-wing forces in the EU and the trade unions well: All actions of the EU institutions such as the COM, the Parliament and the Council, as well as all treaties and agreements of the EU - free trade agreements, directives, restruc-

turing programs as in the "European Semester", subsidies - must be reviewed with regard to human rights![440]

Housing is a human right!
The Europe-wide citizens' initiative Housing for All!, launched in Vienna in 2019, also draws on this potential. Initiators from seven EU countries, including Croatia, Portugal and Spain, fathered it. They cite the largest complex of publicly operated or controlled social housing in the EU, in Vienna.

Against the housing speculation led in the EU by BlackRock, Blackstone & Co, the initiative argues that according to the Universal Declaration of Human Rights, affordable and safe housing is also a human right. "We must radically oppose this speculation! This is destroying our society, this is the breeding ground of the radical right in Europe! We must send a signal!" said the spokeswoman of the initiative. Dozens of national and international initiatives, trade unions, tenants' associations, architectural and student groups and research institutes are participating.[441]

35-hour week! Or better still: 30-hour week
For four years, the trade union Left Bloc GLB has been demanding the 35-hour week for the 125,000 employees in the private health, social and care sector. The GLB was formed within the ÖGB.

Sick system, sick state budget, sick employees
Employees are poorly paid, overworked, often sick - in the soul, in the muscle and bone system. The health, care and social system as a whole is underfunded in the public sector, outshone by a better private system. Government agencies bring in even more poorly paid doctors and nurses from impoverished neighboring countries, but also, for example, from the Philippines.

The nine regional health insurance funds were merged into one Austrian Health Insurance Fund ÖGK - in order to cut 1,500 jobs and make further cuts in the process. The previous self-administration was abolished, and the business associations now have the upper hand.

The private companies - including Caritas and Diakonie - have already been trimming their facilities for profit for three decades. The employees are harassed in a highly unchristian way. As the GLB has documented many times, only 30 percent have full-time jobs; 70 percent have various part-time positions. In addition, many are on mobile assignments, dashing from one job site to the next on assignments lasting minutes. Many give up after only a few years. The bosses enforce temporary work, fixed-term employment and pseudo self-employment. Shift work and marginal working hours tear families apart. Education and training are cut back. Old-age poverty among those who retire - many prematurely because of exhaustion and illness - is widespread.

Seven rounds of negotiations, strikes, demonstrations
For the sake of simplicity and in order to highlight the problem, the GLB concentrated on one demand: 35-hour week with full wage and personnel compensation! This also applies proportionately to part-time employees.[442]

The employers rejected the demand in seven rounds of negotiations. Their last offer was a general wage increase of 2.35 percent.

Therefore, in the four years, the GLB has held 120 works meetings with strike resolutions, has organized demonstrations in Vienna, Innsbruck, Graz along with other public actions. At the end of 2019 and in January 2020, employees in 280 facilities went on strike. The ÖGB, by no means eager to strike, also gave the go-ahead for the strike on Jan. 30, 2020 - according to the state constitution, a strike is only legally permissible if the ÖGB so decides.

30-hour week!?
To overcome the multiple health and social emergencies, the 35-hour week would not be enough. Therefore, the GLB is also demanding that state funding be increased.

But even all this would not be enough. That is why the GLB is also demanding the abolition of the various forms of precarious employment such as temporary work and pseudo self-employment. And because women are particularly affected here, free and all-day childcare is on the list of demands, which must be co-financed by the companies.

Hence, the 30-hour week is also being demanded.[443] The GLB is also fighting here on behalf of the EU-wide emergency in care for the elderly.[444]

4.
Ex-Yugoslav states

Firstly, Yugoslavia was one of the emerging countries that, under a socialist leadership, was able for the first time to free itself from a dependent periphery and develop and industrialize its national economy. Secondly, a free public sector for education and health was established. Thirdly, previously hostile ethnic groups were peacefully united in a multi-ethnic state. The EU and NATO have destroyed all this.

First into NATO, then into the EU
The Western way of globalization works best when states are first broken up into as many small states as possible: The smaller, the easier to control.

Thus, the West financed nationalist hatred, nationalist wars - the BND cooperated as early as the 1970s with the remnants of the fascist Ustasha hibernating in Germany. US-led NATO waged a war in violation of international law. This leads on to the establishment of US military bases, NATO and EU membership and aspirations. The IMF and Western buyers destroyed the economy.[445]

The six Balkan states not admitted to the EU are becoming desolate: A third of the younger people, especially from the middle classes, are emigrating, leaving behind the old and the poor. Clique rule is also promoted by the EU.[446] According to the "Western Balkans Regulation", these states are allowed to send an annual contingent of 25,000 migrant workers to Germany. In Kosovo, separated from Serbia in violation of international law, the US expanded the second largest foreign US military base, Camp Bondsteel, named after a Vietnam veteran. Tiny, poor Montenegro became a pleasure spot for oligarchs from Britain, France, Egypt and Azerbaijan.[447]

Backyard sale
By the end of 1990, 2,435 factories with 1.3 million employees had already become insolvent as a result of import liberalization in accordance with the IMF's shock "therapy". After that, Western buyers plundered the remaining enterprises and mostly closed them down, for example all tex-

tile and car factories. Western car companies sell Western cars, Western supermarkets import Western products.[448]

There are almost no local banks anymore, but Austrian, US, Italian, French ones. Coca Cola and other beverage producers from Germany and France exploit the water sources, Austrian companies have bought up forests and export the wood to Western Europe. For education, especially for higher education, as well as for medical treatments, which were free in Yugoslavia, you now have to pay dearly. If you want to study, you have to go into debt.[449]

Tourism instead of industry: Seasonal work
Instead of industry, the EU primarily promoted tourism, in Croatia, for example, through toll highways built by the US corporation Bechtel. Investors from the Gulf States and the USA are building real estate complexes with condominiums, hotels and swimming pools on picturesque beaches. Seasonal work for three months - these are the new jobs.

Minimum wages in the two states that are EU members rank at the lower end, at EUR 5.10 (Slovenia) and EUR 2.92 (Croatia). Unemployment officially ranges from 30 percent in Kosovo to 8.9 percent in Croatia. However, firstly, youth unemployment is higher, secondly, marginally employed persons are also counted as "working" and, above all, thirdly, the figure would be twice as high on average if emigrants were included.

Reappraisal of fascism
Especially in the EU's favorite states of Slovenia, Croatia and Serbia, EU-subsidized neoliberal governments are organizing "the worst kind of historical revisionism. The anti-fascist struggle that liberated the region - the first victory against the Nazi regime in Europe - is being reinterpreted. One can no longer speak publicly there about the victory of anti-fascism".[450]

In Croatia, Serbs, Roma, lesbians, gays and Serbian Orthodox Christians are bombarded with hate slogans, the Council of Europe's anti-racism commission found. Croatian national soccer players chanted songs with Ustasha slogans during the 2018 World Cup. Without criticism from the EU, however, Croatia was able to assume the 2020 EU Council presidency.[451]

When EU leaders simultaneously uphold the "memory of the Holocaust" in solidarity with Israel, they exhibit extreme hypocrisy.

Stirrings
Nevertheless: "Direct democracy movements are organizing all over the Balkans. Factory occupations are taking place, resulting in self-managed factories like the one in Tuzla. In Serbia, an alliance of workers and free-lance journalists who have lost their jobs has emerged," reports Croatian philosopher Srecko Horvat, a member of the Democracy in Europe 2025 Movement (DIEM).[452] The situation is similar in the other neighboring countries Albania, Slovenia, Montenegro, Kosovo.[453]

North Macedonia:
A voice for women textile workers!
The former Yugoslav Republic of Macedonia has been associated with the EU since 2000 and has been a candidate country since 2005, but has not yet been admitted. In preparation, the deindustrialized, desperately poor country is being developed by the EU and Western investors as a location for professionalized low-wage labor.

Still an EU candidate, but already a NATO member
The US, assisted by the EU and the German chancellor, pushed through accession to NATO in 2019: Enemy target, Russia. This had been pre-pared for years by joint maneuvers and the deployment of Macedonian soldiers in Afghanistan. For NATO accession, Macedonia was renamed North Macedonia to ensure Greek agreement.

The EU grants Macedonia aid (pre-accession assistance) from the Western Balkans program. The capital Skopje has been transformed into a nationalist Disneyland: A glorious past is evoked with expensive monu-ments and buildings for the Greek conqueror Alexander the Great and his father Philip.

Upgrading to "Bangladesh" in the EU
The State Agency for Foreign Investment and Export Promotion advertis-es generous competitive advantages:
Member of NATO, EU candidate country
- profit and income tax 10 percent, the lowest rate in Europe
- tax rate on reinvested earnings: 0 percent
- tax holidays up to 10 years
- grants on purchase of insolvent companies
- fast registration

- "abundant competitive workforce"
- low minimum wage
- government wage subsidies.[454]

Investors from Austria, Greece, France, the Netherlands bought up the main state-owned companies: Banks, telecommunications, industry. Philip Morris and Pepsi opened branches. Above all, suppliers to Western car, chemical and textile companies are taking advantage of the state incentives.[455]

From Germany, automotive suppliers such as Kromberg & Schubert, Marquardt, Lenze Antriebstechnik and Schmitz Cargobull opened branches. Marquardt had laid off 600 employees at its German site in Rietheim for this purpose. The chemical sector is represented by Bayer, Linde Gas, Gerresheimer and Messer Gas, while the electrical engineering sector is represented by Kessler and Swarco. Gerresheimer praised the "ideal location, good cost and infrastructure" on opening its branch in 2020 - manufacturing prefillable syringes for the healthcare system.[456] Dekra has staff placement to itself. Because the products are transported to Western Europe for finishing or sale, the big players in transport logistics are also represented: Deutsche Post DHL, Sixt, DB Schenker.

EU: No criticism of labor rights violations
The COM affirms: The Roma minority "continues to be exposed to social exclusion, marginalization and discrimination". The EU also notes "inadequate state aid control" and ineffective tackling of corruption.[457] But with subsidies for road expansion in the context of pan-European networks and for businesses, the EU is turning the country into the Bangladesh of Europe.

The unions are sorely weakened and membership is low. The employers make it clear: Membership in a union is not welcome here! Even in the case of unpaid overtime, the extorted employees keep quiet: This is not criticized by the EU.[458]

German entrepreneurs: No increase in the minimum wage!
The sugarcoated unemployment rate is officially 26.3 percent. The average monthly wage is EUR 529 gross. Managers sent from Western companies earn several times that amount.[459]

The government most recently set the monthly minimum wage for the touted "abundant competitive workforce" at EUR 283 gross or EUR 198 net. The German Chamber of Commerce and Industry DIHK in Skopje argues against an increase in the minimum wage: "We believe that an increase at this moment will negatively affect the attractiveness of the investment location."[460]

"The voice of women textile workers"
In the face of criticism of the conditions in Bangladesh, Western European textile companies are increasingly having production carried out in Eastern Europe and Northern Macedonia. In addition, the transport routes are shorter and cheaper.

Low-wage work for western customers in 1,100 textile plants
The town of Stip was the center of the Yugoslav textile industry. The largest factory was Makedonka with 9,000 employees. They produced 90 percent for the domestic market and 10 percent for export. After the breakup of Yugoslavia, the plant was closed and all employees were laid off. The buildings are rotting away.

Especially in Stip, then also in Kocani and Delcevo, 1,100 new textile companies are now registered. Most of them are local small businesses and subcontractors with up to 50 employees; only five percent have more than 250 employees. Production is practically only for export. Customers are high-end brands such as Versace, MaxMara and Gucci from Italy, Seidensticker, BOSS and Escada from Germany, Jack&Jones from Denmark, Barnett&Barnett and La Salle from the Netherlands and Ahlers from Belgium.

Only two German companies have work done in their own branches: Lutex from Wallheim, specializing in home textiles such as pillows and tablecloths; then Adler Modemärkte AG from Halbach with 178 fashion stores in Germany, Luxembourg, Austria and Switzerland: In northern Macedonia, Adler produces work clothes for the Malteser Hilfsdienst and police uniforms.[461]

Most of the workers cannot afford the clothes made here. In the outlet stores of Skopje, a shirt sold by Seidensticker in Germany for EUR 60 still costs EUR 10. The population therefore goes to the cheap markets, where comparable shirts from Bangladesh can be had for EUR 4.99, while the local nouveau riche are happy to pay Western European prices in the BOSS boutique.[462]

"Those who protest are fired"
"We have to work through. The bosses are constantly pushing us. We don't get bathroom breaks. There's no heating in the winter, and it's too hot in the summer. Some textiles contain acids that are washed out only after sewing. Dust everywhere. Some workers are allergic, get red spots on their body and face. They have to buy medicine. Overtime is not paid... Those who protest are fired." This is what the seamstress "Svetlana", whose name has been changed, reports to the former seamstress Kristina Ampeva. "Svetlana" works at the Paltex factory. She does at least get EUR 220 a month.

"If my employer knew I was working with Kristina, I wouldn't get another job at Paltex or anywhere else in Delcevo," says "Svetlana". Paltex - a Taiwanese company specializing in the organization of global low-wage labor. From Germany, Strellson and Seidensticker are among its customers.

Kristina Ampeva: The former seamstress builds a network
The seamstress Kristina Ampeva could not stand the working conditions anymore. When she complained, she was fired. "I couldn't form a works council. The other workers didn't even know what it was. The only option was to form a self-help organization that would finally begin to fight against the exploitation of women workers," Kristina describes.

She looked around. She came across the Olof Palme International Center in Stockholm on the Internet. This foundation of Swedish trade unions supports the development of organizations of dependent workers in Southeast Asia, Africa - and in the Balkans. This enabled Kristina, in a small office, to build a network of textile workers, co-workers and supporters from home and abroad. The initiative is called *Glasen Tekstilec*: Voice of Women Textile Workers. In the poster, a fist stretches upward beneath a modern sewing machine.[463]

Glasen Tekstilec documents labor injustice: the working conditions described by "Svetlana", the extortionate exclusion of the weak unions out of the factories, the frequent non-payment of even the low minimum wage, forced work on holidays, unpaid overtime, the understaffed, complicit to corrupt labor inspectorate.

Kristina passes on some of the numerous complaints to the authorities. Supported by her husband, she still knows about the conditions in Yugoslavian times: The textile complex Makedonka belonged to the employees, the boss got 30 percent more, there was a kindergarten, own cinema and other cultural activities. The profits were distributed to everyone.

(A few) entrepreneurs also want improvements
In 2019, the initiative organized the two-day conference "Textiliada": an art student produced a comic strip with the ironic heroine "Supertextilka". A photo exhibition documented situations in the textile industry.

Two entrepreneurs also came: CEO Zonev, who extricated himself from the sweatshop Paltex and is introducing better working conditions in his new company MMC Progres, e.g. hot food for the female workers. Then there is Angel Dimitrov, head of Casa Moda, chairman of the North Macedonian Employers' Association. Both entrepreneurs have introduced improvements, pay 150 percent of the minimum wage, but want to change the overall situation. They cannot venture too far because of the ruthless competition: the reality is that Esprit and Marc O'Polo pay only EUR 3 for a shirt.

Representatives of initiatives from Albania, Serbia and Kosovo also came to the Textiliada. A representative of the otherwise invisible labor inspectorate also showed up. Even the new Minister of Labor, Mila Karovska, came: She affirmed that her government wants to break away from the corrupt nepotism of the previous government and raise the minimum wage.

"The workers should be proud of themselves"
In the meantime, the virtuous Swabian textile retailer Olymp from Bietigheim has terminated the supply contract for 40,000 shirts a month with the textile company Stobi because not even the minimum wage had been paid. Stobi shut down. A dismissed worker explains: "This is bad for us workers. But it is good: the employers are made aware that they are dependent on us, dependent on the women workers. Labor rights need to be improved."

Kristina Ampeva proposed a monument to mark the Textiliada: a 5-meter-high sewing needle was erected in Stip. On the plaque, next to the raised fist, it says: Dedicated to women textile workers. The mayor came and expressed his gratitude. Kristina Ampeva: "We must all stand together, for good working conditions, for respect for labor and human rights. The workers should be proud of themselves. And that they are important for this town and for the whole country."

Croatia:
Shipyard workers - strikes and hopes pinned on China

Croatia became the second full member of the EU among the former Yugoslav states after Slovenia. Only 30 percent of eligible voters had voted in favor of accession in the 2012 referendum. Only 20 percent took part in the subsequent election to the European Parliament. But that was well in line with the EU's democracy criteria.

Fascist currency in the EU

This "success" had been prepared for 10 years during the candidate status: State enterprises - banks, businesses, forests - had to be sold. Deutsche Telekom bought the majority of the telephone company. Lactalis from France bought the largest dairy farm. The EU subsidized the development of tourism. Upon accession, unemployment was high, nationalism and corruption flourished, and even more subsidies were on hand.[464]

The explicit recourse to the fascist past did not stand in the way of accession: With the founding of the separate state in 1991, the government had introduced the kuna as the national currency. It had been the Croatian currency for four years in the national history otherwise invoked as 1000 years old, namely during World War II, when the fascist Ustasha movement under Ante Pavelic, installed by Hitler and Mussolini, was in government and carried out extremely brutal massacres of Jews, Serbs and Communists.[465] The kuna (HRK) remains the Croatian currency to this day and is pegged to the euro.

"Mainland sword of the US in Southeastern Europe"

The integration of the impoverished state with the West was driven primarily by the USA. For NATO's leading power, Croatia represented "a kind of mainland sword" in the northern flank of Southeastern Europe: Because of its geographic location and because of its anti-communist, Catholic-ethnic fortified potential. That is why retired US generals trained the Croatian army shortly after the state was founded. "Croatian Defense Minister Gojko Susak was flown in a special US Defense Department plane to Washington's Walter Reed Hospital, the US government's celebrity hospital, for lung surgery.... He was classified in Washington according to protocol as is usually only the case with the closest allies of the USA", the German Springer press approvingly reported.[466]

Four years before EU entry, Croatia was maneuvered into NATO (2009), along with the even smaller mini-state of Albania, which became an EU candidate in 2014.

EU entry cuts trade relations with neighboring countries

The EU took in an over-indebted state with high unemployment. The employment rate stood at 40 percent. Soldiers of the 1991-1995 war of secession and other cronies were given large pensions: "Quite a few so-called veterans never saw the front - estimates put the number at 150,000."[467] As a result, the number of pensioners doubled. 1.2 million pensioners have to be co-financed by 1.5 million contributors – that was the situation when the country joined the EU. And another reason why the IMF pushed through cuts in social and health benefits.[468]

After the establishment of the separatist states, Croatia's trade with the other separatist states revived. The division of labor practiced in Yugoslavia was gradually resumed. But this fragile recovery was largely destroyed by EU accession: These relations, "which had been extremely important for Croatia until then, are being made more difficult and more expensive". The EU erected new customs barriers against Serbia and Bosnia-Herzegovina.[469]

Bulwark against refugees: "Europe's lawless border"

Croatia's most important role in the EU at present is warding off refugees. For this, Croatia's nationalist governments do not have to be wooed first.

The Croatian police uses brute force against refugees. 35,000 illegal deportations have been documented - the government denies this, but does not launch any investigations. The EU wants to keep its external border closed by all means. "We don't ask you how you do it" - this is how former Interior Minister Ranko Ostjic describes the attitude of EU officials.[470] "Croatian police are beating migrants back to Bosnia. In the German Chancellery, the breach of law is tacitly tolerated."[471]

EU promotes "yellow" unions

Before Croatia was allowed to join the EU, the state had to fulfill conditions imposed by the IMF and the World Bank: In 2012, the social democratic government passed the Employment Promotion Act: More fixed-term employment contracts, more flexible working hours, easier dismissal.

The rights of the trade unions were also severely interfered with. They had enjoyed state protection in Yugoslavia. As in Greece, industry-, occupation- and business-friendly unions were encouraged. Associations that did not charge membership dues were also treated the same as unions.[472]

Under pressure from the EU, the unions were integrated into a government-run system of "social dialogue" in a tripartite table with business associations and the state. Collective bargaining agreements are also approved there. The unions were broken down into about 600 individual unions with three umbrella organizations. Most are "house unions" supported by employers.

Unemployment, emigration, seasonal work
The employees still in the country are blackmailed into staying quiet by the dismantling of industrial remnants and with the help of high unemployment. The younger workers let themselves be sent abroad.[473]

From 1992 to 2018, emigration reduced the population from 4.7 million to 4 million. This process accelerated with EU accession and, in EU circles, is expected to continue.[474]

Every second Croat between the ages of 20 and 30 is unemployed. 80 percent of new hires are temporary. The monthly minimum wage is HRK 3,750 gross (EUR 503), HRK 3,000 net (EUR 402); it can be lowered through collective agreements. Temporary work and all forms of precariousness are legalized, and the frequency of non-payment of wages by insolvent entrepreneurs is even higher than in Western countries. However, the prices of most groceries in Lidl, Kaufland and Billa supermarkets are similar to those in Germany and Austria.

The government promotes temporary posting to other EU countries. This mainly involves construction workers. At the same time, Croatian contractors bring in construction workers from even poorer countries, from Pakistan, Bangladesh and India. For the tourist season, hoteliers and restaurants bring in about 80,000 cooks, waitresses, bartenders and chambermaids from neighboring Serbia, Montenegro, Kosovo and Bosnia-Herzegovina every year.[475]

The biggest strikes since the new-found freedom
Over the past few years, defensive struggles have been on the rise, in a wide variety of areas.

Universities occupied in protest against university "reform"
Some young people are fighting back for the first time, spontaneously, without organization. This was the case with the 2012 university "reform", when the over-indebted state was no longer able or willing to finance the ailing education system. The government introduced tuition fees in accordance with EU requirements.

A local strike quickly became a nationwide strike. Students occupied universities across the country. But it was in vain. They lacked the powerful organization and the experience to stand up to a demagogically shrewd government.

Studies in the social sciences and humanities now cost between EUR 800 and 2,200 a year, in engineering EUR 3,000, and in medicine EUR 3,600. The government promotes student loans.[476]

All unions oppose the pension "reform"
In 2019, for the first time, all umbrella organizations and most individual unions joined forces against the government. Here, too, the government had proposed a pension "reform" in line with EU requirements. Although the average pension is only EUR 300, it needed to be reduced by raising the retirement age to 67 and reducing it by four percent per year in the case of early retirement.

The unions also involved other population groups and initiatives in their actions. 600,000 protest signatures were collected for a referendum. Politicization increased. The government was criticized not only for the pension cuts, but in general. "After school, unemployment; after work, the grave", banners read. But again, it was no use.

Largest labor dispute since the founding of the state: The teachers
20,000 teachers, who had been on strike for a month for better pay and conditions, gathered in the central square of the capital Zagreb on Nov. 25, 2019. They protested against the dilapidated school buildings and against the low salaries, which are on average EUR 1,200, lower than elsewhere in the public sector. The public sector has swelled to 240,000 employees due to party cronies and fake war veterans.

The nationwide strike had been well prepared, with individual strikes at different schools in different cities on different days. Eventually, 90 percent of the school system's 68,000 employees participated at the same time. Other unions, including those of police and journalists, supported the strike and rally. Other public sector workers supported the various actions, and parents also went along: This purposefully organized amplification of a labor dispute was new.

Religion teacher Marin Miletic proclaimed at the rally: "We stand up for fair wages for workers, for our pensioners. We want a society where we can stay and not have to emigrate." The president of the teachers' union Sanja Sprem shouted, "This is also a fight against our children leaving for Germany and Ireland. We are fed up with our children's future being destroyed. We have been silent for too long."[477]

The political content of the strike was also evident in the protest against the reactionary alliance of the neoliberal government and the Catholic Church. The separation of church and state, which is customary in a democracy, was demanded. The influence of the Zagreb archbishop on school textbooks was criticized, as were the "unacceptable, corrupt relations" with the Vatican.[478]

Shipyard workers: Strikes - and hopes pinned on China
The two largest shipyards in Rijeka and Pula, formerly successful state-owned enterprises, had to be privatized in accordance with EU requirements before EU entry. The state still holds 20 percent of the shares. But the neo-liberal players were unable to break the 50 percent participation of the employees in the Yugoslavian tradition; there was too much support in the company. 10,000 jobs at suppliers still hinge on the current 4,500 shipyard jobs.

In 2018 and 2019, the shipyard workers repeatedly went on strike. The management did not pay wages for up to 6 months, with the justification: We are threatened with insolvency; because we do not have enough capital, we are losing orders. Hundreds of striking workers protested in Zagreb in front of the company's headquarters, the Uljanik Group. Then, after a delay, the wages were paid in arrears after all. A test of nerves that also erodes the efficiency and international image of the shipyards.[479]

The state repeatedly pumped in subsidies, but too little, and the EU put the brakes on. In 2019, the EU rejected a requested subsidy of EUR 96

million. This means that the necessary technological innovation cannot be
initiated; further training for the employees also falls flat: death in installments.

Savior China?
The end of the shipyards would be a disaster for the coastal region. The
government does not want to prop up a company that still has so many
elements of Yugoslav socialism such as employee co-ownership. And the
EU has issued the maxim for Croatia: Promote tourism, new marinas,
luxury apartments, hotels, cultural events for the young cosmopolitan
elite.

There's only one potential savior: The People's Republic of China.
What the EU has promised, such as the construction of infrastructure, but
which is not worthwhile for Western investors - China delivers, incidentally in all Eastern and Southern European EU Member States and
candidate countries.[480] Currently, Chinese companies are building the 2.4
km long bridge near the Peljesac peninsula. At the "largest business meeting in Croatia's history" in Dubrovnik in 2019, a further 10 projects with
China were agreed, also within the framework of the "New Silk Road".
Huawei has been involved in Croatia's telecom infrastructure for over a
decade.[481]

Because of the shipyards, the government contacted Beijing at the end
of 2019. "I asked the Prime Minister", there could be a visit by Chinese
Premier Li Keqiang very soon, Prime Minister Andrej Plenkovic let it be
known.[482]

5.
Scandinavian states

The Scandinavian states of Sweden, Norway, Denmark and Finland are known for their Nordic welfare model, combined with a strong status of social democracy. The preconditions had been created by militant leftists with and in the trade unions before World War II. After the war, leftist organizations and trade unions in Scandinavia were also cleansed of communist elements.[483] Finnish trade union officials were still financed by the CIA and through the ICFTU until the 1970s.[484]

Nazi collaboration and guilty conscience
The second precondition for the welfare state was the guilty conscience of the ruling class of the bourgeoisie, aristocrats, military folk, bankers and entrepreneurs. They had cooperated with the Nazis during the war, especially in militarily neutral and unoccupied Sweden:

- Finland fought with the Wehrmacht against the Soviet Union, the Einsatzkommando Finland committed massacres of Jews, Soviet prisoners of war and communists, the Wehrmacht maintained 100 prison camps in Finland.[485]
- Denmark had concluded a trade agreement with Germany in 1934, which was expanded under the German occupation; Danish temporary workers were dispatched to German companies.[486]
- In occupied Norway, the leader of the fascist National Union, Vidkun Quisling, provided a puppet government; the Norsk Hydro corporation supplied heavy water for the development of the atomic bomb in Germany.[487]
- Swedish companies and banks, especially those of the Wallenberg Group, supplied wartime essentials to Nazi Germany: iron ore, ball bearings, stainless steel. Enskilda Bank, which belonged to Wallenberg, sold looted shares for the benefit of the Hitler regime, camouflaged German holdings in Swedish companies.[488] The resources of the Scandinavian countries necessary for German warfare had been explored by the Kiel Institute for the World Economy before the war.[489]

Quisling was executed in 1945, but the collaborators, bourgeoisie, aristocrats and the Wallenberg accomplices remained unscathed. Thus, the communist-cleansed parties and unions were granted the welfare state. The enduring, lavishly funded monarchies in Norway, Denmark and Sweden also contribute to the colorfully clad amnesia to this day.

Welfare state at home - exploitation abroad
Sweden, as a particularly vaunted welfare state, still shows its double face particularly drastically today. While the big companies in Sweden appear friendly, they act unsocially abroad, including in EU countries, for example when it comes to working conditions and tax evasion. The Swedish textile chain H&M had its employees in Germany, who were kept in a "climate of fear", spied on and dossiers compiled with data on illnesses, marital disputes, vacation experiences.[490]

The energy company Vattenfall is sueing the German state for closing a nuclear power plant. The furniture company Ikea exploits low-wage workers in Eastern Europe. The "locust" firms EQT and IK of the Wallenberg Group tear apart corporations abroad, currently Thyssen/Krupp. The Norwegian state fund Norges takes good care of Norwegian pensioners, but as a major shareholder of Deutsche Post DHL harms German pensioners.[491]

The Danish slaughter company Danish Crown agrees collective wage agreements in Denmark, pays an hourly wage of EUR 25 to the mostly Danish meat cutters, adheres to the daily working time of 7.4 hours, pays overtime - while in Germany it participates in the exploitation and fraud system shaped by the German market leader Tönnies many thousands of times over: No collective agreements; minimum wage of EUR 9.35, which is also circumvented by unpaid overtime; multiple exploitation of mostly Eastern European workers through fraudulent work contracts, deductions for "misconduct" and for daily transportation to and from the overpriced mass accommodations.[492]

Nobel Prize in Economics
Sweden's representative during WW2 in the Wall Street-led money-laundering bank BIS, Per Jacobssen, worked after the war with CIA chief Dulles and with EU founding commissioner Monnet, was responsible for the Marshall Plan at BIS until 1956, and headed the IMF from 1956 to 1963. The Swedish Riksbank, building on Jacobssen's ideas, established

the Nobel Prize in Economics in 1968 and subsequently attached it to the prestigious Nobel Prize: The latter contributed significantly to the global spread of the neoliberal heresy, for example through the prizes awarded to the dictator-friendly gurus Friedrich von Hayek and Milton Friedman.

Unions: Their ambivalent strength
Today, the Scandinavian trade unions still have the highest degree of organization in an EU comparison: 74 percent in Finland, 70 percent in Sweden, 67 percent in Denmark and 52 percent in Norway. It is higher in the public sector and lower in the private sector.[493] However, this is the snapshot of a "slow decline" that began in the 1990s.[494]

Of the Scandinavian states, Denmark was the first EU member by a long way, mainly for two reasons: First, because of its convenient location on the doorstep of the GDR for Western espionage led by the CIA and the BND[495]; second, because of the US military base at Thule in what was then the Danish colony of Greenland. The small kingdom was a founding member of NATO in 1949. Despite popular resistance, Denmark was maneuvered into the EU in 1973. To this day, Denmark's vassal status vis-à-vis the US is particularly pronounced, for example in the fight against the Nordstream 2 gas pipeline and against the new enemy China.[496] The largest shipping company, Denmark-based Maersk, has its largest standing order with the US military.

Sweden and Finland did not follow into the EU until 1995. In Norway, a narrow majority rejected the Social Democratic government's accession proposal.

Both social democratic and conservative parties implemented the neoliberal program: Privatization of kindergartens and housing, pension reform, deregulation. To some extent, the unions countered with a political concept, especially in Norway in 2004 with their campaign against neoliberalism. But their binding force declined. They could not prevent temporary work and other forms of precariousness.[497] Nor were they able to halt the drift to the right.[498]

While the unions remained comparatively strong in their core areas, dependent employees were impoverished by the state and investors: through rising rents and expensive health services, through the highest VAT rates in the EU: Sweden and Denmark 25 percent, Finland 24 percent - only Hungary is higher at 27 percent. Private households in Sweden, the showcase country, are heavily indebted by international standards.[499]

No EU minimum wage!

The Scandinavian countries are among the six EU states that do not have a statutory minimum wage.

There were once good reasons for the statutory minimum wage. In Roosevelt's New Deal, it was part of an overall package: State protection for unions, criminal liability of companies for obstructing unions, public investment in infrastructure such as schools, city halls, water supply - not least with the promotion of progressive, politically motivated art in public spaces, on public buildings.[500]

Such an overall package does not exist anywhere in the EU. On the contrary: At the same time as the minimum wage, trade unions are being weakened, precarious forms of work are being promoted, and public infrastructure is deteriorating.

The Scandinavian trade unions have prevented a minimum wage. They are now resisting the COM's plan for the EU minimum wage: "Salaries must be set through collective bargaining. A statutory minimum wage undermines the collective bargaining system."[501]

The resistance is also supported by the trade unions of Austria and Italy, which are among the least conformist trade unions in the EU. Austria and Italy also have no minimum wage.

But unions too weak to control the minimum wage

At the latest in the face of expanding decentralized wage setting and new labor migration, the Scandinavian model is coming to its end. For example, Sweden's largest union, Kommunal, has negotiated a minimum wage for seasonal berry pickers from Thailand and has the right to control it - but it doesn't have the staff to do so. The government does not care. Employers undermine the agreed wage, for example by paying by the kilo and not paying overtime.[502]

The Scandinavian trade unions champion a good principle, but can no longer implement it. But at least they are highlighting the dubiousness of the EU minimum wage.

6.
Eastern European states

The three most important Eastern European countries, Hungary, Poland and the Czech Republic, were initially admitted to NATO in 1999. EU membership also followed simultaneously for these countries, in 2005. Slovakia was not admitted to NATO until 2004, at the same time as it was admitted to the EU.

Public property was sold to Western capitalists, and many of the unemployed were highly skilled. Therefore, industrial groups, mainly from the EU core states, the USA and Japan, set up branches and a deep network of supplier factories. Wages, labor and union rights were low, and EU subsidies were high even before EU entry. National subsidies to investors are also extremely high. Here, in a comparison of EU states, wages and labor productivity diverge the most, to the detriment of employees: High skills, high productivity - but proportionately the lowest labor income,[503] and the fewest collective labor rights.

Lowest labor rights, highest EU subsidies
The development of the national economies as a whole does not play a role. Gross national product grew. But this also included the cost of living: Rents rose for the now privatized apartments, for goods in Western supermarket chains. Hospitals and government agencies charged fees or bribes. Social spending was cut. Public sector schools and hospitals decayed. Private schools for the rich flourish, Western corporations qualify the few local specialists themselves. As a result, millions of unemployed, low-wage workers, including teachers, engineers and doctors, emigrate and work in the West.

For all the EU's criticism of the nationalist, corrupt governments of Hungary, Poland, and the Czech Republic, they are the logical products of Western subsidies. Poland and Hungary receive by far the most EU subsidies per capita, Poland first, Hungary second.

Governments are taking authoritarian action against protests, which began to intensify around 2015. Nevertheless, criticism and collective action are on the rise.

Hungary 2019: Workers suddenly realize their strength

The "reform socialism" in Hungary, praised by the West as early as the 1980s, promised more. You could smell it: Capitalism was on the horizon. That is why George Soros founded a branch of his Open Society Foundation (OSF) in Budapest in 1984. The speculator had founded the aggressive hedge fund Quantum in the deregulated banking world of the USA. He used the profits to finance "human rights activists" in the socialist states. "Open society" - the deliberately vague demand for "openness" could be used for all sorts of things (within the capitalist framework).

Soros rears Orban

The OSF awarded scholarships to elite British and US universities to a group of Hungarian students, including spokesman Viktor Orban. He received a scholarship to Oxford. In 1988, they founded the Fidesz party. The term alludes to Latin fides, loyalty, faith. Fidesz saw itself as "liberal" in the sense of "free market" as practiced by Soros. The party was admitted to the Liberal International, in which the German FDP plays a leading role.

That did not promise success; it was not populist enough. Therefore, Fidesz renamed itself a "conservative" party. The ideologically opportunistic party leaders, such as Orban, added the "Christian" to this a few years later and switched to the European People's Party, where the CDU and CSU play a leading role, as well as to the Christian Democratic International, where Orban became vice president.[504] In 2011, the Fidesz government changed the constitution: Republic was removed from the name "Republic of Hungary", the reference to God was inserted, the country was declared part of "Christian Europe".[505]

The overlapping schools of thought, liberal, conservative and Christian, belong to the political spectrum of Western capitalist democracy and its populist variants. Orban shows: They are compatible with nationalism and right-wing radicalism or can merge into them.

Open for Western investors

After the collapse of socialism, parties calling themselves social democratic and liberal initially ruled. They sold state-owned enterprises, housing cooperatives, land and hotels to foreign investors at knockdown prices. Deutsche Bank, Morgan Stanley and Daiwa from Japan granted long-term loans. Car companies such as Audi/VW, Mercedes, BMW, Opel, Suzuki and the tire manufacturer Hankook from South Korea set up factories with tens of thousands of well-trained low-wage workers starting in 1993. The factories are surrounded by a deep chain of domestic sub-subcontractors. The Bertelsmann and WAZ media groups snapped up domestic media, Tengelmann and Lidl opened supermarkets, Deutsche Telekom took over the majority of telephone services, and Austrian banks dominate the financial sector.

The governments became so unpopular that only the Christian nationalist demagogues of Fidesz could still spread hope. During their first term in government from 1998 to 2002, loans in the foreign currencies of euros, Swiss francs and US dollars were allowed for the purchase of apartments; this was considered chic and modern. Interest rates were lower than in the domestic currency, the forint. But precisely because of this, the forint fell, interest rates rose, tens of thousands of borrowers were suddenly over-indebted and lost their apartments. The price of condominiums quadrupled in just a few years.

Prices in Western supermarkets and for Western goods were also at Western European levels. Wages remained low. Automobile workers at Mercedes and Audi earn between EUR 400 and 800 a month, gross, as do doctors, judges, nurses. Universities have to gather assignments from companies to survive. Only a small middle class flourishes. Slums in the cities are standard, and at the bottom are the Roma, who are also ethnically discriminated against.

Since the economic crisis of 2007, at least 700,000 Hungarians have emigrated. Economist Szilard Kalmar even speaks of "1.5 million disappeared workers".[506]

Fidesz even more servile for BMW & Co
The discontent brought Fidesz back into government in 2010, and for the long term. In particular, the car companies from Germany, Japan and France demanded new measures: The "skilled worker gap" that they themselves had caused must be closed! At the same time, labor should become even cheaper, although it still costs only a quarter compared to Germany - for industrial workers, EUR 9 per hour including social security contributions versus EUR 34 (as of 2017, Eurostat and OECD).[507]

In 2012, Fidesz fulfilled some investor wishes in a first round with the new labor law:

- On-call workers may be employed by more than one employer at the same time
- Unions now only have the right to receive information, but no say in the matter
- "small collective agreements" at the level of individual companies are promoted
- The employee must also represent the good image of the company in his free time.[508]

This failed to spark the hoped-for revival in investment. The "skilled worker gap" continued to grow. Hungary was caught in the trap created by the investors themselves with state aid.[509] The decisive new push was made possible by e-mobility, which is now being pushed forward frantically. It requires lower qualifications for many jobs: The complicated gasoline engine is completely eliminated.

New benefits for investors - legal and covert
In 2017, Fidesz fulfilled (almost) all investors' wishes through legislation and other measures:

- Profit tax (corporation tax) is reduced to 9 percent, the lowest in the EU
- Social security contributions are reduced from 27.5 to 19.5 percent - the lowest level in the EU
- House unions given preference for collective bargaining agreements
- New vocational schools to be established on a group-wide basis
- New workers to be recruited from even poorer countries such as Romania and as far away as Asia
- Land is sold even cheaper

Since then, mainly German car companies and their suppliers have been stepping up investment again: Audi, with 12,900 employees the second largest industrial company in the country, then Daimler with 3,500 employees, Schaeffler, Continental, Bosch, ThyssenKrupp, Siemens, BMW. Schaeffler celebrated its 20th anniversary in Debrecen in 2019: there were 49 employees there when it was founded, and the number is expected to reach 2,000 in 2020.[510] A large part of the new e-car production is being relocated to Hungary.

IG Metall, which cooperates with the Hungarian trade union Vasas, notes that "German car companies dictate laws abroad".[511] In addition to the statutory gifts, the government enters into special agreements with individual investors. The BMW spokesman is as satisfied as he is cagey: The two sides have "agreed to maintain mutual silence about the specific subsidies from the Hungarian government".[512]

State economy and cronyism: Subsidized by the EU
The socialist "planned economy" is still portrayed as an ugly antithesis. But, as in Poland, Hungary's "open" and "free market" economy is a very different state economy because of extremely high state and EU subsidies. The state interventions are also combined with corrupt cronyism: Well-paid jobs only for Fidesz members: here the charge of "state economy" coined for socialism is fulfilled, including extensive nepotism. The EU's anti-fraud office OLAF has known for years about the continuous fraud with EU subsidies in favor of rich oligarchs and the Orban clan, including Orban's son-in-law: The subsidies continue.[513]

For example, the largest company is a hundred percent state-owned group: The holding company MOL, with 34,000 employees, has oil and gas under its control, and is the market leader not only in Hungary itself, but also in Slovakia, Croatia and Bosnia-Herzegovina. For the development of plastic disposal, MOL has bought up the recycling company Aurora in Germany, operates 2,000 gas stations as service and shopping centers and organizes carsharing.[514]

Highest VAT in the EU - dereliction of public infrastructure
With the lavish spending in favor of private investors and low labor incomes, state revenues are low. Revenues from the lucrative state corporation MOL cannot make up for this. The state collects by far the most revenue by further impoverishing the lower strata of the population: At 27 percent, VAT is the highest in the EU.

In order for the state to comply with EU requirements from the European Semester, cuts are being made in social spending such as unemployment benefits. State and public authority employees who have not emigrated are poorly paid. School, university and hospital buildings are being repaired only in a makeshift fashion, unless these facilities are privatized and services are made more expensive.

Soros/Orban: Cads' fighting, when ended, is soon mended
In 2018, Soros withdrew the 100 employees of his OSF from Budapest to Berlin. The European Central University he had run there since 1991, with 1,500 students and 400 staff, will also be moved to the West, to Vienna, in 2020. OSF had also financed newspapers, institutes and associations.

The animosity between Orban and his sponsor began in 2008. The latter had bet with his Quantum fund against the largest Hungarian bank OTP, with a profit of USD 675,000. The regulator imposed a fine of EUR 1.5 million on Quantum. Soros regretted the bet, saying he personally had nothing to do with it. But it violated Hungary's sovereignty. Then came the refugees: Soros was in favor of accepting refugees, Orban against. The anti-Semitism virulent in Fidesz since its founding had not bothered Soros, who is of Jewish origin. Now, suddenly, it did bother him.[515]

Surprised themselves: The workers realize their strength
"We were really scared because no one had done this before us in Hungary," said György Csalogany. He belongs to the independent trade union AHFSZ at Audi Hungaria in Györ. It had called a strike in January 2019, for the first time. They themselves were surprised that virtually all 12,000 workers went on strike, for a full week. "We organized the strike as a small team of nine, but the workers were behind us the whole time. It was uplifting."[516]

The first strike, a complete success
And they were successful: the management, which was also surprised, immediately agreed to the demanded wage increase of 18 percent, for the next 15 months. There had never been such a strike and such a wage increase in Hungary before.

Without being precisely planned with that aim, the strike had also hit the sore spot: Engines from the factory in Györ, Europe's largest engine plant, are delivered just in time to the German Audi plants in Neckarsulm and Ingolstadt, to the Porsche plant in Leipzig and to the VW plant in Bratislava. There, assembly quickly came to a standstill. Group management had to act.

Swelling protest, new coalitions

The strike was all the more important and courageous because it was prohibited under the new labor law, which had been in force since January 1, 2019. Strikes at other companies followed, such as at tire manufacturer Hankook. Teachers went on strike in four of the 60 school districts, and for the first time the government conceded a pay raise to them as well. The strikes also aroused great interest among broad sections of the population, for the first time.[517]

Protests against the looming labor law had already been organized in previous years. In 2018, 70 company and sector unions joined forces for the first time in the "Initiative from Below" alliance. Their broad slogan was "For democracy, social security and preservation of human and workers' rights". Thousands of demonstrators marched through the main streets of Budapest and besieged the parliament. Students also joined in. Calls for a general strike were heard.

The protests were

- against the restriction of the right to strike,
- against the ban on unions supporting their members in court,
- against forced labor for Roma,
- against the abolition of protection against dismissal for older employees and pregnant women.

The law was denounced as a "slave law". There were protests against the even more radical flexibilization of working hours. Up to 400 hours of overtime per year were to remain unpaid. The compensation period for overtime was to be extended to three years. The protests prevented these new regulations. However, the government has by no means abandoned the plan.[518]

EU against refugee policy, but for labor injustice

The EU only criticizes the Orban government for not accepting refugees.

However, the EU does not criticize the blatant labor injustice, which in many cases deeply violates EU directives.

Nor does the EU criticize the "economically successful" country for impoverishing the majority of its citizens and for being at the bottom of the EU rankings in per capita consumption.

"Eastern Europeans on the barricades for higher wages"
The surprising, widespread, successful strike at Audi Hungary was only the tip of the iceberg that finally emerged under the long-extorted silence of authoritarian state and corporate rule. Strikes were also suddenly organized in related industries in neighboring Czech Republic, Romania and Slovakia, and they were also comparatively successful: At Skoda, a 12 percent wage increase and a one-time payment of no less than EUR 2,600 were quickly forced through.

"Eastern Europeans on the barricades for higher wages," German business newspapers report in a mixture of astonishment and doubt: Can the oligarch regimes keep their show on the road?[519]

Labor injustice on the public agenda for the first time
The strikes and the politically broad-based protests against Orban's new "slave law", which resonate with large segments of the population and have even been successful in some cases, represent a watershed.

Agnes Gagyi and Tamas Geröcs of the University of Gothenburg and the Hungarian Academy of Sciences sum up the situation as follows: "The outrage over the slave law marks a moment when the issue of labor has reached the surface of public political discourse at an unprecedented level since the regime change. The struggles against the law are building coalitions and organizational capacity that may become important in the future. But the capacity to act that comes from resisting the law is countered by the weight and inertia of a collapsing global system."[520]

Poland: Internationally networked against Amazon
The independent trade union Solidarnosc, founded in 1980, was good to overthrow socialism with the slogan of freedom. For this it was supported by Catholic bishops and Polish Pope Wojtyla, John Paul II, the CIA and Western trade unions and "human rights activists". Hence, Solidarnosc became a member of the (a)social trialogue with the nationalist Catholic government and the big Western investors like Amazon: Solidarnosc now manages the labor injustice even of its own members.

Military and economic "integration with the West"
Due to its pronounced anti-communist and anti-Russian potential as well as its territorial size and central location, Poland was particularly signifi-

cant for the USA - comparable to Adenauer's Federal Republic after World War II.

Immediately in 1990, the American Chamber of Commerce in Poland was established. Christine Lagarde, as president of Baker McKenzie, the most important US law firm in foreign policy at the time, and Zbigniew Brzezinski, the Polish-born foreign policy advisor to several US presidents, developed the strategy for the economic-military development of Poland on behalf of the US government starting in the mid-1990s.[521]

This included early admission to NATO. Poland became the center of "Eastern NATO" under US Presidents Bush, Obama and Trump. These are the countries that cooperate particularly closely with the US and form a belt against Russia from the Baltic Sea to the Black Sea. It is also called the Intermarium: Revisiting the 1930s concept of anti-Semitic Polish dictator and Hitler ally Josef Pilsudski directed against the Soviet Union. He, in turn, had nostalgically harkened back to Polish rule in Eastern Europe during the 16th to 18th centuries.[522] The Catholic oligarchs today have been begging for the US's anti-Russia medium-range missile defense system, Aegis, to be located here.

It was no coincidence that at the 2016 NATO summit in Warsaw Obama affirmed: the alliance is directed against the aggressor Russia, the European NATO members must increase their military budget to two percent of gross national product, joint maneuvers will be conducted. In 2018, most Eastern NATO countries already met the two percent target: Poland, Lithuania, Latvia, Estonia – with Romania just below at 1.9 percent.[523]

EU subsidies for highways for military use
A large chunk of the EU subsidies went towards the construction of 3,300 kilometers of highway. These are intended in particular to promote truck traffic for the production, service and supply chains of Western investors.[524] This applies, for example, to Amazon's logistics centers built at highway interchanges, whose catchment and delivery area extends to both Western and Eastern Europe.[525]

At the same time, coordinated with NATO, the north-south and east-west highways also serve to transport military equipment and troops, such as the east-west 670 kilometers from Görlitz to the Ukrainian border. In the US strategy, Ukraine is the key state to attack Russia.

All Poland a special economic zone

The EU celebrates Poland as the most successful economy among the ex-socialist states with its five percent growth rates over many years. Special economic zones (SEZs) are an important factor: no other state has so many. Better put, Poland developed into a single SEZ. Initially, the government set up 14 SEZs. They attract investors with numerous subsidies: In addition to EU subsidies, there are tax exemptions, free access to highways, free energy, water/sewage connections, subsidized energy costs, concessionary loans.

The 14 SEZs are industrial parks that maintain 300 additional outposts. In the meantime, however, Western corporations can choose the location of a branch themselves, independent of an SEZ. When the supermarket chain Lidl wanted to set up its new logistics center at a new location where there was no SEZ, the authorities declared the site a new SEZ without further ado. The Passauer Neue Presse managed to have the site it had selected for a large printing plant declared an SEZ.[526]

For example, the automotive and supplier groups VW, Daimler, MAN, Bosch, FIAT, General Motors, Opel/PSA, Toyota, KIA and Hyundai (South Korea), the electrical multinationals Siemens, Samsung (South Korea) and Sharp (Japan), the logistics groups Deutsche Post DHL, UPS and Girteka (Lithuania), and the chemical groups BASF and Henkel have built and are building highly subsidized branches. Lufthansa operates a maintenance center for aircraft with General Electric. Kaufland and Lidl are opening more and more supermarkets. Auto suppliers such as Festo, Sitech (VW), ABM Greiffenhagen and Lenze also have operations here. Sub-subcontractor chains of local medium-sized and small businesses are clustered around them.

IMF, Western banks, corporate lobby

In addition to the tax subsidies granted by the Polish state, there is also tax evasion. For instance, most investments and loans - especially from the USA - pass through the EU financial havens of the Netherlands and Luxembourg for tax purposes.[527]

The US Chamber of Commerce in Poland represents 300 US companies and banks, including 80 from the list of the 500 largest US corporations. It sees itself as "the leading voice of international investors in Poland". Together with the US Embassy, it maintains "close relations" with the Polish authorities. The government repeatedly awards representatives of the Chamber of Commerce with the highest civilian decoration.[528] In second place as a lobbyist is the Chamber of Foreign Trade from Germany.

"Large Western corporations have come to Poland and basically do what they want here, without regard for the Polish context and local conditions," said Andrzej Szabaj, a professor of political philosophy at the University of Torun.[529]

At the car company during the day, delivering packages in the evening
Core staff numbers in the branches of the foreign corporations are low, and in no other EU country is the proportion of temporary workers - who can be dismissed on a weekly basis - so high. The leading temporary employment vendors in the West, Adecco, Manpower and Randstad, operate large branches here.

In the affiliated subcontractors, all forms of temporary and fragmented work dominate: Here, you can consider yourself lucky if at least the minimum wage of EUR 3.50/hour (as of 2020) is paid correctly, even if not for all overtime. "The fact is that in Poland the number of precarious (short-term) jobs is the highest in the whole EU," attests even the business rag FAZ.[530]

Even those who work full time directly for a car company do not earn enough to cover the high cost of living. Earning slightly above the minimum wage at Toyota during the day and delivering parcels for Deutsche Post DHL in the evening - this second job pattern is widespread.[531]

Subsidies and law violations for low-wage work
The state subsidizes the corporations via
- topped-up wages
- reimbursement of costs for newly installed and retrofitted workstations
- grants for training programs
- reimbursement of social security contributions on hiring of unemployed persons
- permission for unpaid internships up to 12 months without an employment contract.[532]

At the same time, the state allows companies to violate the low standards. This was not ascertained by the EU, but by the German trade union verdi, for example. The Polish labor inspectorate covers up the non-payment of overtime, working hours of over 16 hours and the violation of protective regulations.[533]

Privileges for state workers: Promoted by the EU
As in Hungary, there is a large state sector. This includes the oil company Orlen and, with PGG, the large coal-fired power plants and mines that supply coal and lignite. PGG is the largest coal company in the EU. 80 percent of Poland's energy comes from coal.

The state promotes this outdated, toxic energy. It passes it on to investors at a reduced price. The EU subsidizes this: in 2019, it approved subsidies so that "large energy consumers" can benefit from "tax reductions". This is supposed to serve the "global competitiveness of energy-intensive industries".[534] EU and Green Deal?

In this capitalist "state economy", cronyism flourishes. Employees here have unusual privileges: secure and permanent jobs, generous salary increases of 12 percent in both 2019 and 2020, plus quarterly bonuses that add up to a 14th month's pay.

In this way, the government props up a domestic oligarchy, as in Hungary and the Czech Republic. It also provides itself with profits, which it uses to finance special projects for other cronies,[535] but also child benefits and a housing program for the lower middle class: these are important voters.[536]

EU agricultural subsidies: Small farmers become unemployed
The EU subsidizes agriculture: grants of up to 50 percent and premiums for modernization. From 2014 to 2020, this amounted to EUR 8.6 billion, the largest agricultural program per capita in the EU. But the subsidies are out of reach for the many small farmers; a large proportion suffer from mounting rents due to the land grabbing of well-funded investors - local old owners and Western agribusiness.

Thus, Poland became the largest exporter of poultry. The government pays generous social benefits to the unemployed and landless farmers, since they are an important constituency. This is more or less enough to live on, but unemployment and impoverishment in the villages are growing.[537]

Emigrate, immigrate

2.5 million Poles have emigrated permanently, while others work as seasonal workers in the West on a weekly or monthly basis. At the same time, the immigration of millions of even poorer people is encouraged.

From Ukraine, highly extoled and impoverished by the EU and NATO, over a million commuters and migrants now work in cheap jobs in Poland, as domestic and cleaning help and as seasonal workers for agricultural companies. The government wants to bring back as many of the 900,000 Poles from Britain as possible, but they don't want to return.[538]

In 2004, 10,000 haulage companies were registered in Poland. In 2017, there were 30,000. Truck drivers- about 300,000 - hired through temporary-work agencies are also increasingly coming from Ukraine, Lithuania, Belarus, Moldova and also Sri Lanka. Here, too, the labor inspectorate assists in the violation of labor and other laws: The submitted documents on the drivers' residence, license, insurance are accepted without verification.[539]

The nationalist government promotes the cohesion of society and the value of the family with Christian-painted populism. The cult of Mary, the Mother of God, is ubiquitous. But the forced, also organized emigration and immigration tears apart millions of families, Europe- and worldwide.

Growing stirrings: Stifled - but not completely

The over-indebted location state has "slimmed down" the public administration, except for the central ministries: this affects labor inspectorates, schools, hospitals.

Doctors on hunger strike

Hospitals are not only understaffed. The doctors, nurses and midwives who have not emigrated are poorly paid. In many cases, they are only employed on a temporary basis. Many have a fee-for-service contract as pseudo-self-employed. Hospital doctors open their private practice for a few hours after work. Doctors in training earn EUR 500 a month.

In December 2017, the lingering discontent erupted. 200 doctors, above all assistant physicians, went on hunger strike for four weeks. That had never happened before. More than 1,000 doctors simultaneously cancelled their opt-out clause: in order to earn a little more, they had taken on an additional 15-20 hours per week on top of their 48-hour week. They now worked to rule, without overtime. They took to the streets.[540]

In January 2018, the assistant physicians followed suit, refusing to work extra hours and shutting down operations at several clinics. This was all a first, made a big splash. It was even reported abroad (a little). The Minister of Health was replaced. Success seemed close at hand. The government held out the prospect of improvements and salary increases. Salaries were topped up a bit. But no new jobs were created.

Great disillusionment set in, frustration. "It was very easy to get all the anger that was fermenting beneath the surface onto the streets." But, "After our courageous hunger strike, I am really surprised how little we achieved," said 31-year-old activist Dr. Filip Dabrowski, a gynecologist.[541] No solidarity from Solidarnosc.

Teachers 2019: Largest strike since system change
Like the health care system, the public-sector school system is in a state of disrepair. There are too few teachers, most of them are over 50 years old, and only 7 percent are under 30. In addition, the few who do work are poorly paid: the state pays EUR 420 a month for newcomers to the profession, and EUR 1,250 gross after 15 years in the job. The buildings are decaying. There are too few rooms because dilapidated buildings have to be closed. As a result, classes are overcrowded with up to 40 pupils. In some schools, the government has therefore ordered shift teaching. Many teachers can only keep their heads above water with private lessons: In a perverse logic, the ramshackle system creates the demand.[542]

Government sends in priests as strike breakers
In April 2019, the phony truce broke. The two teachers' organizations, ZNP and FZZ, had been preparing for an indefinite strike for three years - 90 percent of members had voted in favor of the strike. Four-fifths of the teachers participated. Janitors and kindergarten teachers also joined in. Rallies were held in the major cities.

As with the doctors, there was a demand for a salary increase of 15 percent in the current year and another 15 percent the following year. They also demanded better equipment for schools. The population was divided, as was Polish society in general: half was in favor of the strike. The other half was against it - mainly PiS voters. The government's counter-proposal: You can increase the number of teaching hours per week from 18 to 24, then you can also earn more, namely 9.6 percent.[543]

At the same time, the government called on school principals to report the names and details of the strikers. Where exams were threatened with cancellation, the government ordered 9,000 nuns, priests, foresters, fire-fighters, retired teachers and even prison guards into the schools.

Solidarnosc with government for poor working conditions
Solidarnosc had forbidden its members to take part in the strike. But it negotiated with the government without consulting the two teachers' organizations: a five percent salary increase, a special allowance for newcomers to the profession, training assistance starting at EUR 80 per month. And teacher training is shortened.

ZNP and FZZ ended the strike with reservations, saying that there would be further strikes in the fall. But there was no further strike. Overall, the general education system remains decrepit - without replacement.

Internationally networked against Amazon
Amazon, with 650,000 employees worldwide - with "corona" there are 170,000 more - is one of the most important laboratories of digitally organized labor for the struggle for human rights:

- Amazon not only cooperates closely with the US military and impoverishes numerous states through tax fraud.
- Amazon spreads hatred worldwide against unions and any form of collective representation of workers.
- Amazon promotes all forms of precarity and the all-around, all-time control of labor, including at night and on Sunday.
- Amazon also uses all forms of digitalization and artificial intelligence to squeeze, monitor, discipline dependent employees.

With EU subsidies, Amazon maintains four logistics centers, a center for software development and a location for the cloud storage service Amazon Web Services (AWS) in Poland. There are 15,000 permanent employees working there - the number of others is not known, changes constantly anyway.

Start: A go-slow strike
In June 2015, Amazon bosses at the Poznan Fulfillment Center (FC) ordered at short notice: The shift will now last an hour longer! Several employees responded with a go-slow. The reason for the order: Workers at the German FC Bad Hersfeld were striking again.

The independent grassroots trade union Inicjatywa Pracownicza (IP) with only 300 members had not organized the go-slow itself, but to some extent had prepared the ground. It had already been in contact with verdi activists in Bad Hersfeld for some time and had distributed leaflets about the situation there in Poznan. They therefore knew that they were meant to serve as strikebreakers in Poznan.[544]

10.5-hour shift with unpaid break
Work is performed in shifts of 10.5 hours with an unpaid half-hour break and in blocks of four working days each. There are no, or at most minimal, bonuses for night shifts and Sunday work. Video surveillance, even in the locker rooms, is standard. Amazon pays the minimum hourly wage determined by the government: Since 2015, this has been gradually increased from EUR 2.94 gross to EUR 4.36 by 2019.

IP organized a ballot for a real strike the following year. However, the 2,000 votes for this were not enough under Polish labor law: for a strike, all employees must be consulted, not just union members, and at least 50 percent must vote in favor of the strike. Management had warned against participating in the strike ballot in prescribed works meetings. After the go-slow, the bosses had already summoned several employees for individual questioning, urged them to sign severance agreements, had them sign statements saying whether they had participated in the go-slow and by whom they had been asked to do so. Some left the work hell "voluntarily".[545]

International network
Solidarnosc is recognized by Amazon as the responsible trade union. The yellow, pro-government union was ultimately unable to ignore the pressure unleashed by IP, and its own members were threatening to walk away. Hence, Solidarnosc and IP jointly set out demands in 2019. These included an increase in the hourly wage to between EUR 5.89 and 8.01, i.e. almost double.

Solidarnosc now also participates in the international networking meetings of Amazon workers. The meetings, which have so far taken place in Brussels, Dublin and Berlin, are now attended by 23 initiatives and trade unions from 19 countries, including the USA, Pakistan, Egypt, Brazil. They started in 2013 in the wake of the first strikes in the German FC Bad Hersfeld. Strikes in France, Spain, Italy followed. Because Amazon is one of the biggest air polluters due to excessive air and truck transports, 3,000 US workers participated in the Global Climate Strike on September 20, 2019.

"One of the most important labor struggles"
The trade union UNI Global Union takes over the coordination. This union was founded in 2000, has its headquarters in Switzerland, has adapted to the new global working conditions and is now present in 150 countries. In Poland, it has set up the COZZ Organizing Center in consultation with IP and Solidarnosc.

"The fight against Amazon's corporate greed is one of the most important labor struggles in recent history," sums up Christy Hoffman of UNI Global Union.[546]

7.
Baltic States

The Baltic states of Estonia, Latvia and Lithuania are the region in the EU that has undergone the most radical neoliberal transformation. The three states entered the EU at the same time, in 2004, and into NATO: a complete package. The three states - Lithuania in the lead - combine this with the most direct dependence on the USA, with extreme nationalism and racism, and as pioneers of digitalization.

"Radical capitalism":
US military, nationalism, digitalization, low wages
"Radical capitalism" was the program of Mart Laar, twice prime minister of Estonia, who also filled such seemingly disparate roles as defense minister and head of the central bank's supervisory board. He received the Milton Friedman Prize for Advancing Liberty from the Washington think tank Cato.[547] The Lithuanian Free Market Institute LFMI is also ultra-neoliberal: It was founded in 1990 by Petras Austrevicius, after he had completed training at Stanford University and then became Lithuania's first foreign minister and negotiator for EU accession.

Money laundering and shadow economy
- The Baltic states have, with differences, the most capital-friendly financial supervision. International money laundering into the EU is flourishing, organized through the branches of Swedish and Danish banks (SEB, Danske Bank, Nordea). Since EU membership, this has become increasingly true.[548]
- Most investments go via the financial havens of the Netherlands and Cyprus.
- The shadow economy accounts for about one-fifth of gross domestic product in Lithuania.[549]

State racism
- Largely irrespective of the name of the ruling parties: "radical capitalism" is common doctrine.
- Right-wing extremist, nationalist, racist parties or "conservative" parties with such currents are routinely involved in governments.[550] Traditions of complicity with German fascism and membership in the SS are nurtured. Every year, Latvia hosts the March of the Legionnaires, accompanied by priests, to commemorate the Latvian Waffen SS.[551] Germany helped with pension payments for Latvian SS veterans.[552]
- Foreigners, refugees, Jews, especially Russians are discriminated against. In Latvia, 220,000 citizens of Russian origin have been expatriated, are not given Latvian passports, and are listed as "non-citizens". They are not allowed to vote and are banned from state-related professions.[553]

In the grip of the USA and NATO
- Until joining the euro, Lithuania's currency was pegged to the US dollar. US advisors have been frequent visitors here. The most frequent visitor was US Senator John McCain. Leading politicians receive visiting professorships at elite US universities, such as Toomas Ilves, ex-head of state of Estonia.
- The three countries, together with Poland, form the core of Eastern NATO, are the site of numerous large-scale US and NATO maneuvers (Defender 2020). Estonia hosts the NATO Cyber Center, Lithuania the NATO Center for Energy Security and the NATO Center for Strategic Communications (Stratcom).

- The Baltics host four multinational combat forces from the US, UK, Canada, and Germany.
- Militarization of work and school life: Managers must undergo regular training for the "invasion case". Air-raid drills are mandatory in schools. Hatred of the mortal enemy Russia is state doctrine.[554]
- The Baltic states were the first to meet the two percent US military budget target.

Digital services for foreign investors
- The Baltic states are considered digital prodigies: fast online start-ups, online elections, highest Internet speeds in the EU, digital services for Western investors and for NATO.
- This is cheap and convenient for outsourced branches and subcontractors of Western corporations such as Google, Uber (cab services), Schaeffler (car supplier), Barclays and Western Union (banking services), Microsoft, IBM, Siemens, Philip Morris (cigarettes, also for smuggling), PWC and EY (auditors/tax advisors) and Moody's (rating agency) as well as for information technology (shared service center).

Employees largely without rights
The three countries have dutifully ratified all eight core standards of the ILO, such as equal pay for men and women, the right to independent trade unions and to collective bargaining agreements. However, these rights are being deliberately violated:
- The difference in labor income between men and women is extremely high; discrimination on the basis of ethnic, social and gender affiliation is normal.[555]
- This is where the lowest level of collective wage bargaining prevails: Only between 2 and 8 percent of all wages. Most wages are negotiated individually with the bosses.[556]
- The degree of unionization is 7 to 9 percent (US level).

Poverty, wealth
- The Baltic States offer low minimum wages: Lithuania EUR 3.72, Estonia EUR 3.48, Latvia EUR 2.54 (as of 2020). Ten years earlier they were, in this order: EUR 1.40, EUR 1.73 and EUR 1.68.

- That's why haulage companies, German and Swiss automotive suppliers set up here alongside digital corporations.[557] IKEA has wood processed here.
- After the financial crisis, pensions, unemployment benefits and their duration, and public sector salaries were cut.
- The cost of living is just below the EU average, VAT is high: 21, 21 and 20 percent.
- One-third of the population - including many elderly and pensioners, some of whom live in slums and rural areas - is considered poor.
- Alongside working-poor incomes, a few tens of thousands of software specialists in the rising middle class and owners of subcontracting firms earn many times more.

Mass emigration
While the populations grew until 1989, emigration began in 1991, especially of young qualified people. The reasons were unemployment, low wages and racism.
- Latvia: Out of 2.4 million people, 0.5 million have emigrated to date.
- Estonia: Out of 1.5 million, 150,000 emigrated.
- Lithuania: Out of 3.7 million, 900,000 emigrated.

Highest suicide rate
The second wave of emigration began after EU accession. Lithuania, which was particularly praised by the EU, produced the lowest life expectancy in the EU for its population, as well as the highest suicide rate among men in the world: it is 3.5 times higher than the EU average for ages 30 to 60.[558]

Industrial action in the public sector
Teachers and doctors earn between EUR 500 and 900 a month, buildings and technical equipment are in a state of disrepair. The too few and too poorly paid teachers and doctors maintain a kind of emergency operation in dilapidated schools and hospitals.

In Latvia, for example, teachers have been protesting since 2014. They are demanding not only an increase in their salaries, but also in the education budget. A rally of 7,000 teachers in 2014 was one of the largest rallies in decades.[559] Similarly for freelance and hospital doctors, midwives, carers and social workers in 2019.[560]

In Estonia, teachers, university and kindergarten employees have been organizing strikes repeatedly since 2012.[561] But the successes have been few and far between.

In 2019, 5,000 teachers went on indefinite strike at 230 schools in Lithuania. They demanded an increase in the average gross salary of EUR 800 a month. A third of the teachers work only part-time, sometimes less than 9 hours a week. The strike ended after almost two weeks. The government's promises remained unclear.[562] Likewise, for many years doctors have repeatedly gone on strike.[563]

Lithuania:
Logistics center of the EU

It is true that "growth" is reflected in GDP. But the share of labor income, at 40 percent, is the lowest in the EU. The EU success state produces the greatest labor injustice and the greatest labor and pension poverty.

Lithuania has the most special economic zones after Poland, in fact it is a single special economic zone itself. Tax exemption, state and EU subsidies, and arbitrariness on the part of entrepreneurs prevail here. There are practically no sectoral collective agreements. Joint wage and salary negotiations take place for only five percent of employees. With the European Social Fund, the EU promoted "social dialogue" between business associations and trade unions, but to no avail: The entrepreneurs were not interested, the trade unions were too weak.[564]

EU report: Social disaster reigns in Lithuania!
In 2019 the COM summed up the labor and social situation as follows:

- The minimum wage of 2008 – EUR 1.40 – was not increased until 2018.
- "The pension system cannot effectively protect the elderly from poverty and social exclusion."
- Unemployment is "about 20 percent".
- "Income inequality is among the highest in the EU and is driven primarily by income growth among top earners."
- "Old-age poverty remains a serious challenge."
- "The risk of poverty among people with disabilities is growing."
- "Poor health care is an ongoing challenge."

- "Lithuania has one of the highest rates of households unable to heat their homes in the winter and suffering from other rental costs."
- "High levels of homelessness persist."[565]

A center of the new EU labor injustice

On June 21, 2016, the Lithuanian Parliament adopted the new labor law. It was based on the proposals of the COM within the framework of the "European Semester". In no other EU state have the lowest standards of the ESSR, which breach human rights, been enforced as one-to-one as in Lithuania. The goal was to stop emigration, primarily by creating tens of thousands of new low-cost jobs.

As a result, since January 2017, dependent labor can be further disenfranchised, flexibilized, cheapened:[566]

- Introduction of the zero-hour contract.
- On-call work: Only actual working time is paid.
- Employment contract for project work: The employment relationship, which is not defined in terms of time, ends with the end of the project.
- Employees may enter into employment agreements with multiple employers at the same time.
- The daily working time may be increased to 12 hours.
- The overtime limit of previously 4 hours on two consecutive days can be increased to 12 hours per week. Collective agreements may further increase this figure.
- Annual leave is no longer calculated according to calendar days as before, but according to actual working days.
- Employees are liable for up to 6 months' salary for any damage they cause.
- Terms of notice and severance entitlements are reduced.

Protests against the labor law

A few hundred activists and members of the union of forest and wood workers LMPF protested against the labor law. They stayed overnight in tents in central squares in Kaunas and Vilnius. They distributed flyers. A few activists from other Eastern European countries, including Bosnia-Herzegovina, joined in solidarity.[567]

The General Secretary of the Building and Woodworkers International BWI, Ambet Yuson, came to Vilnius. Founded in 2005, BWI now has 365 affiliated unions and 12 million members from 127 countries, has its headquarters in Geneva and is involved with the ILO. Yuson expressed support for the protests. He made clear that most of Lithuania's workers are among the more than 50 percent working poor of dependent employees.

The Filipino trade unionist stated, "You should continue your protest and we will do our best to support it and make it known around the world. Workers around the world must unite."[568]

Employer practice: Even worse than the law
As elsewhere in the EU, employers undercut even the lowest standards, with impunity. For example, the Turkish construction company Kayi has been building a new soccer stadium on behalf of the city of Kaunas since March 2019. The 100 construction workers were brought in from Turkey.

In December 2019, some construction workers dared to go public: we are still not getting the agreed wage, but only EUR 200 a month, so that we can just survive somehow. As a result, Kayi paid some of them their wages and sent them back to Turkey. The other workers continue to be treated as before.

These conditions resemble those on construction sites in the sheikdom of Qatar, according to the construction union in the umbrella organization LPSK:

* no written contract
* only one day off in three weeks
* daily working time of 12-14 hours
* Kayi confiscates passports.[569]
* Government, labor inspectorate, COM – no protest.

The migrant army of truck drivers
The EU is turning Lithuania into an EU logistics center. The new labor law also serves this purpose: Tens of thousands of truck drivers have to be cheap, willing and voiceless. Digital platforms of the haulage companies monitor all trucks during their weeks-long journeys between Norway, Spain and Belarus and, prohibited under EU law, arrange as many further intermediate and additional jobs as possible in a timely manner.[570]

Girteka: Largest freight company in the EU
Hovering over the hundreds of small and medium-sized freight companies, mostly subcontractors, is Girteka Logistics, by its own account "Europe's largest full-service freight company". The current 7,400 trucks are to be expanded to 10,000 by 2021. The number of drivers is to be doubled from around 10,000 to 20,000 over the same period.[571]

The drivers are recruited from Eastern European and Asian countries and housed in collective accommodation for which they have to pay. Girteka has branches in other countries, for example at the Amazon site in Poznan, Poland. With the help of the Lithuanian location, the group is trying to undercut the previously dominant freight companies in the EU, such as UPS and Deutsche Post DHL.

EU money for the oligarch
Girteka is the largest of the 34 companies in the Me Investicija holding. The 90 percent shareholder and chairman of the board is the country's second richest man, Mindaugas Raila. (The richest, Numavicius, owner of supermarket chains in the Baltic States, Poland and Bulgaria, resides in London and pursues real estate business there.) In ten years, he increased his private fortune from EUR 50 to 750 million now. The empire includes financial services companies, the SIRIN company with real estate throughout Europe, and the Novaturas tour operator.[572]

From 2018 to 2021, the EU subsidized the oligarch's freight company to the tune of EUR 914,568 from the Regional Development Fund. This was used to develop a "real-time transport planning algorithm" for the group. Vilnius University received part of the funding for this. The algorithm is intended to optimize the current real-time monitoring, controlling and loading of freight vehicles across Europe.[573] This is also a tool for circumventing EU directives, e.g. on cabotage.

First aid for truckers
The 89,000 or so drivers who work for haulage companies based in Lithuania are attracted from Ukraine, Belarus, Poland and many even poorer countries such as Kazakhstan. They do not speak Lithuanian. They sign contracts they do not understand. They usually do not know how long they will be employed. They come without family and are happy when they get a place in collective accommodation. They don't dare to join a

union, that would be an obstacle to employment - nobody says that publicly, but everybody knows it.

Falsified pay slips

Audrius Cuzanauskas, president of the Lithuanian Trade Union Alliance, is busy documenting concealed employment and helping drivers who self-report. Contractors routinely falsify documents. "The written contracts can be very accurate. But I have a contract here: wages EUR 3,870 for 64.5 days. Correct. But we see: penciled in afterwards the deductions. Paid out at the end: EUR 600 euros."[574] Deductions for accommodation, penalties, placement fee, expenses - the exploitation fantasy knows no bounds, all under the protection of the EU.

Other violations of the law:
- In posting orders for EU and third countries there is nothing about duration and place of posting.
- Only some truck stops have drinking water, toilets and showers.
- Drivers are sometimes not allowed home for three to four months - but they don't know that at the beginning.
- Employers impose unpaid leave, which can last up to a year.

In Lithuania, there was outrage when the usual cartel of silence was disrupted by the interviews of a ZDF team. Cazanauskas reported from his information office, which the union has set up for truck drivers, "None of the 89,000 drivers get the correct pay, none. Most of them don't know anything about laws and minimum wages."[575]

Cazanauskas describes further fraudulent practices. In addition to the initially agreed freight order, additional orders are placed during the journey. They are organized via Internet exchanges and transmitted to the drivers by satellite. This circumvents cabotage: According to this, a foreign transporter would only be allowed to take on three additional orders within 7 days, for example. But the drivers are kept on the road abroad much longer and get many more additional orders. In case the drivers are caught, they get enough cash up front from the employer to pay the fine as soon as possible. The EU Member States are supposed to control cabotage, but everywhere it is only enough for a few spot checks - a practiced mechanism.

For the drivers, union membership is practically impossible. Therefore, Cazanauskas & colleagues have only first aid left: documenting violations of the law, supporting complaints and, in the best case, a lawsuit in court: "We have 500 cases in court."

8.
Associated states

The EU intervenes in many other states, for example through trade agreements and military relations. Not considered here are the relations with states outside Europe:

- European Economic Area EEA: The 27 EU states with Iceland, Norway, Liechtenstein.
- official candidate states: Serbia, Northern Macedonia, Albania, Montenegro, Turkey
- potential candidate countries: the protectorates of Kosovo and Bosnia-Herzegovina
- Eastern Partnership: Ukraine, Moldova, Armenia, Azerbaijan, Georgia, Belarus.

We have already dealt with Northern Macedonia. There is still room here for Switzerland: it is formally the least involved, but is particularly important.

Switzerland:
"We went on strike against our invisibility"

Switzerland is considered "neutral", but it is firmly integrated into Western capitalism and the EU, both above and below ground, as a financial haven, as an intelligence base, as a participant in US-led wars, as the site of the Bank for International Settlements BIS (Central Bank of Central Banks), as a location for corporations with numerous sites in the EU such as Nestlé, Novartis, the banks UBS and Julius Baer, Zurich Insurance, the state-owned arms company RUAG, the temporary employment company Adecco.

The financial haven is also a popular location for global organizations such as the Red Cross, FIFA, the International Olympic Committee and the World Economic Forum. The traditional stronghold of numbered accounts and shell companies enables tax evasion, corruption, illegal financing of pro-capital parties, fraud, arms trading and environmental pollution on a global scale in the middle of Europe - the EU does not mind.[576]

In 2001, the Swiss voted 77 percent against EU membership in a referendum. However, the liberal and conservative governments want their clientele to have the most direct access possible to the EU's internal market. To this end, the EU and Switzerland have concluded bilateral agreements. The protection of dependent employees is not among them.

Against the EU: "Protect wages, not borders"

Since 2014, the COM has been demanding that Switzerland renegotiate the existing agreements. However, the Swiss Federation of Trade Unions (SGB) has put its foot down, refusing to go along with the further weakening of wage protection demanded by the COM. The negotiations are stagnating - a good sign for the influence of a union. The new COM President von der Leyen has lost patience. At the World Economic Forum 2020 in Davos, she met with Swiss Federal Council President Sommaruga. They want to make a new start.[577]

German construction companies demand: Relax wage protection!
Construction companies from Austria and Baden-Württemberg have been exerting pressure for years: They want to send construction workers and craftsmen to large construction sites in Switzerland via subcontractors, under illegal conditions, as documented by the Swiss trade union UNIA.[578]

Entrepreneurs complain about "too much bureaucracy", Swiss authorities control too much: Are they dealing with pseudo self-employed? Is the EU Posted Workers Directive being observed, according to which Swiss wages must be paid?

UNIA: Union investigates fraudulent entrepreneurs
This much rule of law is too much for German and Austrian entrepreneurs. They are used to getting away with fraud. But in Switzerland, more and more breaches of the law are being uncovered. The UNIA trade un-

ion, in particular, is uncovering a lot; it is more active than the competent authorities.

UNIA member Christa Suter set up a specialist unit to prevent wage dumping. She put together an investigative team, and some members got themselves hired as construction workers. Suter also investigated the working conditions at the Austrian building contractor Goger. He was involved in prestigious buildings, an art academy, a museum, and the Atlantis luxury hotel.

Suter compiled testimony from Hungarian workers. But Goger had ace attornies pick their oral testimony apart in court. Suter therefore traveled to Hungary to get written statements from laid-off workers there: Goger, through his subsidiary Goger Swiss, had prepared correct pay stubs for the Hungarian workers, but had forced the workers to subsequently pay back a portion in cash. In addition, he had deducted SFR 600 a month for their accommodation, while he himself paid much less in rent for the accommodation. Suter was also able to prove that Goger had not paid SFR 3.4 million for overtime. He has since fled to Austria and is wanted on a Swiss arrest warrant.[579]

Most breaches of the law will probably never be uncovered. This is because public and private clients are also interested in low construction costs. UNIA made it plain to the authorities: The usual examination of written documents is not enough! This goes too far for the EU. The COM wants to repress this "bureaucracy" in the new treaty with Switzerland.

Against the EU: "Protect wages, not borders"
With its campaign "Protect wages, not borders!" the SGB opposes the EU. The European Trade Union Confederation ETUC supports the campaign. They demand controls and sanctions against wage dumping. Also because of wage dumping, poverty has spread in "rich" Switzerland – one in twelve is officially poor, in reality there are more. Wage dumping affects many women.

The campaign has European significance, explains ETUC General Secretary Luca Visentini: "If wage protection falls in Switzerland, this would also have consequences for workers in other EU countries. The majority of construction workers who are members of the UNIA union have foreign passports anyway. The fight against wage dumping is also a fight against nationalism."[580]

12,000 construction workers took part in a UNIA survey on working conditions, occupational safety, deadline pressure, health, occupational accidents, leisure and family, and breaches of the law by employers. Every year, employers tolerate 20 fatal accidents. Since February 2020, UNIA has been organizing decentralized meetings throughout Switzerland with the survey results: Construction workers share their experiences, formulate their demands together.[581]

"We went on strike against our invisibility"

Trade unions in Switzerland were strong after World War II. Until 1948, they fought for wage increases and new rights in numerous strikes - the bad conscience of Swiss banks, companies and also the government because of their collaboration with Nazi Germany had an effect.

But with Switzerland's involvement in Western anti-communism, the unions were weakened. The low point was in the 1980s. However: At least legally, the right to strike was not touched "as long as it was a matter of teaching the regimes of the Eastern bloc lessons in freedom," according to SGB President Paul Rechsteiner. But after the collapse of socialism, the employers got cocky.

After a while, the unions found their way back to resistance. In the late 1990s, they succeeded in getting the right to strike included in the new constitution. In 2002, 15,000 construction workers went on a nationwide strike for the first time in half a century, blocking tunnels and transport hubs. One of their successes was early retirement from the age of 60 - it still applies today.[582]

Grassroots democracy with particularly fierce oppression of women

In Switzerland, vaunted for its grassroots democracy, women were the last in Europe to be granted the right to vote, in 1971. The purchase of women for sexual services flourishes particularly lavishly here, with both luxury, normal and cheap prostitutes from all over the world. Labor discrimination and the displacement into unpaid and poorly paid work has been further exacerbated in the course of the neoliberal reign.[583]

A strike committee therefore spent months preparing a women's strike in 2019. The climax was July 14, 2019, when more than half a million women took part in a wide variety of actions: extended strike and coffee breaks in administration bodies and companies, car corsos, baby buggy demonstrations, even church bells began to ring just as the strike began.

Women from a wide variety of professions participated, young and mid-dle-aged and older, local and foreign. Farmers' wives and rural women also joined in, three quarters of them are not covered by social security.

Largest nationwide women's strike in history
The climax was the closing rallies in numerous cities. The turnout reached unprecedented levels for Switzerland: 160,000 in Zurich, 60,000 in Lausanne, 40,000 each in Bern and Basel. In smaller cities, up to 10,000 women came together - historically unparalleled.

Back in March 2019, the strike collective had already published a manifesto with 17 demands, including:

- Controls and sanctions on fraudulent employers and subcontractors.
- Joint employment contracts in industries with a high proportion of women
- Work in private households and on farms must be brought under the general labor law
- Subsistence pensions
- More time and money for care work
- End of on-call work
- Penalization of sexual violence in the workplace
- Reduction in gainful employment to 30 hours a week.

The actions, strikes and rallies were enlivened by variously printed T-shirts, buttons, scarves, individual and group banners.

"That's how we drew attention to ourselves that day - we were striking against our invisibility," summed up Nadine Swan, a volunteer member of the strike coordination team in Bern.[584]

Abbreviations

ACUE	American Committee on United Europe (Allen Dulles/CIA)
ACUSE	Action Committee for the United Staates of Europe (Jean Monnet)
AFL/CIO	American Federation of Labour/Congress of Industrial Organizations
BDA	Confederation of German Employers' Associations
BDI	Federation of German Industries
BetrVG	Betriebsverfassungs-Gesetz (Works Constitution Act)
BIS	Bank for International Settlements
CEO	Corporate Europe Observatory
CIA	Central Intelligence Agency
COM	European Commission
DGB	German Trade Union Confederation
DLF	Deutschlandfunk
EC	European Community
ECB	European Central Bank
ECHR	European Convention on Human Rights
ECJ	European Court of Justice
ECtHR	European Court of Human Rights
ECSC	European Coal and Steel Community
EEA	European Economic Area
EEC	European Economic Community
ESF	European Social Fund
EPSR	European Pillar of Social Rights
ETUC	European Trade Union Confederation
ETUI	European Trade Union Institute
EU	European Union

FAZ	Frankfurter Allgemeine Zeitung
FC	Fullfillment Center
FTUC	Free Trade Union Committee
GAMFA	Google Apple Microsoft Facebook Amazon
GDP	Gross domestic product
GLB	Gewerkschaftlicher Linksblock (Österreich)
HB	Handelsblatt
ICFTU	International Confederation of Free Trade Unions
ILO	International Labor Organization
ITF	International Transport Workers' Federation
NATO	North Atlantic Treaty Organization
NYT	New York Times
OECD	Organization for Economic Cooperation and Development
OLAF	European Anti-Fraud Office in the COM
OSS	Office of Strategic Services (predecessor of the CIA)
PWC	Price Waterhouse Coopers
SEZ	Special Economic Zone
SZ	Süddeutsche Zeitung
UNIA	Largest union in Switzerland
WIIW	Vienna Institute for International Economic Studies

Glossary

Action Committee for the United States of Europe (ACUSE): Organization for (Western) European unification headed by Jean Monnet from 1955.

Action Committee on United States of Europe (ACUE): Organization for (Western) European unification headed by CIA chief Allen Dulles from 1948.

Binding Treaty: Framework obliging companies to respect human rights in their cross-border supply and service chains reinforced with sanctions; blocked by the EU and the USA.

Capitalist bureaucracy: Coordination of the interests of, above all, the powerful capitalists by a non-transparent, privileged state or state-like bureaucracy such as the COM.

Capitalist democracy: Democracy directly and/or indirectly influenced or dominated by capital, especially through a combination of government parties permanently financed by corporations, assumption of public tasks by corporate foundations, private perma-consulting of authorities, ministries and governments, professional corporate lobbying as well as revolving door mechanisms: ex-politicians as paid agents of influence. Freedom of expression primarily owned by private and state media, including "social" media owned by private digital corporations.

Dependent employees: All those working under the instructions of private and state employers, from the bottom (illegal, precarious, unemployed) to almost the top (managers, consultants, senior civil servants). Variously and contentiously lumped together in the working class.

Directive: Supra- and extra-legal directive, preferred legal instrument of the EU.

Disenfranchisement: Legal and extralegal degradation or downgrading

Economy: "The economy" = populist disguise for capitalists and capitalism. Coded term for "the companies" to the exclusion of dependent employees.

European Pillar of Social Rights EPSR: Temporally last codification of EU labor injustice. Recognizes all forms of precariousness including zero-hour contracts.

Exploitation: Illegal appropriation of third-party resources, such as labor, nature, property, data, in excess of common needs

Fair labor conditions: This EU-typical demand, most recently in the EPSR, is characterized by 1. legal fuzziness, 2. legally unregulated procedures, 3. accord aimed at current accord with the "employers".

Flexicurity: Concept of the COM, according to which flexibility could be combined with security.

Free trade treaty: Promotes transnational private investment. The rights of large investors are enforceable in private arbitration tribunals; the rights of dependent employees are not.

Globalization: Cover-up term for the US-led global expansion of Western capitalists (including from Japan, Taiwan, and the Gulf States), also associated with rights violations and global labor exploitation.

Human rights: According to the EU mind, civil rights such as freedom of assembly and expression, protection of minorities and sexual freedom of choice, but exclusion of UN and ILO social and labor rights. Propagates advancement of women to leadership positions while simultaneously promoting the exploitation of the majority of women in the workforce.

Industrial society: Cover-up term for capitalist society; similar: consumer, service, and risk society.

International Labor Organization (ILO): Institution of the League of Nations granted in the wake the uprisings and revolutions of the workers' movement after World War 1. At that time with rights such as 8-hour day and freedom of trade union self-organization. Since 1946 sub-organization of the UN. Like the UN, the ILO was disempowered by the representatives of Western "globalization".

Labor injustice: 1. Violation of labor rights in Article 23 of the UN Declaration of Universal Human Rights, 2. violation of International Labor Organization ILO conventions, 3. violation of EU directives and national laws of EU Member States.

Populism: When entrepreneurs, consultants, politicians, media promise jobs, prosperity, security, peace, sufficient pensions and environmental protection, but cannot, should not, will not, are not allowed to realize them because they directly or indirectly serve hidden interests of private minorities.

Vassal: Person or state contractually or extra-contractually obligated to a suzerain for military contributions and economic privileges, but with liberties to dominate and exploit its own subjects or citizens.

Bibliography (selection)

Alleva, Vania/Andreas Rieger (Hg.): Streik im 21. Jahrhundert. Zürich 2017

Anderson, Elizabeth: Private Government. How Employers Rule Our Life and Why We Don't Talk About It. Princeton 2017

Backes, Ernest/Denis Robert: Das Schweigen des Geldes. Zürich 2003

Balanyá, Belén u.a.: Europe Inc. Regional and Global Restructuring and the Rise of Corporate Power. London 2000

Berghahn, Volker: The Americanization of West German Industry 1945 – 1973. New York 1986

Blanke, Thomas: Die Entscheidungen des EUGH in den Fällen Viking, Laval und Rueffert. Oldenburger Studien zur Europäisierung und zur transnationalen Regulierung Nr. 18/2008

Böwe, Joern/Johannes Schulten: Der lange Kampf der Amazon-Beschäftigten, Berlin 2019

Booker, Christopher/Richard North: The Great Deception. A Secret History of the European Union. New York/London 2003

Bossuat, Gérard: La France, l'aide américaine et la construction européenne 1944 – 1954. Paris 1992

Branco, Juan: Crépuscule. Emmauel Macron et ses amis. Massot Éditions 2019

Carew, Anthony: American Labour's Cold War Abroad 1945 – 1970. Edmonton 2018

Clauwaert, Stefan/Isabelle Schömann (ETUI): The crisis and national labour law reforms. Brussels 2012

Corporate Europe Observatory (CEO): Accounting for Influence – how the Big Four are embedded in EU policy-making on tax avoidance, Amsterdam 2018

Däubler, Wolfgang: Die Entwicklung des Arbeits-Völkerrechts, in: Monika Schlachter u.a. (Hg.): Arbeitsvölkerrecht, Tübingen 2019, p.5 - 36

Damjanovski, Gjorgji: Overview of Foreign Direct Investment Strategies of Multinational Companies – The Case of Western Macedonia, Ljublyana Sept. 2016

EFFAT: Covid-19 outbreaks in slaughterhouses and meat processing plants in Europe, Brüssel 30.6.2020

Egger de Campo, Marianne: Seniorensitterinnen? Globale Dienstbotinnen? Personenbetreuerinnen! ApuZ 38-39/2015

Europäischer Wirtschafts- und Sozialausschuss: Die wirtschaftliche und soziale Lage in den baltischen Staaten, Brüssel 2013

European Commission: Flash Reports on Labour Law, Brussels 2019

Europäische Kommission: Grünbuch - Ein moderneres Arbeitsrecht für die Herausforderungen des 21. Jahrhunderts, Brüssel 2006

Fischer-Lescano, Andreas: Austeritätspolitik und Menschenrechte. Rechtspflichten der Unionsorgane beim Abschluss von Memoranda of Understanding, Wien 2014

Francisco, Trillo u.a.: Offensive contre le droit du travail et les syndicats en Espagne, in: Gresea Echos 88/2016, S. 23-30

Friedrich Ebert-Stiftung: Der lange Weg nach Europa – Kroatiens EU-Beitritt, Bonn Juli 2013

Gagyi, Agnes/Tamas Geröcs: Die politische Ökonomie des neuen ungarischen „Sklaven-Gesetzes", in: IG Metall: transnationale einblicke, Januar 2019

Gewerkschaftslinke Hamburg (Hg.): Das System Tönnies – Organisierte Kriminalität und moderne Sklaverei. Berlin 2020

Gillingham, John: Zur Vorgeschichte der Montanunion. Westeuropas Kohle und Stahl in Depression und Krieg, Vierteljahresheft für Zeitgeschichte 3/1986

Hartz, Peter: Job-Revolution. Wie wir neue Arbeitsplätze bekommen können. Frankfurt/Main 2001

Heinisch, Brigitte: Satt und sauber? Eine Altenpflegerin kämpft gegen den Pflegenotstand. Vorwort von Werner Rügemer, Einbek/Berlin 2008

Hellmann, Rainer: Amerika auf dem Europamarkt. US-Direktinvestitionen im Gemeinsamen Markt. Baden-Baden 1966

Hogan, Michael: The Marshall-Plan. America, Britain and the reconstruction of Western Europe 1947-1952. New York/Melbourne 1987

Horvat, Srecko: Der Zerfall Jugoslawiens und die Krise der EU, in: David Goeßmann/Fabian Scheidler: Der Kampf für globale Gerechtigkeit, Wien 2019

Investigate Europe: Race to the Bottom: Europe's Precariat, 12.9.2018

Jenkins, Simon: Thatcher & Sons. London/New York 2006

Labour Party: It's time for real change. Labour Party Manifesto 2019

Lacroix-Riz, Annie: Industriels et Banquiers sous l' Occupation. La
  Collaboration Économique avec le Reich et Vichy, Paris 1999

Lebor, Adam: Tower of Basel. New York 2013

McCabe, Conor: Sins of the Father. The decisions that shaped the irish economy.
  Dublin 2013

Meier, Stefan: Nähen zum Hungerlohn. Billigtextilien vom Balkan, arte-TV
  13.1.2020

Monnet, Jean: Mémoires. Paris 1976

OECD: Who Cares? Attracting and Retaining Car Workers for the Elderly, Paris
  2020

Opitz, Reinhard (Hg.): Europastrategien des deutschen Kapitals 1900 – 1945,
  Köln 1977

Panitch, Leo/Sam Gindin: The Making of Global Capitalism. London 2013

Pauwels, Jacques: Big Business avec Hitler, Brussels 2013

Rasnaca, Zane/Magdalena Bernaciak (Hg.): Posting of workers before national
  courts. ETUI, Brussels 2020

Richter, Hedwig: Die Komplexität der Integration. Arbeitsmigration in die
  Bundesrepublik Deutschland von den 50er bis in die 70er Jahre.
  www.zeitgeschichte-online.de

Rügemer, Werner: Strukturveränderungen in der Lebens- und Arbeitssituation
  abhängig Beschäftigter in den USA, WSI-Mitteilungen 6/1986

Rügemer, Werner: RatingAgenturen. Einblicke in die Kapitalmacht der
  Gegenwart. 2. Auflage Bielefeld 2012

Rügemer, Werner: Travail et non-travail dans l'Union Européenne, in: Les
  Possibles 11/2016

Rügemer, Werner/Elmar Wigand: Die Fertigmacher. Arbeitsunrecht und
  professionelle Gewerkschaftsbekämpfung. 3. erweiterte Auflage, Köln 2017

Rügemer, Werner: Commerzbank: „America First". Bundesregierung missachtet
  deutsches Arbeitsrecht, arbeitsunrecht.de 20.11.2017

Rügemer, Werner: Das charmante Gesicht der Ausbeutung Europas. Christine
  Lagarde wird Präsidentin der EZB, www.nachdenkseiten.de 4.11.2019

Rügemer, Werner: Friede braucht Gerechtigkeit. ILO – vor 100 Jahren Gründung der Internationalen Arbeitsorganisation, ver.di publik 3/2019

Rügemer, Werner: Arbeitsrechte – Blindstelle im Grundgesetz, https://arbeitsunrecht.de 23.5.2019

Rügemer, Werner: Unternehmer als straflose Rechtsbrecher, in: K.-J. Bruder u.a. (Hg.): Gesellschaftliche Spaltungen, Gießen 2018, S. 207 – 222

Rügemer, Werner: Das „System Tönnies" endlich stoppen! arbeitsunrecht.de 12.9.2019

Rügemer, Werner: The Capitalists of the 21st Century. An Easy-to-Understand Outline on the Rise of the New Financial Players, tredition 2020

Rügemer, Werner: Covid-19: Korrumpierte Wissenschaft, nachdenkseiten.de 6.5.2020

Shaxson, Nicholas: The Finance Curse, London 2018

Thum, Horst: Mitbestimmung in der Montanindustrie. Der Mythos vom Sieg der Gewerkschaften. Stuttgart 1982

U.N. Human Rights Council: Spain – Report on extreme poverty and human rights, Genf Juli 2020 A/HRC/44/40/Add.2

WIIW: Decoupling of Labour Productivity Growth from Median Wage Growth in Central and Eastern Europe, July 2020

Villiers, Philippe de: J' ai tiré sur le fil du mensonge et tout est venu, Paris 2019

Wahl, Asbjörn: The Rise and Fall of the Welfare State. London 2011

Wirtschaftskammer Österreich: Österreich in der EU, Wien, Jänner 2020

Ziegler, Jean: Die Schande Europas. Von Flüchtlingen und Menschenrechten. München 2020

Annotations

[1] europa.eu/european-union/topics/health_en, downloaded 04.17.2020

[2] Werner Rügemer / Elmar Wigand: Die Fertigmacher. ArbeitsUnrecht und professionelle Gewerkschaftsbekämpfung, 3., erweiterte Auflage, Köln 2017, p.211ff.

[3] Rügemer / Wigand: Die Fertigmacher, loc. cit., p.214f.

[4] Medizinökonomen gehen von rund 1,6 Millionen aufgeschobenen Operationen aus, aerzteblatt.de, downloaded 04.29.2020

[5] Gemeinsame Presseerklärung der externen Experten des Bundesinnenministeriums 05.11.2020, abendzeitung-muenchen.de, downloaded 06.05.2020

[6] Das Sterben der anderen, Der Spiegel 24/2020, p.26-32

[7] European Observatory on Health Systems: Diagnosis-Related Groups in Europe, Berkshire / New York 2011

[8] Werner Rügemer: Covid-19: Korrumpierte Wissenschaft, nachdenkseiten.de, 05.06.2020

[9] www.ghsindex.org, downloaded 03.25.2020

[10] Rügemer: Covid-19 – Korrumpierte Wissenschaft, loc. cit.; the Charité and the Robert-Koch-Institut also receive donations from the Bill and Melinda Gates Foundation.

[11] Emma Clancy: Austerity Kills. EU Commission Demanded Cuts to Public Health Care Spending 63 Times from 2011 – 2018, braveneweurope.com, 03.28.2020

[12] »Ohne Vorerkrankung ist an Covid-19 noch keiner gestorben«, Hamburger Morgenpost, 04.03.2020

[13] Klaus Püschel: Tote schweigen nicht. Faszinierende Fälle aus der Rechtsmedizin. Hamburg 2020

[14] Die soziale Infektion. Darüber entscheiden auch Vermögen und Bildung, Der Spiegel, 06.20.2020

[15] Amerikas Armutszeugnis, FAZ, 06.03.2020; Is the pandemic waning or raging? New York Times (NYT), 06.03.2020; A vast inequality in risk, NYT, 04.29.2020

[16] When Covid-19 deaths are analyzed by age, America is an outlier, Economist, 06.24.2020

[17] The food chain's weakest link: Slaughterhouses, NYT, 04.20.2020

[18] The top US hot spots are all Indian lands, NYT, 06.04.2020

[19] A small hospital's struggle with the coronavirus, NYT, 08.06.2020

[20] Elizabeth Williamson i.a.: Open SAFELY – factors associated with COVID-19 related hospital deaths in the linked electronic records of 17 million adult NHS patients, Nature, 07.08.2020

[21] Werner Rügemer: BlackRock & Co, der Schlachtkonzern Tyson und die USA in Zeiten der Pandemie, arbeitsunrecht.de, 05.28.2020

[22] Jens Berger: Wer Menschen dauerhaft ausgrenzt, kann nicht auf deren »Selbstverantwortung« pochen, nachdenkseiten.de, 06.05.2020

[23] de.wikipedia.org/wiki/Covid-19-Pandemie_im_Landkreis_Tirschenreuth, downloaded 06.05.2020

[24] Studie: Arbeitslose haben höheres Risiko für Corona-Klinikaufenthalt, neues deutschland, 06.16.2020

[25] Werner Rügemer: Hoch-Risikogruppe Fleischarbeiter, nachdenkseiten.de, 05.13.2020

[26] WDR-TV extra 06.17.2020, 20.15h

[27] Sorge wegen Arbeitskräften aus dem Ausland, Handelsblatt (HB), 03.30.2020

[28] Ministerium für Arbeit, Gesundheit und Soziales des Landes NRW: Abschlussbericht der Überwachungsaktion »Faire Arbeit in der Fleischindustrie«, 01.20.2020

[29] Abbasali Kaseinasab i.a.: Respiratory Disorders among Workers in Slaughterhouses, Safety and Health at Work 08/2017, p.84-88

[30] European Federation of Food, Agriculture and Tourism Trade Unions (EFFAT): Covid-19 outbreaks in slaughterhouses and meat processing plants, Brussels 06.30.2020

[31] Werner Rügemer: Werkverträge in der Fleischindustrie abschaffen? Das vordergründige Skandal-Management der Bundesregierung – Lügen inbegriffen, nachdenkseiten.de, 06.05.2020

[32] Werner Rügemer: Infektionsschutz-Gesetz: Warum fehlen die Unternehmen? www.nachdenkseiten.de 11.25.2020

[33] Irgendwie offen bleiben, Die Zeit, 08.27.2020

[34] https://s-f.com/wirbleibenzuhause-scholz-friends-kommuniziert-in-der-coronakrise-fuer-das-bmg

[35] Die Arbeitslosigkeit – nicht wegen Corona, FAZ, 07.31.2020

[36] Interview mit Vorstandsmitglied der Arbeitsagentur Daniel Terzenbach, FAZ, 07.27.2020

[37] Kurzarbeit: Belastung für Arbeitnehmer, Gewinn für Unternehmen, Kontraste/ARD, 06.04.2020

[38] Werner Rügemer: Die staatliche Lufthansa-Rettung – Eine Schmierenkomödie,

mehrfach, nachdenkseiten.de, 06.29.2020
[39] Europas brutaler Kampf um Ärzte, FAZ, 07.21.2020
[40] Mehr privatisieren. Studie von Charité Global Health und Bill & Melinda Gates Foundation, corodok.de, 06.04.2020
[41] Solider Mittelstand in Existenznot. Schon vor der Pandemie schwächelte jedes dritte Unternehmen, HB, 04.20.2020
[42] Siehe: Jahresüberschüsse der DAX-Mitglieder 2000 – 2019, Handelsblatt, 07.08.2020
[43] Automarkt im Wandel, HB, 04.27.2020
[44] Cum-Ex-Fälle drohen zu verjähren, tagesschau.de, 24.03.2020
[45] Kohleausstieg: Viel Geld für wenig Klimaschutz, Monitor/ARD, 07.09.2020
[46] Mehr Geld für Deutschland und Frankreich, FAZ, 08.03.2020
[47] Öl- und Kohle-Investor BlackRock soll EU bei Nachhaltigkeitsthemen beraten, ecoreporter.de, 04.15.2020
[48] On EU dependence on GAMFA even before "corona" see Werner Rügemer: Die Kapitalisten des 21. Jahrhunderts. Gemeinverständlicher Abriss zum Aufstieg der neuen Finanzakteure, 3. Auflage, Köln 2021, p.153ff. with updated introduction on corona, the system winner China and on the military buildup of the US-led West
[49] Big Tech, eager to get bigger, seizes the moment, NYT, 06.15.2020
[50] Interview mit dem Datenrechtler Peter Hense, SZ, 07.27.2020
[51] Big Tech: Digitaler Kolonialismus, HB, 06.03.2020
[52] Krankenhäuser retten – Schließungen stoppen! www.gemeingut.org, 05.22.2020
[53] Mausebär und Schneewittchen im Großherzogtum, in: Werner Rügemer: Bis diese Freiheit die Welt erleuchtet, Köln 2017, p.139ff; Werner Rügemer: Das wahre hässliche Gesicht der EU, lunapark21.net, 03.20.2020
[54] Die Linke im Europaparlament: Eine Kriegskasse namens Friedensfazilität, 06.03.2020
[55] Coronavirus could make US gun problem even deadlier, NYT, 06.15.2020
[56] Jung, am Leben verzweifelt, Welt am Sonntag, 06.28.2020, based on a report by the US health authority CDC
[57] Amerikas Offenbarungseid, HB, 06.03.2020
[58] Werner Rügemer: Deutsche Wohnen auf Expansionskurs, ver.di publik 04/2020
[59] Rügemer, Die Kapitalisten des 21. Jahrhunderts, loc. cit., p.235ff.
[60] Cf. Larry Fink's Letter to Shareholders, blackrock.com/corporate/investor-relations, 03.29.2020
[61] Rügemer: Die Kapitalisten des 21. Jahrhunderts, loc. cit., Introduction
[62] Werner Rügemer: Unternehmer als straflose Rechtsbrecher, in: Klaus-Jürgen

Bruder u.a. (Hg.): Gesellschaftliche Spaltungen, Gießen 2018, p.207ff.

[63] Rügemer: Die Kapitalisten des 21. Jahrhunderts, loc.cit., p.31ff

[64] Peter Kossen: EU-Arbeitsmigranten – krasse Ausbeutung und eine Mehrklassengesellschaft auf dem Arbeitsmarkt, in: Das Schweinesystem, Berlin 2020, p.47

[65] Elizabeth Arden: Private Government. How Employers Rule Our Lives and Why We Don't Talk About It, Princeton 2017

[66] Rügemer / Wigand: Die Fertigmacher, loc.cit., p.65ff.

[67] WIIW: Decoupling of Labour Productivity Growth from Median Wage Growth in Central and Eastern Europe, July 2020

[68] Werner Rügemer: Friede braucht Gerechtigkeit. ILO – vor 100 Jahren Gründung der Internationalen Arbeitsorganisation, ver.di publik 3/201

[69] www.ilo.org/berlin/arbeits-und-standards.de

[70] Wolfgang Däubler: Die Entwicklung des Arbeitsvölkerrechts, in: Monika Schlachter u. a. (Hg.): Arbeitsvölkerrecht, Tübingen 2019, p.5-36

[71] Werner Rügemer: Arbeitsrechte – Blindstelle im Grundgesetz, arbeitsunrecht.de, 05.23.2019

[72] Allgemeine Menschenrechte der UNO, www.menschenrechtserklaerung.de

[73] European Pillar of Social Rights, ec.europa.eu/commission/sites

[74] ilo.org/wcmsp5/groups/public, downloaded 01.07.2020

[75] Werner Rügemer: Das Transpazifische Freihandelsabkommen TTIP: Augenwischerei bei den Arbeitsrechten, DGB Gegenblende, 12.10.2015

[76] Werner Rügemer: Strategien zur Belegschaftsübernahme. Eröffnungsrede zur Konferenz Workers' Buy Out, Berlin 21./22.6.2020, arbeitsunrecht.de, 06.24.2020

[77] »Europa steht am Scheideweg«, bundesregierung.de/breg-de/aktuelles/-europa-steht-am-scheideweg, 06.04.2018; the Commission published its white paper on the future of Europe in 2017

[78] Wikipedia: List of countries by public debt, auf Grundlage von CIA: The World Factbook, downloaded 06.05.2020

[79] Rügemer: Die Kapitalisten des 21. Jahrhunderts, loc.cit, p.231ff.

[80] Jean Ziegler: Die Schande Europas. Von Flüchtlingen und Menschenrechten, München 2020

[81] Wanderarbeiterkonvention.de

[82] See lieferkettengesetz.de

[83] United Nations Declaration on the Rights of Peasants and other People Working in Rural Areas (UNDROP), UN-Resolution 73/165 of 12.17.2019

[84] ilo.org/ilc/ILCSessions/108, June 22, 2019

[85] Didier Eribon: Linke Bewegungen wie Podemos und Nuit Debout klingen oft wie Rechtsradikale, Die Zeit online, 07.04.2016

[86] Anthony Carew: American Labour's Cold War Abroad 1945 – 1970, Edmonton 2018

[87] Reinhard Kühnl / Eckart Spoo (Hg.): Was aus Deutschland werden sollte. Konzepte des Widerstands des Exils und der Alliierten, Heilbronn 1995

[88] Das Manifest von Ventotene, www.cvce.eu/de/obj/das_manifest_von_ventotene_1941

[89] Adam Lebor: Tower of Basel. The Shadowy History of the Secret Bank that Runs the World, New York 2013

[90] Reinhard Opitz (Hg.): Europastrategien des deutschen Kapitals 1900 – 1945, Köln 1977, p.581

[91] Opitz, Europastrategien, loc.cit., p.629

[92] Annie Lacroix-Riz: Industriels et Banquiers sous l'Occupation. La Collaboration Économique avec le Reich et Vichy, Paris 1999; Ingolf Gritschneder /Werner Rügemer: Hehler für Hitler. Die geheimen Aufträge der Firma Otto Wolff, WDR/ARD 2001

[93] Leo Panitch / Sam Gindin: The Making of Global Capitalism, London 2013, p.89ff.

[94] Adam Lebor: Tower of Basel, New York 2013, p.140ff.

[95] Werner Rügemer: NATO – Die Gründungslüge, nachdenkseiten.de, 04.04.2018

[96] Judith Jeffrey: Ambiguous Commitments and Uncertain Politics. The Truman Doctrine in Greece 1947 – 1952, New York 2000

[97] Heinz Richter: Griechenland 1940 – 1950. Die Zeit der Bürgerkriege, Mainz 2012, p.156ff.

[98] Mira Wilkins: The Maturing of Multinational Enterprises. American Business Abroad from 1914 to 1970, Cambridge/Mass. 1994, p.330

[99] Rainer Hellmann: Amerika auf dem Europamarkt. US-Direktinvestitionen im Gemeinsamen Markt, Baden-Baden 1966, p.43ff.

[100] Kurt Viermetz: Magie der Märkte. Meine Geschichte als internationaler Banker, Hamburg 2014, p.56ff

[101] Hellmann: Amerika auf dem Europamarkt, loc.cit., p.52f.

[102] Hellmann, ibid., p.53

[103] Hellmann, ibid., p.54

[104] Ernest Backes / Denis Robert: Das Schweigen des Geldes. Die Clearstream--Affäre. Zürich 2003, p.332

[105] Luxleaks whistleblower sentenced again, EU Observer, 15.3.2017, downloaded 05.10.2020

[106] Backes / Robert, loc.cit, p.332

[107] Hellmann, loc.cit., p.211

[108] Hellmann, ibid., p.164

[109] Hellmann, ibid., p.84

[110] Werner Rügemer: Strukturveränderungen in der Lebens- und Arbeitssituation abhängig Beschäftigter in den USA, WSI-Mitteilungen 6/1986, p.394ff.

[111] Werner Rügemer: Donald Trump. Presidente des Estados Unidos – la Vision de Europa, Mundo Siglo XXI (Mexiko) Nr. 41/2017; ders.: Clinton/Trump – Varianten des Populismus, Ossietzky 24/2016

[112] Werner Rügemer: Privatisierung in Deutschland – Eine Bilanz. Von der Treuhand zu Public Private Partnership. 4., erweiterte und aktualisierte Auflage, Münster 2008, p.38ff.

[113] Rügemer: Die Kapitalisten des 21. Jahrhunderts, loc.cit., p.153ff

[114] Melvyn Leffler: The Struggle for Germany and the Origins of the Cold War. German Historical Institute, Washington D.C., Occasional Paper No 16/1996, p.51f.

[115] Walter Lippmann: US Foreign Policy. Shield of the Republic, Boston 1943, deutsche Übersetzung: Die Außenpolitik der Vereinigten Staaten, Spiegel Verlag, Zürich 1944, p.120ff.

[116] Gérard Bossuat: La France, l'aide américaine et la construction européenne 1944 – 1954, Paris 1992, p.356 and 380

[117] Christopher Booker / Richard North: The Great Deception. A Secret History of the European Union, New York 2003, p.38

[118] Seymour Hersh: CIA Said to Have Aided Plotters Who Overthrew Nkrumah in Ghana, NYT, 05.09.1978

[119] Nicolas Lewkovicz: The German Question and the International Order 1943 – 48. London 2010, p.55 and 61; Kai Bird: The Chairman John McCloy. The Making of the American Establishment, New York 1992, p.292

[120] Leffler: The Struggle for Germany, loc. cit., p.56

[121] Bossuat: La France, loc. cit., p.484ff.

[122] Bird: The Chairman, loc. cit., p.296

[123] Wolfgang Reinhard: Die Unterwerfung der Welt. Globalgeschichte der europäischen Expansion 1415-2015, München 2016, p.1139f.

[124] Werner Rügemer: Grönland – US-Militär gegen chinesischen Ausbau der Infrastruktur, nachdenkseiten.de, 10.16.2018

[125] Volker Berghahn: The Americanization of West German Industry 1945 – 1973, New York 1986, p.267ff.

[126] Carlton Hayes: Wartime Mission to Spain 1942-1945, New York 1946, p.287 and 310

[127] Reinhard: Die Unterwerfung der Welt, loc. cit., p.1198f.

[128] Reinhard, ibid., p.1138ff.

[129] Bossuat: La France, loc. cit., p.501ff.

[130] Cf. Daniele Ganser: Illegale Kriege. Wie die NATO-Länder die UNO sabotieren, Zürich 2016

[131] Deutscher Bundestag, Wissenschaftlicher Dienst: Umfang und Standorte der in Deutschland stationierten US-Streitkräfte, 01.18.2017

[132] Atommacht Europa?, IMI-Analyse 2019/13

[133] Jürgen Wagner: PESCO: Das militaristische Herz der Europäischen Verteidigungsunion, Brüssel September 2019

[134] Streitthema NATO, Verteidigungsausgaben 2019, HB, 01.24.2020

[135] IWF gewährt Ukraine im Wahljahr 2019 neuen Milliardenkredit, Die Welt, 10.19.2018

[136] Rügemer: Die Kapitalisten des 21. Jahrhunderts, loc. cit., p.256f.

[137] Cf. Marie-Janine Celic: Tito. Der ewige Partisan. Munich 2020, p.128ff. and 167

[138] Jörg Becker / Mira Beeham: Operation Balkan – Werbung für Krieg und Tod, Baden-Baden 2008, p.92-126

[139] Lacroix-Riz: Banquiers et Industriels sous l'Occupation, loc. cit., p.146.ff.

[140] John Gillingham: Zur Vorgeschichte der Montan-Union: Westeuropas Kohle und Stahl in Depression und Krieg, in: Vierteljahreshefte für Zeitgeschichte 3/1986, p.401

[141] Gritschneder / Rügemer: Hehler für Hitler, loc. cit.

[142] Lacroix-Riz: Industriels et Banquiers sous l'Occupation, loc. cit.

[143] Gillingham: Zur Vorgeschichte der Montanunion, loc. cit., p.401f.

[144] Eric Kresse: Die deutschen Ford-Werke im »Dritten Reich«. Universität der Bundeswehr, München 2012

[145] Gillingham, loc. cit., p.396

[146] 141   Horst Thum: Mitbestimmung in der Montanindustrie. Der Mythos vom Sieg der Gewerkschaften, Stuttgart 1982, p.96

[147] Gillingham, loc. cit., p.404

[148] Jean Monnet: Mémoires, Paris 1976, p.364ff.

[149] Booker/North: The Great Deception, loc. cit., p.48

[150] Michael Hogan: The Marshall Plan, Cambridge / New York 1987, p.375

[151] Booker/North: The Great Deception, loc. cit., p.49

[152] The following details, unless otherwise noted, are taken from Eric Roussel: Jean Monnet, Paris 1996; Jean Monnet: Mémoires, Paris 1976; Bossuat: La France, loc. cit.

[153] Werner Rügemer: Der neue Systemkonflikt zwischen dem US-geführten Westen und der Volksrepublik China, isw-Report 119, München December 2019, p.22

[154] Philippe de Villiers: J'ai tiré sur le fil du mensonge et tout est venu, Paris

2019, p.93f.

[155] De Villiers, loc. cit., p.110

[156] Brief von Monnet an Harry Hopkins, Berater Roosevelts, quoted from: Villiers, ibid., p.112

[157] Hogan: The Marshall Plan, loc. cit., p.433

[158] De Villiers: J'ai tiré sur le fil du mensonge, loc. cit., p.66f.

[159] Monnet: Mémoires, loc. cit., p.124, 184f, 202ff., 321, 364, 420ff., 518

[160] Roussel: Jean Monnet, loc. cit., p.645f.

[161] De Villiers, loc. cit., p.120f.

[162] clearygottlieb.com, »Wofür stehen wir?«, downloaded 12.18.2019

[163] Ernest Backes / Denis Robert: Das Schweigen des Geldes, Zürich 2003, p.213ff.

[164] Jacques Attali: Sir Siegmund Warburg – Un homme d'influence, Paris 1985, p.345

[165] Backes/Robert: Das Schweigen des Geldes, loc. cit., p.325

[166] Attali: Sir Siegmund Warburg, loc. cit., p.346f.

[167] Belgien/Kohlekrise – Das Ende der Schonzeit, Der Spiegel, 02.25.1959

[168] Ambrose Evans-Pritchard: Euro-federalists financed by US spy chiefs, Telegraph, 09.19.2000

[169] Hogan: Marshall-Plan, loc. cit. p.339

[170] Werner Abelshauser: Deutsche Wirtschaftsgeschichte. Von 1945 bis zur Gegenwart, München 2004, p.242f.

[171] Monnet: Mémoires, loc. cit., p.458f.

[172] Horst Thum: Mitbestimmung in der Montanindustrie, loc. cit., p.100

[173] Frank Deppe i.a.: Geschichte der deutschen Gewerkschaftsbewegung, Köln 1977, p.335ff.

[174] Monnet: Mémoires, loc. cit., p.478

[175] Johannes-Dieter Steinert: Migration und Politik. Westdeutschland – Europa – Übersee. Ein Vergleich, Schwalbach 2008, p.307

[176] Hedwig Richter: Die Komplexität der Integration. Arbeitsmigration in die Bundesrepublik Deutschland von den fünfziger bis in die siebziger Jahre, zeitgeschichte-online.de

[177] Monnet, loc. cit., p.415

[178] Roussel: Jean Monnet, loc. cit., p.646

[179] Monnet: Mémoires, loc. cit., p.483-488

[180] Monnet, ibid., p.491

[181] De Villiers, loc. cit., p.149

[182] clearygottlieb.com, »Wofür stehen wir?«, downloaded 12.18.2019

[183] Werner Rügemer: Commerzbank: »America First«. Bundesregierung

missachtet deutsches Arbeitsrecht, arbeitsunrecht.de, 11.20.2017

[184] De Villiers, loc. cit., p.121ff.

[185] De Villiers, ibid., p.182

[186] Werner Rügemer: Philosophische Anthropologie und Epochenkrise. Studie über den Zusammenhang von allgemeiner Krise des Kapitalismus und anthropologischer Grundlegung der Philosophie am Beispiel Arnold Gehlens, Köln 1979, p.92ff.

[187] De Villiers, loc. cit., p.194

[188] De Villiers, ibid., p.196

[189] Werner Rügemer: arm und reich, Bielefeld 2002, p.28f.

[190] Bundesarchiv N 1266-1569, quoted from: de Villiers, loc. cit., p.197

[191] Wikipedia: Walter Hallstein, downloaded 12.15.2019

[192] David Rockefeller: Erinnerungen eines Weltbankiers, München 2008, p.564ff.

[193] Hellmann: Amerika auf dem Europamarkt, loc. cit., p.55

[194] Hellmann, ibid., p.43ff.

[195] Viermetz: Magie der Märkte, loc. cit., p.56ff.

[196] Hellmann, ibid., p. 52f.

[197] Hellmann, ibid., p.53

[198] Hellmann, ibid., p.54

[199] Backes/Robert: Das Schweigen des Geldes, loc. cit., p.332

[200] de.statista.com, downloaded 12.12.2019

[201] Backes/Robert, loc. cit., p.332

[202] Hellmann, loc. cit., p.211

[203] Hellmann, ibid., p.201

[204] Hellmann, ibid., p.164

[205] Hellmann, ibid., p.84

[206] Rügemer/Wigand: Die Fertigmacher, loc. cit., p.79ff. and 169ff.

[207] Hellmann, loc. cit., p.174

[208] Saul K. Padover: Experiment Germany, New York 1946, only 50 years later in German: Lügendetektor. Vernehmungen im besiegten Deutschland 1944/45, Frankfurt/Main 1999, p.189-192

[209] Monnet, ibid., p.551; de Villiers, loc. cit., p.174

[210] Bruessel.eu.diplo.de/blob/, downloaded 12.15.2019

[211] Martin Schirdewan: Überwachen und Strafen: Das Ende des Wegs für den Stabilitäts- und Wachstumspakt der EU, dielinke-europa.eu/se, 02.05.2020

[212] »Meine Vision ist die politische Union«, SZ, 01.26.2012 (Merkel); Europa: »Perfekte Lösungen brauchen lange«, Der Spiegel 26/2012 (Schäuble)

[213] Rügemer: Die Kapitalisten, loc. cit., p.233f.

[214] EU Urged to Exclude Israeli Arms Firms from Research Funds, peoplesdis-

patch.org, 07.06.2018

[215] Tür nach Europa, SZ, 01.22.2020

[216] M.E. Levine / J.L. Forrest: Regulatory Capture, in: Journal of Law Economics & Organization 6/1990, p.167ff.

[217] Nicholas Shaxson: The Finance Curse, London 2018, p.163ff. and 187

[218] Werner Rügemer: RatingAgenturen. Einblicke in die Kapitalmacht der Gegenwart, 2. Auflage, Bielefeld 2012, p.139ff.

[219] Pleiten, Pech und Pannen. Wirtschaftsprüfer, Ratingagenturen, Aufseher im Wirecard-Fall, SZ, 06.30.2020

[220] Forscher attestieren EU hohen Handelsüberschuss – mit sich selbst, Der Spiegel, 01.07.2020

[221] Tatjana Mischke / Valentin Thurn: EU – gekaufte Agrarpolitik? Arte TV, 04.29.2019

[222] EuGH Juni 2018: Deutschland wegen zu hoher Nitratbelastung und Verletzung/Nichtumsetzung der Gülle-Richtlinie verurteilt, kontextwochenzeitung.de, 12.18.2019; Deutschland droht Strafe wegen Nitratbelastung, SZ, 07.26.2020

[223] Europäischer Rechnungshof: Sonderbericht 13/2020: Biodiversität landwirtschaftlicher Nutzflächen, eca.europa.eu/de, 06.05.2020

[224] »Unterfinanziert, unterbesetzt, unterkompetent«, SZ, 07.27.2020

[225] Werner Rügemer: Das System Tönnies endlich stoppen!, arbeitsunrecht.de, 09.12.2019

[226] Das süße Leben im EZB-Steuerparadies, FAZ.net, 03.22.2014

[227] Bayer entschuldigt sich für Geheimlisten bei Monsanto, SZ, 05.12.2019

[228] Vicky Cann / Belén Balanyá: Captured States: When governments are a channel for corporate interests, Brussels February 2019

[229] Belén Balanya i. a.: Europe Inc. Regional and Global Restructuring and the Rise of Corporate Power, London 2000

[230] Shaxson: The Finance Curse, loc. cit., p.281ff. and 301

[231] Corporate Europe Observatory: Accounting for Influence – how the Big Four are embedded in EU policy-making on tax avoidance, Amsterdam 2019

[232] Western Advisers Helped an Autocrat's Daughter Amass and Shield a fortune, www.icij.org, 01.19.2020

[233] Werner Rügemer: Cross Border Leasing. Ein Lehrstück zur globalen Enteignung der Städte, 2. Auflage, Münster 2005

[234] Werner Rügemer: »Heuschrecken« im öffentlichen Raum. Public Private Partnership – Anatomie eines globalen Finanzinstruments, Bielefeld 2012, p.59ff. and 143ff.

[235] Blut im Piranha-Becken, Der Spiegel, 01.18.2020, p.57ff.
[236] Werner Rügemer: Die Kapitalisten, loc. cit., p.133ff.
[237] Rügemer, ibid. p.16ff.
[238] Rügemer: RatingAgenturen, loc. cit., p.170ff.
[239] Werner Rügemer: Das charmante Gesicht der Ausbeutung Europas. Christine Lagarde als neue Präsidentin der EZB, nachdenkseiten.de, 11.04.2019
[240] Ist Christine Lagarde die richtige EZB-Präsidentin?, Wirtschaftswoche, 07.12.2019
[241] Michael Ignatieff: Empire lite. Die amerikanische Mission an den Grenzen der Macht, Hamburg 2003
[242] Rügemer: Die Kapitalisten, loc. cit., p.64ff.
[243] Troika attackiert Tarifsysteme, Böckler impuls 2/2014
[244] Florian Rödl: EU im Notstandsmodus, Blätter für deutsche und internationale Politik 5/2012, p.8
[245] Adam Lebor: Tower of Basel. The Shadowy History of the Secret Bank that runs the World, New York 2013
[246] Rügemer: RatingAgenturen, loc. cit., p.33ff.
[247] Rügemer: Die Kapitalisten, loc. cit., p.31f.
[248] Shaxson: The Finance Curse, loc. cit., p.164.
[249] Hermann Ploppa: Die Macher hinter den Kulissen. Wie transatlantische Netzwerke heimlich die Demokratie unterwandern, Frankfurt/Main 2014
[250] Rügemer: Die Kapitalisten, loc. cit., p.229
[251] www.aktion-coke-eu.foodwatch.de
[252] EU-Ratspräsidentschaft: Deutschland muss Sponsoring-Verbot durchsetzen, foodwatch.org/de, 06.19.2020
[253] Werner Rügemer: Privatisierung in Deutschland. Eine Bilanz, 4. Auflage, Münster 2008, p.77
[254] Corbyn's nationalisation plans for energy sector to collide with EU law, The Guardian, 11.28.2019
[255] Rügemer: Die Kapitalisten, loc. cit., p.88ff.
[256] Neufassung der Trinkwasser-Richtlinie bringt nur einzelne Verbesserungen, press release ver.di, 01.31.2018
[257] See ec.europa.eu/competition/state_aid/legislation
[258] The Money Farmers: How Oligarchs and Populists Milk the E.U. for Millions, NYT, 11.03.2019
[259] Rügemer: Die Kapitalisten, loc. cit., p.165, 188, 254
[260] Steigen die Gebühren stärker an?, FAZ, 06.23.2020
[261] Oxfam: Trapped between Aid Policy and Migration Politics, London 01.29.2020

[262] EU-Fördergeld für Zwangsarbeit?, HB, 01.28.2020

[263] The Money Farmers: How Oligarchs and Populists Milk the E.U. For Millions, NYT, 11.03.2019

[264] Der Milliardenwahnsinn mit den EU-Subventionen, Wirtschaftswoche, 02.05.2014

[265] Werner Rügemer: Des sächsisch-christlichen Ministerpräsidenten Angst vor den Fremdvölkern, nachdenkseiten.de, 08.30.2018

[266] Werner Rügemer: Treuhand und die Folgen, SoZ – Sozialistische Zeitung 10/2019

[267] Rügemer: »Heuschrecken« im öffentlichen Raum, loc. cit., p.70f.

[268] Hartz IV: Staat stockte 2018 Löhne um fast 10 Mrd. Euro auf, Redaktionsnetzwerk Deutschland, 11.13.2019

[269] Europas dreckige Ernte, die story/ARD, 07.09.2018

[270] Werner Rügemer: Das jüngste Weltgericht, Hintergrund, 01.14.2015

[271] bindingtreaty.org/global-interparliamentary-network-for-the-binding-treaty-side-event-at-the-un-gva-14-oct-2019

[272] dejure.org/gesetze/AEUV/153.html

[273] www.echr.coe.int

[274] Cf. Rügemer: Cross Border Leasing, loc. cit.; id.: Privatisierung in Deutschland, loc. cit.; id.: »Heuschrecken« im öffentlichen Raum, loc. cit.; id.: Die Kapitalisten des 21. Jahrhunderts, loc. cit., p.43ff.

[275] Wolfgang Däubler: Das Arbeitsrecht, Reinbek 2006, p.320ff.

[276] See www.coe.int

[277] Charter of Fundamental Rights of the EU (2010/C 83/02), Official Journal of the EU 03.30.2010

[278] Stefan Clauwert/Isabelle Schömann: The Crisis and national labour law reforms. Annex to working paper 2012.04. Country by country analysis, Brussels 2016

[279] Marianne Egger de Campo: Seniorensitterinnen? Globale Dienstbotinnen? Personenbetreuerinnen!, in: APuZ [Aus Politik und Zeitgeschichte] 38-39/2015, p.17ff.; in the wake of the "corona" scandal in EU meat factories, this is meant to change.

[280] Zane Rasnaca / Magdalena Bernaciak (Hg.): Posting of workers before national courts. European Trade Union Institute (ETUI), Brussels 2020, p.14

[281] Lkw-Fahrer – die Sklaven der globalisierten Welt, Der Tagesspiegel, 05.01.2018

[282] Christian Bock: Sklaven der Straße. Lohndumping in der Logistikbranche, ZDF Zoom, 02.12.2020

[283] etf-europe.org/activity/bus-and-coach-road/

284 Wirksamere Kontrollen gefordert, ver.di publik 4/2019
285 Rasnaca/Bernaciak: Posting of workers before national courts, loc. cit., p.14
286 ilo.org/wcmsp5/groups/public/normativeinstruments/wcms_c097_de.htm
287 Wolfgang Däubler / Michael Kittner: Geschichte der Betriebsverfassung, Frankfurt/Main 2020, p.576
288 IG Metall: Solidarität ohne Grenzen. Themenheft Globalisierung, Frankfurt/Main 2015, p.29ff.
289 General Motors. US-Autoriese zieht sich aus weiteren Märkten zurück, HB, 05.18.2017
290 Can anybody hear us? An overview of the 2018 survey of EWC and SEWC representatives, ETUI Brussels 2019, p.100f.
291 Rügemer/Wigand: Die Fertigmacher, loc. cit., p.155ff.
292 Die Kommission der Europäischen Gemeinschaften: Gemeinsame Grundsätze für den Flexicurity-Ansatz herausarbeiten: Mehr und bessere Arbeitsplätze durch Flexibilität und Sicherheit, Brüssel 06.27.2007, p.23ff.
293 Green Paper – Modernising labour law to meet the challenges of the 21st century (2006/708) p.5
294 Werner Rügemer: Die Mär vom Jobwunder bei den Nachbarn, die tageszeitung 04.22.1997
295 Werner Rügemer: Travail et non-travail dans l'Union Européenne, in: Les Possibles 11/2016
296 Harald Schumann/Elisa Simantke: Europas neue Reservearmee, Der Tagesspiegel 09.12.2017
297 Werner Rügemer: Das System Tönnies stoppen! arbeitsunrecht.de 12.12.2019; Europas dreckige Ernte, die story/ARD, 07.09.2018
298 Diskriminierung: Deutschland hat fast die größten Lohnunterschiede in der EU, Der Spiegel, 03.07.2018
299 »Unser Wirtschaftssystem wird sich verändern«, SZ, 04.08.2020
300 Charly Kowalczyk: Aufklärer unter Verdacht, DLF, 01.28.2020
301 anstageslicht.de/themen/whistleblower, abgerufen 01.10.2020
302 www.whistleblower-net.de, downloaded 01.10.2019
303 Nach Skandal neuer Spitzenjob, Wiener Zeitung, 10.23.2002, updated 04.07.2005, downloaded 01.10.2020
304 Jacques Santer: Volksnaher Politiker und zukunftsweisender Europäer, DLF, 06.29.2017
305 Martin Höpner: Lohndumping unter dem Schutz des Europarechts, makroskop.eu, 01.07.2020
306 Rügemer/Wigand: Die Fertigmacher, loc. cit., p.131 und 165f.
307 Deutsches Rotes Kreuz: Warum war das DRK für den Schwarzen Freitag

13. Oktober 2017 nominiert?, arbeitsunrecht.de/freitag13/drk
[308] Arbeitszeiterfassung: Suche nach dem Königsweg, HB, 01.14.2020
[309] Rügemer: Unternehmer als straflose Rechtsbrecher, loc. cit.
[310] Porträts und Aktivitäten von Rieble und Thüsing siehe Rügemer/Wigand: Die Fertigmacher, loc. cit., p.135 and 131
[311] Arbeitszeiterfassung: Suche nach dem Königsweg, HB, 01.14.2020
[312] Brigitte Heinisch: Satt und sauber? Eine Altenpflegerin kämpft gegen den Pflegenotstand. Vorwort von Werner Rügemer, Reinbek/Berlin 2008
[313] Heinisch vs. Deutschland: Urteil 28274/08 vom 07.21.2011; www.whistleblower-netzwerk-net.de/blog, 07.22.2011
[314] Altenpflegerin erhält 90.000 Euro, Der Tagesspiegel, 05.25.2012
[315] Wolfgang Bittner: Verfassungsfeindlichkeit zur Disposition, in: Manfred Funke (Hg.): Extremismus im demokratischen Rechtsstaat, Bundeszentrale für politische Bildung, Bonn 1978
[316] Berufsverbote verstoßen gegen Menschenrechte – Urteil vom 09.26.1995, berufsverbote.de/index.php/EUGM.html
[317] See the website of the initiative fighting for public rehabilitation to this day: berufsverbote.de
[318] https://ec.europa.eu/commission/priorities/european-pillar-social-rights-20-principles.en
[319] European Commission, https://ec.europa.eu/social/main.jsp?catld=1313&langld=en
[320] Rügemer: Die Kapitalisten, loc. cit., p.55f.
[321] Jens Berger: BlackRocks Angriff auf die Rente, Telepolis, 01.14.2020
[322] ec.europa.eu/eures, downloaded 01.03.2020
[323] Osha.europa.eu/en
[324] ec.europa.eu/social/main
[325] Committee on Employment and Social Affairs: Activity Report 8. Legislative term 2014-2019, europarl.europa.eu/committees/en/empl
[326] Berichte über die 8 Förderperioden von 1958 bis 2020, esf.de/portal/DE/ueber-den-ESF/geschichte-des-ESF
[327] faire-mobilitaet.de/
[328] Werner Rügemer: Werkverträge in der Fleischindustrie abschaffen? Das vordergründige Skandal-Management der Bundesregierung – Lügen inbegriffen, nachdenkseiten.de, 06.05.2020
[329] Berichte u. a. aus Automobilwoche, 9.1.2019: Tschechien – Kampf um qualifizierte Arbeitskräfte wird härter; Neue Zürcher Zeitung, 11.03.2019: Die verschämten Einwanderungsländer im Osten der EU; Der Spiegel, 12.09.2019: Das Ende des Projekts »Optimus«; Der Spiegel, 08.04.2018: Ausländische

Arbeitskräfte – Wen Polen ins Land lässt, und wen nicht; Die Welt, 09.15.2016: Ungarns Wirtschaft sucht den perfekten Einwanderer

[330] Investigate Europe: Race to the Bottom: Europe's Precariat, www.journalismfund.eu/news/race-to-the-bottom-europes-precariat, 09.12.2018

[331] Nähen zum Hungerlohn. Billigtextilien vom Balkan, arte TV, 01.13.2020

[332] Brüssel erwägt EU-Mindestlohn, HB, 01.13.2010

[333] Ein Rahmen für Europa, HB, 11.27.2019

[334] WIIW: Decoupling of Labour Productivity Growth from Median Wage Growth in Central and Eastern Europe, Research Report 448, July 2020

[335] Asbjörn Wahl: The Rise and Fall of the Welfare State, London 2011

[336] Cf. Werner Rügemer: Die Kapitalisten des 21. Jahrhunderts. Gemeinverständlicher Abriss zum Aufstieg der neuen Finanzakteure. 3. Auflage Köln 2021, with foreword on the progress of "corona" policy. The English edition "The Capitalists of the 21st Century" (tredition 2019) and the French edition "Les Capitalistes du XXIème Siècle" (tredition 2020) have now also been published.

[337] Werner Rügemer: Aus der Defensive gegen das Kapital, arbeitsunrecht.de, 01.03.2020

[338] David Graeber: Bullshit Jobs, New York 2018; 4. Auflage, Stuttgart 2019

[339] Characteristic for this confusion are for example the publications of Guy Standing: The Precariat. The New Dangerous Class. London 2011

[340] Dorothea Brummerloh: Man hat wieder Personal, DLF Kultur, 10.14.2019

[341] Werner Rügemer: Strategien zur Betriebsübernahme, https://arbeitsunrecht.de 06.24.2020

[342] Joseph McCatin: Collision Course. Ronald Reagan, the Air Traffic Controllers and the Strike that Changed America, Oxford 2011

[343] Pit Wuhrer: Dreißig Jahre Bergarbeiterstreik. »Jetzt hungern die Leute wieder – wie damals«, Die Wochenzeitung (Zürich), 08.26.2014

[344] Anthony Carew: American Labour's Cold War Abroad, loc. cit., p.61ff.

[345] Wuhrer: Dreißig Jahre Bergarbeiterstreik, loc. cit.

[346] Simon Jenkins: Thatcher & Sons. A Revolution in Three Acts, London / New York 2006

[347] Owen Jones: Prolls. Die Dämonisierung der Arbeiterklasse, Mainz 2013, p.105ff.

[348] Zero-hour contracts: 5.5m Britons are on deals offering little guaranteed work, The Guardian, 09.08.2013

[349] It's the weekend. Are you working?, Financial Times, 01.25.2020

[350] UK austerity has inflicted great misery on citizens, UN says, The Guardian, 11.16.2018

[351] Solomon Hughes: Who funds the Brexit Party?, Morning Star, 09.12.2019

[352] Arron Banks: Brexit was a war. We won, The Guardian, 04.02.2017

[353] Wealthy US donors gave millions to right wing UK groups, The Guardian, 11.29.2019

[354] Richard Wolff: Capitalism's Political Servants: Trump and Johnson, CounterPunch, 02.11.2020

[355] Der Abräumer, Die Zeit, 01.16.2020

[356] Brexit: 10 ways the EU protects workers' rights, The Independent, 01.17.2017

[357] It's time for real change. Labour Party Manifesto 2019, labour.org/uk/manifesto

[358] Paul Mason: Postkapitalismus. Grundrisse eine kommenden Ökonomie, Berlin 2016

[359] How much Does it Cost to Study in the UK?, topuniversities.com

[360] Major NHS Trust forced to terminate use of private contractors, uvwunion.org.uk/news, 01.30.2020

[361] UCL cleaners and academics to picket together in first ever joint strike, iwgb.org.uk, 12.03.2019

[362] ISS HMRC cleaners take strike action over pay and conditions, pcs.org.uk, 11.20.2019

[363] Campaign: Justice for Workers, soas-unison.org.uk, downloaded 01.20.2020

[364] Angry Workers of the World: For working class inquiry, https://angryworkersworld.wordpress.com/about

[365] Mensakas: APP de comida a domicilio responsable, en.goteo.org/project/mensakas; Entlassene Deliveroo-Fahrer gründen Kooperative in Barcelona, de.labournet.tv, 2018

[366] First-ever international meeting of app-based transport workers to develop global strategy to challenge platform companies, wgb.org.uk, 01.28.2020

[367] Lloyd's of London bedauert Rolle im Sklavenhandel, FAZ, 06.19.2020

[368] On Italy see introduction in Werner Rügemer: I Capitalisti del XXI Secolo, Roma 2020

[369] Harald Schumann: Arrogante Kritik aus der Steueroase, Der Tagesspiegel, 07.27.2020

[370] Taxjustice.net/country-profiles/Luxembourg

[371] https://www.vangard.de December 2016

[372] Cf. Isaf Gün u. a. (Hg.): Gegenmacht statt Ohnmacht. 100 Jahre Betriebsverfassungsgesetz, Hamburg 2020

[373] Werner Rügemer: Arbeitsrechte? Die Blindstelle im Grundgesetz, arbeitsunrecht.de, 05.23.2019

[374] Werner Rügemer: Kölner IHK lässt Kammer-Kritiker überwachen, arbeitsunrecht.de, 12.06.2017

375 Rügemer/Wigand: Die Fertigmacher, loc. cit., p.177f.
376 Werner Rügemer: Travail et Non-Travail dans l'Union Européenne, Les Possibles 11/2016 (attac Frankreich)
377 Peter Hartz: Job-Revolution. Wie wir neue Arbeitsplätze bekommen können, Frankfurt/Main 2001
378 Rügemer/Wigand: Die Fertigmacher, loc. cit., p.38ff. and 167ff.
379 Rügemer: Unternehmer als straflose Rechtsbrecher, loc. cit.
380 Gutachten: EU-Mindestlohnplan verstößt gegen Verträge, FAZ 27.1.2021
381 Eurostat press release 38/2018 on International Women's Day 03.07.2018
382 Frauen in Führungsetagen: Deutschland unter EU-Durchschnitt, destatis.de/Europa, downloaded 06.22.2020
383 Werner Rügemer: Das System Tönnies muss gestoppt werden!, arbeitsunrecht.de, 09.12.2020
384 Fleischbranche vor Zeitenwende, HB, 06.24.2020
385 Betriebsratswahlen erleichtern, aktive Beschäftigte besser schützen, Deutscher Bundestag Drucksache 19/1710, 04.18.2018
386 Rügemer/Wigand: Die Fertigmacher, loc. cit., p.48ff.
387   Hinweisgeberschutz: www.transparency.de/themen/hinweisgeberschutz, downloaded 06.22.2020
388 Sieben Jahre Streiks: ver.di erneuert Kampfansage gegen Amazon, heise.de, 05.14.2020; Petra Welzel: Der Schein trügt. Amazons Image als Arbeitgeber ist angekratzt, verdi publik 8/2020
389 Mehr von uns ist besser für alle, klinikpersonal-entlasten/verdi.de
390 Rügemer: Das System Tönnies, loc. cit., and further reports on arbeitsunrecht.de
391 Die Amputation. »Wir sind mehr wert als das«, ver.di publik 4/2016
392 Juan Branco: Crépuscule, Paris 2019
393 Macron unter Druck, Deutschlandfunk, 07.03.2020
394 Rügemer: Die Kapitalisten, loc. cit., p.140ff.
395 See the breadth of demands: Par le peuple, pour le peuple! giletsjaunes-coordination.fr
396 Streiken bis die Rente bleibt, ver.di publik 1/2020
397 Qu' est-ce que „la convergence des luttes"?, francetvinfo.fr/economie/transports/sncf/
398 Des cheminots grévistes manifestent au siège de BlackRock à Paris, lexpress.fr/actualité 01.07.2020
399 Rügemer: Ratingagenturen, loc. cit., p.142ff.
400 Carlton Hayes: Wartime Mission to Spain 1942–1945. New York 1946; the same applies for Portugal.

[401] Hannes Bahrmann: Francos langer Schatten, Berlin 2020

[402] See the Initiative Asociación para la Recuperación de la Memoria Historica, ARMH

[403] Jon Larreategi: Documentos secretos de la CIA senalan que Felipe González creó los GAL, gasteizberri.com, 06.15.2020

[404] Oliver Neuroth: Spaniens Geisterflughäfen und Autobahnruinen, DLF, 01.23.2019

[405] U.N. Human Rights Council: Spain – Report on extreme poverty and human rights, Geneva July 2020 (A/HRC/44/40/Add.2)

[406] Alfredo Jalife-Rahme: Die Korruption in der spanischen Volkspartei und der Sturz von Präsident Rajoy, voltairenet.org, 06.14.2018

[407] Institut für Medien- und Kommunikationspolitik: Länderporträt Spanien, mediadb.eu/europa/spanien.html, downloaded 01.27.2010

[408] Trillo Francicso i.a.: Offensive contre le droit du travail et les syndicats en Espagne, in: Gresea Echos 88/2016, p.23ff.

[409] Die Bahn sucht Lokführer in halb Europa, Kölner Stadt-Anzeiger 01.30.2020

[410] Las practicas non laborales sustituyen unos 300.000 puestos de trabajo al ano, ugt.es, 01.24.2020

[411] https://laskellys.wordpress.com/quienes-somos

[412] Historic addressment ends long-running strike in the elder care sector, epsi.org/de/search/policies, 11.27.2017

[413] geographyfieldwork.com: Agribusiness Cluster in Almeria, downloaded 01.20.2020

[414] Sergen Canoglu: Almeria – Kämpfe in Europas Gemüsegarten, diefreiheitsliebe.de, 03.30.2019

[415] Europas dreckige Ernte, ARD, 07.09.2018

[416] http://sindacatoandaluz.info

[417] https://www.interbrigadas.org

[418] On Ireland's financial and corporate history: Conor McCabe: Sins of the Father. The Decisions that Shaped the Irish Economy, Dublin 2013

[419] Nicholas Shaxson: The Finance Curse, London 2018, p.118ff.

[420] Apple is Ireland's largest company, Irish Examiner, 05.09.2019

[421] US Billionaire Wilbur Ross cashes out Bank of Ireland stake, Reuters, 06.10.2014

[422] Memorandum of Understanding on Specific Economic Policy Conditionality (Ireland), 11.28.2010, p.5f.

[423] EuGH kippt EU-US-Datenschutzvereinbarung, zdf.de/nachrichten, 07.16.2020

[424] Apple is Ireland's largest company, Irish Examiner, 05.09.2019

[425] Hier feiern sich Apple und Irland gegenseitig, manager magazin, 01.21.2020

[426] Eine Insel der Seligen? FAZ 01.22.2021

[427] Sebastian Galle / Andrea Schreiber: Fliegen am Limit, ZDF Zoom, 11.13.2019

[428] Gleichstellung. Ehrlichkeit tut weh, SZ 04.05.2018; Lohnungleichheit, Der Spiegel 04.03.2018

[429] Elmar Wigand: Ryanair – Die Hölle friert zu, https://arbeitsunrecht.de 08.08.2018

[430] Ryanair: Wie sich Beschäftigte der ausbeuterischen Fluglinie erfolgreich bessere Löhne und Schutz erkämpfen, ver.di publik 8/2018

[431] § 117 – Aktion Mitbestimmung jetzt!, vcockpit.de/themen-und-positionen/mitbestimmung-jetzt.html

[432] See Wirtschaftskammer Österreich: Österreich in der EU, Vienna January 2020

[433] Rügemer: Cross-Border Leasing, loc. cit., p.109ff.

[434] Blackrock-Chef zum Österreich-Geschäft: »Wir investieren weiter«, Fonds online, 10.08.2018

[435] Voestalpine: ad hoc announcement 05.04.2018; Andritz: ad hoc announcement 01.14.2020

[436] unsere-zeitung.at, 05.09.2018

[437] Rentners Traum, Ein Gespräch mit Bert Rürup, SZ 01.26.2020

[438] Billiglöhner erwünscht. Zuwanderung in den Arbeitsmarkt stieg unter ÖVP/FPÖ-Regierung auf Rekordniveau, nachdenkseiten.de, 06.12.2019

[439] Österreich – Frontalangriffe auf Arbeitsrechte, Initiative zur Vernetzung der Gewerkschaftslinken, 09.27.2018

[440] Andreas Fischer-Lescano: Austeritätspolitik und Menschenrechte. Rechtspflichten der Unionsorgane beim Abschluss von Memoranda of Understanding, Vienna 2014. The report was co-financed by the European Trade Union Institute ETUI in Brussels.

[441] www.housingforall.eu

[442] Resolution: Solidarisch im Kampf für eine 35-Stunden-Woche!, oegb.at/article,02.28.2020

[443] Resolution Prekarisierung, oegb.at/article, 02.28.2020

[444] OECD: Who Cares? Attracting and Retaining Car Workers for the Elderly, Paris 2020

[445] Kurt Gritsch: Krieg um Kosovo. Geschichte, Hintergründe, Folgen, Innsbruck (university press) 2016, p.153ff.

[446] Draußen vor der Tür, FAZ 01.01.2021

[447] Neustart in Montenegro, Le Monde Diplomatique February 2021

[448] Jörg Roesler: Mit oder ohne westliches Geld? Der IWF und die sozialistischen Staaten, in: Welttrends 59/2008, p.85ff.

[449] Srecko Horvat: Der Zerfall Jugoslawiens und die Krise der EU, in: David Goeßmann/Fabian Scheidler: Der Kampf für globale Gerechtigkeit, Vienna 2019, p.103ff.

[450] Srecko Horvat: Der neoliberale Kollaps Jugoslawiens, http://www.kontext-tv.de 04.27.2017

[451] Die nächste EU-Ratspräsidentschaft, https://www.german-foreign-policy.com 11.21.2019

[452] Horvat: Der Zerfall Jugoslawiens und die Krise der EU loc.cit., p.10

[453] Markus Salzmann: Lehrerstreik in Kroatien, https://wsws.org/de 12.03.2019

[454] Investnorthmacedonia.gov.mk, downloaded 01.29.2020

[455] Cf. Gjorgji Damjanovski: Overview of Foreign Direct Investment Strategies of Multinational Companies – The Case of Western Macedonia, Master Thesis Ljublyana, Sept. 2016

[456] https://www.gerresheimer.com, downloaded 01.29.2020

[457] Mitteilung 2019 der Kommission zur Erweiterungspolitik der EU, Brussels 05.29.2019, p.6ff.

[458] Leila Knüppel: Billiglohnparadies Balkan, DLF 01.18.2018

[459] Germany Trade & Invest/GTAI: Lohn- und Lohnnebenkosten Mazedonien, 02.08.2017

[460] AHK/Delegation der Deutschen Wirtschaft in Mazedonien: Pressemitteilung Skopje 02.08.2019

[461] nordmazedonien.ahk.de/katalog/Germanska_Komora, downloaded 01.30.2020

[462] Stefan Meier: Nähen zum Hungerlohn. Billigtextilien vom Balkan, arte TV 01.13.2020; further information comes from the initiative "Voice of Textile Workers".

[463] https://glasentekstilec.wordpress.com

[464] 1. Juli: Kroatien tritt der EU bei, Bundeszentrale für politische Bildung 06.27.2013

[465] Ulrich Schiller: Deutschland und „seine" Kroaten. Vom Ustascha-Faschismus zu Tudjmans Nationalismus. Mit einem Geleitwort von Hans Koschnick, Bremen 2010

[466] USA setzen vor allem auf die Kroaten, Die Welt 04.06.1996

[467] Florian Hassel: Kroatien, schöngeredet, SZ 06.21.2013

[468] Friedrich Ebert-Stiftung: Der lange Weg nach Europa – Kroatiens EU-Beitritt, Bonn Juli 2013, p.6f.

[469] Ibid., p.4

[470] Andrea Beer: „Grenzgewalt ist ein Gerücht". EU-Vorsitz Kroatien ignoriert jede Kritik, tagesschau.de/ausland 01.24.2020

[471] Europas gesetzlose Grenze, FAZ 01.24.2021

[472] Stefan Clauwaert/Isabelle Schömann: Country report: Croatia. ETUI, Brussels 2013

[473] Kroatien: Gewerkschaftsmonitor, Friedrich Ebert-Stiftung May 2019

[474] Kroatien: Gesamtbevölkerung von 1992 bis 2018 und Prognose bis 2024, de.statista.com, downloaded 02.03.2020

[475] European Commission: Flash Reports on Labour Law, Brussels 2019, p.9

[476] College-contact.com/croatia, downloaded 02.03.2020

[477] Over 20,000 people rally for higher salaries for Croatian teachers, xinhua.com 11.26.2019

[478] Novenanews/com 10.21.2019

[479] Croatian shipbuilding workers halt strike after receiving delayed wages, xinhua.net.com 08.31.2018

[480] Werner Rügemer: Die Kapitalisten des 21. Jahrhunderts, p.317ff.

[481] Gipfel in Dubrovnik, Deutsche Wirtschaftsnachrichten 04.10.2019

[482] Uljanik-Werft bald in chinesischer Hand? Hansa-online.de 04.15.2019

[483] Hogan: The Marshall-Plan loc.cit., p.201ff.

[484] Carew: American Labour's Cold War Abroad loc.cit., p.88f.

[485] Finnen kooperierten enger mit den Nazis als gedacht, Die Welt 11.04.2009

[486] Bundesarchiv (Hg.): Europa unter dem Hakenkreuz, Bd. 7: Die Okkupationspolitik des deutschen Faschismus in Dänemark und Norwegen 1940-1945, Berlin/Heidelberg 1992

[487] Berit Reisel/Bjarte Bruland: The Confiscation of Jewish Property in Norway during World War II, Oslo June 1997

[488] Sweden and Jewish Assets, Final Report SOU 1999:20, government.se/legal-documents/1999/03/sou-199920/; Der Spiegel 40/1996, p.200ff. Publicly, reports have to date focused solely on the dissenting family member Raoul Wallenberg, who saved many Jews as a member of the Swedish embassy in Hungary.

[489] Gunnar Take: Forschen für den Wirtschaftskrieg. Das Kieler Institut für Weltwirtschaft im Nationalsozialismus. Berlin 2019

[490] Affäre bringt H&M-Chefin ins Schwimmen, FAZ 02.15.2020

[491] Rügemer: Die Kapitalisten p.107ff. and 37ff.

[492] André Anwar: Fleischindustrie - Tarifverträge und Mindestlohn, Frankfurter Rundschau 06.23.2020

[493] de.workerparticipation.eu, downloaded 01.10.2020

[494] Friedrich Ebert-Stiftung: Die finnischen Gewerkschaften, November 2012, p.1

[495] Christoph Franceschini i.a. (Hg.): Spionage unter Freunden. Berlin 2017 p.228ff.

[496] Werner Rügemer: Grönland – US-Militär gegen chinesischen Ausbau der

Infrastruktur, www.nachdenkseiten.de 10.16.2018

[497] Helge Hvid/Elwind Falkesen: Work and Wellbeing in the Nordic Countries, London 2018

[498] Asbjörn Wahl: The Rise and Fall of the Welfare State loc.cit.

[499] Schwedens heißer Immobilienmarkt, HB 02.21.2020

[500] James Gross: Broken Promise. The Subversion of US Labor Relations Policy, 1947 – 1994, Philadelphia 2002, p.1ff.

[501] https://eufagligt.de/eu 01.20.2020

[502] Traumjob oder Ausbeutung? Thailändische Beerenpflücker in Schweden, arte tv 11.21.2019

[503] WWI: Decoupling of Labour Productivity Growth from Median Wage Growth in Central and Eastern Europe, Research Report 448, Vienna July 2020

[504] Membership in the EPP was suspended in 2019.

[505] Peter Dugar: Orban und Soros – vertraute Feinde, Budapester Zeitung 05.03.2017

[506] Szilar Kalmar: There is no alternative to decent wages, krytykapolityczna 06.21.2016

[507] Ungarn: Gnadenlos günstig, Die Zeit 03.11.2019

[508] Translation of German translation of the 2012 Labor Law: IG Metall: transnationale einblicke 10.23.2017

[509] Hungary migration curbs fuel labour shortages, Financial Times 12.21.2018

[510] Schaeffler erweitert Standort in Debrecen, SCHAEFFLER intern 01/2019, p.27

[511] IG Metall: transnationale einblicke June 2018

[512] Der doppelte Orban, Die Zeit 10.04.2018

[513] Vetternwirtschaft: Wie Victor Orban EU-Subventionen an Freunde verteilt, „Europa heute" DLF 07.24.2020

[514] Ein Ölkonzern wird zum Plastikentsorger, HB 06.03.2019

[515] Peter Dugar: Orban und Soros – vertraute Feinde, Budapester Zeitung 05.03.2017

[516] Audi-Streik: „Es ist ein Wunder, dass dies in Ungarn noch niemand getan hat", portfolio.hu/uzlet/20190130/audi-strajk

[517] Beim größten Reifenhersteller Ungarns geht der Streik weiter, die Beschäftigten im Bildungswesen erringen Erfolge, labournet.de 03.22.2019

[518] Dossier zu Streiks und Widerstand in Ungarn: labournet.de 02.04.2019

[519] FAZ 01.19.2019

[520] Agnes Gagyi/Tamas Geröcs: Die politische Ökonomie des neuen ungarischen „Sklaven-Gesetzes", IG Metall: transnationale einblicke June 2019, p.6f.

[521] Werner Rügemer: Das charmante Gesicht der Ausbeutung Europas loc.cit.

[522] Cf. Clara Weiss: Die Strategie des Intermariums, wsws.org/de 07.06.2016
[523] https://de.statista.com/infografik/4861/militaerausgaben-nato-laender 04.03.2019
[524] EU-Subventionen für Polen, mdr 04.27.2018
[525] Amazon baut fünftes Logistikzentrum in Polen, Deutsche Verkehrszeitung 02.21.2017
[526] Tomasz Konicz: Europa als Sonderwirtschaftszone, DGB Gegenblende 10.17.2012
[527] Bedeutendste Investoren in Polen, HB 04.21.2017
[528] https://amcham.pl/amcham-mission, downloaded 02.11.2020
[529] Sonderwirtschaftszonen in Polen. Am Tropf der Weltkonzerne, DLF 04.23.2017
[530] Die Polen kehren heim, FAZ 02.25.2020
[531] Sonderwirtschaftszonen in Polen. Am Tropf der Weltkonzerne, DLF 04.23.2017
[532] JP Weber: Invest in Poland. Ratgeber für Investoren, Warsaw 2015, p.125
[533] ver.di: Schwarzbuch Lidl Europa, Berlin 2006
[534] European Commission: State aid: Commission authorizes Poland's aid, press release 04.15.2019
[535] Reinhard Lauterbach: Kumpel blockieren Gleise, junge Welt 02.21.2020
[536] Die Polen kehren heim, FAZ 02.25.2020
[537] Die zwei Seiten der Landwirtschaft in Polen. Landwirtschaftliches Wochenblatt 37/2016
[538] Poland's strong economy lures workers back from Britain, Financial Times 12.11.2019
[539] Elisa Schimantke/Harald Schumann: Das schmutzige Geschäft mit LkW-Fahrern aus Osteuropa, Der Tagesspiegel 10.09.2018
[540] Polnische Ärzte fordern Regierung heraus, DLF 12.11.2017
[541] Polnische Ärzte: Keine Verbesserung nach dem Hungerstreik, DLF 02.06.2020
[542] Reinhard Lauterbach: Schulen bleiben zu. Polens Lehrer im Ausstand, Solidarnosc macht den Streikbrecher, junge Welt 04.09.2019
[543] Lehrerstreik in Polen: Bildungssystem vor dem Zusammenbruch, meinwarschau.com 04.09.2019
[544] Joern Böwe/Johannes Schulten: Der lange Kampf der Amazon-Beschäftigten, Berlin 2019, p.23f.
[545] Ralf Ruckus/Jan Podrozny: Amazon Polen – Über 2.000 Beschäftigte wollen streiken, Telepolis 06.26.2016
[546] See Erstes internationales Amazon-Symposium 12.02.2019, handel.verdi.de
[547] Cato.org/blog 05.18.2006

548 Wenn die Kontrollen versagen, SZ 03.29.2019
549 Europäischer Wirtschafts- und Sozialausschuss: Die wirtschaftliche und
   soziale Lage in den baltischen Staaten, Brussels 2013, p.11
550 Estland: Rechtsextreme in der Regierung, wsws.org/de 04.24.2019
551 Lettland: Jubel für SS und Bundeswehr, daserste.ndr.de 03.17.2017
552 daserste.ndr.de 03.29.1993
553 Machtwechsel in Lettland, bpb.de/politik 10.07.2018
554 Baltikum: Verunsicherung durch Donald Trump, Telepolis 08.11.2016
555 Council of the Nordic Trade Unions: Workers' rights in the Baltics, Stockholm
   2017 p.52f.
556 Labor Standards and Working Environment in the New Member States.
   Empirical Analysis of Estonia, Latvia and Lithuania, Brussels October 2019
557 Autozulieferer lieben Litauen, FAZ 08.05.2019
558 Europäischer Wirtschafts- und Sozialausschuss loc.cit., p.3f.
559 https://www.gew.de/aktuelles/lettland-lehrer-demonstrieren-fuer-bessere-
   gehaelter
560 https://bnn-news.com/doctors-to-continue-protesting-in-latvia-with-six-day-
   strike, 11.07.2019; Healthcare trade unions to decide on future protests in
   Latvia, Baltic News Network 11.14.2019
561 https://peoplesdispatch.org/2019/08/18/educational-workers-in-estonia-
   demand-government-funding-for-research
562 https://www.tt.com/Ticker/litauische-lehrer-beenden-unbefristeten-streik
563 Family physicians in Latvia to continue "slow" strike, http://www.baltic-
   course.com 10.27.2017
564 ILO: Talking through the crisis, Geneva 2017, p.176
565 European Commission: Country Report Lithuania 2019, Brussels 02.27.2019
566 Based on the German version of the labor law by the commercial law firm
   Rödl & Partner operating in the Baltics,
   https://www.roedl.de/themen/baltikumsbrief/2016-11, downloaded 02.29.2020
567 Proteste gegen neues Arbeitsgesetz in Litauen, labournet.tv 06.26.2016
568 BMW's Ambet Yuson shows solidarity with the anti-new-labour-protesters in
   Vilnius, bwint.org/de_DE/cms 06.30.2016
569 Call for solidarity with protesting workers of the Kayi Construction Company,
   lpsk.lt/en 02.10.2020
570 Christian Bock: Sklaven der Straße. Lohndumping in der Logistikbranche,
   ZDF Zoom 02.12.2020
571 girteka.eu, downloaded 03.05.2020
572 top.alfa.lt/3/mindaugas-raila, downloaded 03.06.2020
573 girteka.eu/es-projektai.htm, downloaded 03.05.2020

[574] https://www.delfi.lt/news 06.26.2018
[575] Christian Bock: Sklaven der Straße loc.cit.
[576] Cf. Werner Rügemer: Grüezi – Mit welchen Verbrechen können wir behilflich sein? Heilbronn 1999
[577] Bern und Brüssel ringen um einen Rahmenvertrag. Die EU verliert langsam die Geduld, SZ 01.20.2020
[578] UNIA: Der Angriff der süddeutschen Arbeitgeber auf den Schweizer Lohnschutz, Bern September 2019
[579] Lohndumping: Unia-Frau Christa Suter brachte den größten Fall ins Rollen, workzeitung.ch 05.17.2019
[580] Starke Arbeitnehmerrechte gegen Nationalismus und Lohndumping, unia.ch/de 02.25.2019
[581] Wachsende Gefahr Termindruck: Bauarbeiter sagen Stopp! unia.ch/de 02.25.2020
[582] Vania Alleva/Andreas Rieger: Streik im 21. Jahrhundert. Zurich 2017
[583] Therese Wüthrich: Der Frauenstreik – eine Machtdemonstration, lunapark21 46/2019, p.20
[584] „Wir haben unsere Unsichtbarkeit bestreikt", junge Welt 06.19.2019